Manual For The
CHILD BEHAVIOR CHECKLIST

And

REVISED CHILD BEHAVIOR PROFILE

Thomas M. Achenbach
Departments of Psychiatry & Psychology
University of Vermont

Craig Edelbrock
Department of Psychiatry
University of Pittsburgh

Note: Some small changes were made in the 11-88 editions of the CBCL, TRF, and YSR, but these do not affect scoring.

Request for Research and Clinical Papers

The authors would appreciate receiving reports of research and clinical use of the Child Behavior Checklist and related instruments. Please include author's name, address, and telephone number, as well as all available bibliographic information, and send to:

Thomas M. Achenbach
Department of Psychiatry
University of Vermont
Burlington, VT 05401

Proper bibliographic citation for this *Manual:*

Achenbach, T.M., & Edelbrock, C. (1983). *Manual for the Child Behavior Checklist and Revised Child Behavior Profile.* Burlington, VT: University of Vermont Department of Psychiatry.

Related Books

Achenbach, T.M. (1985). *Assessment and taxonomy of child and adolescent psychopathology.* Newbury Park, CA: Sage Publications.

Achenbach, T.M., & Edelbrock, C. (1986). *Manual for the Teacher's Report Form and Teacher Version of the Child Behavior Profile.* Burlington, VT: University of Vermont Department of Psychiatry.

Achenbach, T.M., & Edelbrock, C. (1987). *Manual for the Youth Self-Report and Profile.* Burlington, VT: University of Vermont Department of Psychiatry.

Achenbach, T.M., & McConaughy, S.H. (1987). *Empirically-based assessment of child and adolescent psychopathology: Practical applications.* Newbury Park, CA: Sage Publications.

McConaughy, S.H., & Achenbach, T.M. (1988). *Practical guide for the Child Behavior Checklist and related materials.* Burlington, VT: University of Vermont Department of Psychiatry.

Library of Congress # 83-50450   ISBN 0-9611898-0-0

Published by Department of Psychiatry, University of Vermont, Burlington, VT 05401   15 14 13 12 11 10 9 8 7

USER QUALIFICATIONS

Because the Child Behavior Checklist is designed to be filled out by parents and parent surrogates, no special qualifications are needed for administering it, beyond the tact and sensitivity that are necessary in all dealings with parents. When it is given to a parent, its purpose should be explained in terms of obtaining a picture of the child's behavior as the parent sees it. It is important to tell parents that the Checklist is designed for a wide variety of children and that some of the items may not apply to their child. Whoever gives the Checklist to the parent should be available to answer questions about the meaning of items. Answers to parents' questions should be objective and factual, rather than probing or interpretive.

Whenever possible, it is highly desirable to have the child's mother and father or another adult who lives with the child independently fill out separate Checklists for the sake of comparing their views (see Chapter 10 for further details).

Hand scoring of the Checklist on the Child Behavior Profile requires that the instructions (Appendix A) be followed carefully, including rules for scoring items that request descriptions of behavior. Our interactive computer entry and scoring programs (described in Appendix B) provide instructions that can be followed by users familiar with basic computer procedures.

Although the administration and scoring of the Checklist do not require special skills, proper clinical and research use require knowledge of the theory and methodology of standardized assessment procedures, as well as supervised training in work with parents and children. The training required will differ according to the ways in which the instruments are to be used, but graduate training of at least the master's degree level would ordinarily be expected. However, no amount of prior training can substitute for professional maturity and a thorough familiarity with the procedures and cautions presented in this *Manual*.

All users should understand that our instruments are designed to provide standardized *descriptions* of behavior rather than diagnostic inferences. High scores on our descriptive dimensions of behavior problems should not automatically be equated with any particular diagnosis or inferred disorder. Instead, the responsible professional will integrate parents' Checklist descriptions of their child with other types of data obtained in the comprehensive evaluation of the child and family.

PREFACE

In writing this *Manual*, we had to grapple with two obvious but difficult questions: One is, "Where should we start?" The second is, "Where should we stop?"

The question of where to start raises issues such as the following:

1. The instruments dealt with in the *Manual* have forerunners in our own work and that of other people. Should we review previous work on checklists, parents' ratings, multivariate analyses, and profiles?

2. Behavioral ratings constitute a form of descriptive assessment. Should we compare the epistemological assumptions and implications of descriptive assessment with approaches based on inferences about underlying entities?

3. Multivariate statistics reflect quantitative associations among variables and provide quantifiable dimensions and profiles. Should we compare our multivariate approaches with nosological and psychodynamic approaches to taxonomy?

4. There are many ways to assess behavior disorders of childhood and adolescence. Beside ratings by parents, there are ratings of children by other people, self-ratings, peer reports, interviews, tests, assessment of family systems, and psychodynamic inferences from children's play. Should we compare these with the procedures we have developed?

In order to place the necessary instructions and technical information at the user's finger tips, we decided to forgo detailed expositions of the background of our work and to eschew comparisons with other approaches. We do, however, briefly consider these issues wherever they seem essential and unlikely to obscure the basic information needed by users. The bibliography in Appendix F lists publications that deal more extensively with the background of our work, its conceptual framework, and comparisons with other approaches.

The question of where to stop raises additional issues:

1. We (and others) are engaged in research designed to explore the correlates, the predictive power, and the utility of our instruments in various populations. Should we wait until these studies can be included in the *Manual*?

2. We have developed companion instruments to obtain ratings from teachers, direct observers, and children themselves. Should we wait until we can present a complete array of assessment procedures?

3. Ratings of behavior in natural environments constitute only one aspect of clinical assessment. Should we wait until we can explicitly link all types of data relevant to comprehensive assessment of children?

4. Clinical assessment should benefit the children who are assessed. Should we wait until we can prescribe the optimal means for helping each child on the basis of our assessment procedures?

Unfortunately, this *Manual* would never be finished if we waited until all of the above were accomplished. We have therefore sought to present data essential for use of the CBCL and Profile in assessing children's behavioral problems and competencies. We also present some initial data on companion instruments we have developed, including the Teacher's Report Form, Direct Observation Form, and Youth Self-Report (Chapter 12). To facilitate access to other sources, Appendix F provides a bibliography of reports related to our procedures, but we suggest that users do their own literature searches to obtain additional reports.

We view the instruments we have developed as part of a general approach that will continue to grow and be modified. Our procedures and this *Manual* therefore represent a beginning rather than an end point. Throughout the *Manual,* we have suggested diverse clinical and research applications, but there are many additional possibilities. We hope this *Manual* will encourage users to evolve new applications for themselves.

The *Manual* is written primarily for mental health practitioners, administrators, researchers, graduate students, clinical trainees, and school personnel concerned with behavior disorders of childhood and adolescence. Because not all portions of the *Manual* will be of equal use to all readers, the following guide will help readers locate the sections of most use to them.

Reader's Guide

In preparing this *Manual,* we have benefitted from the help and suggestions of colleagues. G. Dana Baron carried out most of the computer program-
ming and statistical analyses and has aided in countless other ways. Stephanie
Johnson prepared the final manuscript with great care. Drs. Stephanie Mc-
Conaughy and Barry Nurcombe have provided exceedingly helpful critiques of
the manuscript and continual feedback on their own applications of our procedures in their work. By their questions, criticisms, and suggestions, many
others have also spurred the writing of this *Manual* and shaped its final form.
Although we have done our best to be responsive, we know the job has just
begun. We hope, therefore, that they will continue to question, criticize, and
suggest.

                                                            T.M.A.
                                                            C.E.

CONTENTS

LIST OF FIGURES

LIST OF TABLES

Chapter 1
The Child Behavior Checklist

The study and treatment of child and adolescent psychopathology have been handicapped by a lack of standardized procedures for describing the relevant behavior. The lack of standardized descriptions hampers communication about individual cases. This, in turn, hinders the training of new professionals, the formation of subject samples for research, the generalization of research findings, and the collection of epidemiological data. It also makes it hard to assess changes in behavior as a function of time or interventions. Standardized descriptions are not a panacea, but they can at least help practitioners and researchers of different persuasions focus on a common set of phenomena.

SOURCES OF DATA

How should we obtain standardized descriptions of behavior? Unlike adults, children seldom seek mental health services on their own. Instead, they are typically brought by parents or parent surrogates. Furthermore, the main source of data is usually the parent rather than the child. Most referral problems are reported by parents, rather than by the child or directly observed by mental health workers.

Observations of problem behavior can never be totally unbiased. Even trained observers who follow rigidly prescribed procedures, for example, are constrained by the settings in which the child is seen and the observers' impact on the child. Because all observations are susceptible to biases of one kind or another, the question is not how to obtain totally unbiased data, but how to obtain the most useful data despite possible biases.

Although the utility of parent reports varies with the age of the child, such reports are especially crucial from about the age of 4 through 16. During this period, parents' observations offer a better basis for normative assessment of behavior than at earlier or later ages. Prior to age 4, many behavior problems reflect idiosyncratic home conditions to a greater extent than later, when children face a common set of developmental tasks outside the home environment. After age 16, adolescents begin moving out of the home, behavioral norms become less consistent, and parents become less privy to the behavior of their offspring.

We chose parent reports as the cornerstone of our assessment system for the following reasons:

1. Parents are the most universally available informants.
2. Parents are the most knowledgeable about their child's behavior across time and situations.
3. Parents are almost always involved in the evaluation and treatment of their children.

4. Although their reports (like those of all other informants) may be biased, parents' views of their children's behavior are usually crucial in determining what will be done about it.
5. Problems arising in interactions with parents are likely to be especially important for children's long-term adaptation, regardless of what causes the problems.
6. In evaluating outcomes, parents' perceptions of change are important in determining whether further help will be needed or sought.

Parent reports formed the starting point but not the endpoint of our work. As described in Chapter 12 of this *Manual*, we have also developed procedures for obtaining data from teachers, observers, and children themselves.

BEHAVIOR PROBLEMS

What variables should standardized descriptions encompass? Children and adolescents are typically referred for mental health services because of behavior that others view as detrimental to the youngster or to other people. Although views of underlying causes may differ, behavior problems are usually the main source of concern to the significant adults in the youngster's life, as well as to mental health workers. Behavior problems, then, are key candidates for inclusion in standardized descriptions.

In an effort to construct standardized procedures, we started with descriptions of child and adolescent problems that are of concern to parents and mental health professionals. These descriptions were derived from our earlier studies (Achenbach, 1966; Achenbach & Lewis, 1971), the clinical and research literature, and consultation with clinical and developmental psychologists, child psychiatrists, and psychiatric social workers.

We then pilot tested draft versions of the descriptions, instructions, and response scales with parents of children being evaluated in three child guidance clinics in Connecticut. To improve the items, successive drafts of the instrument were discussed with parents and the mental health workers and paraprofessionals who interviewed them. Parents were also asked to add items that were not already included in the draft instrument. We used this feedback in conjunction with analyses of response distributions to improve the item pool.

After successive revisions of the pilot editions, we finalized the 118 behavior problem items shown in Figures 1-1 and 1-2. To permit parents to include items not listed, we left additional spaces for *other physical problems without known medical cause* (Item 56h) and *any problems your child has that were not listed above* (Item 113). Note that items are numbered 1–113, but that Item 56 includes physical problems *a* through *h*; the total number of specific problems listed is thus 118, plus space for "other physical problems" (Item 56h) and "any problems your child has that were not listed" (Item 113).

The final list of items includes a broad range of problems relevant to children's mental health referrals and reportable by parents. We tried to avoid redundancy among items, because we wished to prevent the artifactual correla-

VIII. Below is a list of items that describe children. For each item that describes your child **now or within the past 6 months**, please circle the **2** if the item is **very true** or **often true** of your child. Circle the **1** if the item is **somewhat** or **sometimes true** of your child. If the item is **not true** of your child, circle the **0**. Please answer all items as well as you can, even if some do not seem to apply to your child.

0 = Not True (as far as you know)   **1 = Somewhat or Sometimes True**   **2 = Very True or Often True**

0 1 2	1.	Acts too young for his/her age	16	0 1 2	31.	Fears he/she might think or do something bad	
0 1 2	2.	Allergy (describe): _____					
				0 1 2	32.	Feels he/she has to be perfect	
		_____		0 1 2	33.	Feels or complains that no one loves him/her	
0 1 2	3.	Argues a lot					
0 1 2	4.	Asthma		0 1 2	34.	Feels others are out to get him/her	
				0 1 2	35.	Feels worthless or inferior	50
0 1 2	5.	Behaves like opposite sex	20				
0 1 2	6.	Bowel movements outside toilet		0 1 2	36.	Gets hurt a lot, accident-prone	
				0 1 2	37.	Gets in many fights	
0 1 2	7.	Bragging, boasting					
0 1 2	8.	Can't concentrate, can't pay attention for long		0 1 2	38.	Gets teased a lot	
				0 1 2	39.	Hangs around with children who get in trouble	
0 1 2	9.	Can't get his/her mind off certain thoughts; obsessions (describe): _____					
				0 1 2	40.	Hears things that aren't there (describe):	
0 1 2	10.	Can't sit still, restless, or hyperactive	25			_____	55
				0 1 2	41.	Impulsive or acts without thinking	
0 1 2	11.	Clings to adults or too dependent					
0 1 2	12.	Complains of loneliness		0 1 2	42.	Likes to be alone	
				0 1 2	43.	Lying or cheating	
0 1 2	13.	Confused or seems to be in a fog					
0 1 2	14.	Cries a lot		0 1 2	44.	Bites fingernails	
				0 1 2	45.	Nervous, highstrung, or tense	60
0 1 2	15.	Cruel to animals	30				
0 1 2	16.	Cruelty, bullying, or meanness to others		0 1 2	46.	Nervous movements or twitching (describe):	
0 1 2	17.	Day-dreams or gets lost in his/her thoughts				_____	
0 1 2	18.	Deliberately harms self or attempts suicide		0 1 2	47.	Nightmares	
0 1 2	19.	Demands a lot of attention		0 1 2	48.	Not liked by other children	
0 1 2	20.	Destroys his/her own things	35	0 1 2	49.	Constipated, doesn't move bowels	
0 1 2	21.	Destroys things belonging to his/her family or other children		0 1 2	50.	Too fearful or anxious	65
				0 1 2	51.	Feels dizzy	
0 1 2	22.	Disobedient at home					
				0 1 2	52.	Feels too guilty	
0 1 2	23.	Disobedient at school		0 1 2	53.	Overeating	
0 1 2	24.	Doesn't eat well					
				0 1 2	54.	Overtired	
0 1 2	25.	Doesn't get along with other children	40	0 1 2	55.	Overweight	70
0 1 2	26.	Doesn't seem to feel guilty after misbehaving					
					56.	Physical problems without known medical cause:	
0 1 2	27.	Easily jealous					
0 1 2	28.	Eats or drinks things that are not food (describe): _____		0 1 2	a.	Aches or pains	
				0 1 2	b.	Headaches	
				0 1 2	c.	Nausea, feels sick	
		_____		0 1 2	d.	Problems with eyes (describe):	
0 1 2	29.	Fears certain animals, situations, or places, other than school (describe): _____		0 1 2	e.	Rashes or other skin problems	75
				0 1 2	f.	Stomachaches or cramps	
				0 1 2	g.	Vomiting, throwing up	
		_____		0 1 2	h.	Other (describe): _____	
0 1 2	30.	Fears going to school	45				

Please see other side

Figure 1-1. Behavior problem Items 1–56h of the Child Behavior Checklist.

			0 = Not True (as far as you know)	1 = Somewhat or Sometimes True				2 = Very True or Often True

0	1	2	57.	Physically attacks people	0	1	2	84. Strange behavior (describe): _____
0	1	2	58.	Picks nose, skin, or other parts of body (describe): _____				
				_____ 80	0	1	2	85. Strange ideas (describe):
0	1	2	59.	Plays with own sex parts in public 16				
0	1	2	60.	Plays with own sex parts too much	0	1	2	86. Stubborn, sullen, or irritable
0	1	2	61.	Poor school work	0	1	2	87. Sudden changes in mood or feelings
0	1	2	62.	Poorly coordinated or clumsy	0	1	2	88. Sulks a lot 45
0	1	2	63.	Prefers playing with older children 20	0	1	2	89. Suspicious
0	1	2	64.	Prefers playing with younger children	0	1	2	90. Swearing or obscene language
0	1	2	65.	Refuses to talk	0	1	2	91. Talks about killing self
0	1	2	66.	Repeats certain acts over and over; compulsions (describe): _____	0	1	2	92. Talks or walks in sleep (describe):
					0	1	2	93. Talks too much 50
0	1	2	67.	Runs away from home	0	1	2	94. Teases a lot
0	1	2	68.	Screams a lot 25	0	1	2	95. Temper tantrums or hot temper
0	1	2	69.	Secretive, keeps things to self	0	1	2	96. Thinks about sex too much
0	1	2	70.	Sees things that aren't there (describe):	0	1	2	97. Threatens people
					0	1	2	98. Thumb-sucking 55
				_____	0	1	2	99. Too concerned with neatness or cleanliness
					0	1	2	100. Trouble sleeping (describe):
0	1	2	71.	Self-conscious or easily embarrassed				
0	1	2	72.	Sets fires				
0	1	2	73.	Sexual problems (describe):	0	1	2	101. Truancy, skips school
					0	1	2	102. Underactive, slow moving, or lacks energy
				_____	0	1	2	103. Unhappy, sad, or depressed 60
				_____ 30	0	1	2	104. Unusually loud
0	1	2	74.	Showing off or clowning	0	1	2	105. Uses alcohol or drugs (describe):
0	1	2	75.	Shy or timid				
0	1	2	76.	Sleeps less than most children	0	1	2	106. Vandalism
0	1	2	77.	Sleeps more than most children during day and/or night (describe): _____	0	1	2	107. Wets self during the day
					0	1	2	108. Wets the bed 65
				_____	0	1	2	109. Whining
0	1	2	78.	Smears or plays with bowel movements 35	0	1	2	110. Wishes to be of opposite sex
0	1	2	79.	Speech problem (describe): _____	0	1	2	111. Withdrawn, doesn't get involved with others
					0	1	2	112. Worrying
0	1	2	80.	Stares blankly				113. Please write in any problems your child has that were not listed above:
0	1	2	81.	Steals at home				
0	1	2	82.	Steals outside the home	0	1	2	_____ 70
0	1	2	83.	Stores up things he/she doesn't need (describe): _____ 40	0	1	2	_____
					0	1	2	_____

PLEASE BE SURE YOU HAVE ANSWERED ALL ITEMS.   PAGE 4   UNDERLINE ANY YOU ARE CONCERNED ABOUT.

Figure 1-2. Behavior problem Items 57–113 of the Child Behavior Checklist.

tions that arise when two or more items reflect the same behavior.

For several items, we found that having the parent describe the behavior could help us avoid improperly counting behavior that did not really fit the item or that should be scored elsewhere. An example is Item *28. Eats or drinks things that are not food*: We found that some parents scored this as present to reflect their child's consumption of junk foods, such as candy, rather than true nonfood items, such as paint. The final form of this item requests a description of the specific behavior. As indicated in the scoring instructions (Appendix A), a report of junk foods should not be scored. Similarly, for Item *66. Repeats certain acts over and over; compulsions,* descriptions such as "Won't take no for an answer" or "Keeps hitting brother" would not justify scoring compulsions as present.

Descriptions are also clinically helpful on items that can include a broad range of deviant behavior. For example, the descriptions requested on Items *84. Strange behavior* and *85. Strange ideas* are important to clarify what the parent has in mind. Where parents' descriptions indicate that they have scored an item inappropriately or scored more than one item for a particular behavior, only the item that most precisely describes the behavior is to be counted. (See Appendix A for details of scoring.)

Response Scale for Behavior Problems

A three-step response scale (0,1,2) was chosen because it is typically easier than a *present versus absent* scale for most untrained raters. For each item that describes the child currently or within the last 6 months, parents are to circle the *2* if the item is *very true* or *often true* of their child; the *1* if the item is *somewhat* or *sometimes true* of their child; and the *0* if the item is *not true* of their child. The middle category can be used when mild or ambiguous instances of a behavior would make a forced choice between present and absent difficult.

More finely differentiated response scales were rejected because fine gradations in behavior problems are unlikely to be captured by a questionnaire. Multi-category response scales may also be more vulnerable to untrained raters' tendencies to prefer or shun extreme responses. Furthermore, multi-category response scales have not been found to improve the differentiation of syndromes empirically derived from ratings of behavior problems (see Achenbach & Edelbrock, 1978).

SOCIAL COMPETENCE ITEMS

Mental health referrals are typically prompted by behavior problems, but social competencies may be equally important for assessing children's needs and prognoses. Despite widespread espousal of social competence, however, there was little research to indicate which readily reportable competencies would discriminate effectively between relatively normal children and their behavior-disordered peers.

Following a survey of the existing literature on assessment of social competence in children, we pilot tested descriptions of positive behavioral characteristics in various formats. One approach was to construct bipolar scales with a behavior problem at one end and its opposite at the other end. For example, "kind to animals" is the opposite of "cruel to animals." However, both characteristics might be true of a child: Some children are cruel to some animals but kind to others; or occasionally cruel to a particular animal but otherwise kind to it. A parent aware of both the cruelty and kindness would probably rate a bipolar item in the middle of the scale, thereby obscuring the occurrence of the opposite kinds of behavior.

In other cases, the opposite of a particular behavior problem might also be considered a problem. For example, the opposite of "acts too young for his/her age" would be "acts too old for his/her age."

For some behavior problems, the most appropriate opposite is merely the negation of the behavior problem. For example, the opposite of "fears going to school" is "does not fear going to school." Yet, bipolar items of this sort merely complicate the rating task without adding information about children's competencies.

A second approach is to write favorable items in the same format as the behavior problems but not restricted to opposites of the behavior problems. For example, "has a good sense of humor" is a favorble characteristic for which the negation or opposite is not necessarily a problem. We tested many items of this sort, but found that parents endorsed most of them for most children in clinical as well as nonclinical samples. This probably reflected social desirability effects, plus the fact that it is possible to think of at least *some* evidence for such characteristics in nearly all children.

A third approach is to use items of the type comprising the Vineland Social Maturity Scale (Doll, 1965). These items ask parents to indicate whether or not their child performs age-appropriate tasks, such as dressing, self-care, and making purchases at a store. Although these items are helpful for assessing the type of management needed by the retarded children for whom the Vineland scale was designed, they do not discriminate effectively among children who are not mentally retarded. Being mainly of normal intelligence, children seen in outpatient mental health settings are generally capable of the Vineland items for their age level. Whether they actually demonstrate particular Vineland accomplishments depends more on their opportunities and on their parents' behavior than on their own competence.

A fourth approach is to obtain parents' reports of the actual frequency with which their child engages in specific activities, such as a particular sport or hobby. However, this approach is undermined by the fact that the absolute frequency of each activity is constrained by opportunities to pursue it and may reflect little about a child's preference or skill. For example, some children who are good skiers have few opportunities for skiing. Yet, this type of competency may be at least as important as participating more often but halfheartedly and incompetently in neighborhood games that peers play continually.

To avoid the constraints afflicting the foregoing approaches, we devised the items shown in Figures 1-3 and 1-4. Items I and II ask parents to specify the sports and other activities (up to three each) that their child most likes to take part in. To estimate the quality and amount of the child's involvement in each activity, adjusted for peer group norms as perceived by the parents, parents are asked to indicate how much time the child spends in each and how well the child performs each activity, compared to other children of the same age.

To score the amount and quality of participation independently of the sheer number of activities listed, one score is assigned for the *number* of activities and a second is computed for the mean of the *ratings* of amount and quality of participation. As a result, a child who likes only one sport, for example, gets a low score for number of sports, but can nevertheless get a high score for participating more often or more effectively in that sport than his/her peers do. Similar principles apply to the scoring of the child's participation in organizations, jobs and chores, and friendships (see Appendix A for specific scoring instructions).

Additional competence items include the parent's rating of how well the child gets along with siblings, other children, and parents, how well the child plays and works by himself/herself, and school performance. Parents are also asked if the child is in a special class, has ever repeated a grade, and has any other school problems.

The CBCL can be filled out by most parents whose reading skills are at a fifth grade level or higher. Some parents can complete it in as little as 10 minutes, although the average is about 15–17 minutes. It is desirable for someone familiar with the CBCL to be available in case parents have questions. However, questions about items should be answered in a factual manner aimed at helping the parent describe the child's behavior, rather than at making inferences about the parent or child. If a parent cannot read, an interviewer can read the CBCL aloud and enter the parent's responses.

SUMMARY

The Child Behavior Checklist is designed to record in a standardized format the behavioral problems and competencies of children aged 4 through 16, as reported by their parents or others who know the child well. The items and format were refined through successive editions that were pilot tested with parents of children referred for mental health services. Each of the 118 behavior problem items is scored on a 3-step response scale. The 20 social competence items obtain parents' reports of the amount and quality of their child's participation in sports, hobbies, games, activities, organizations, jobs and chores, and friendships; how well the child gets along with others and plays and works by himself/herself; and school functioning. The CBCL is designed to be self-administered but can be administered by an interviewer if necessary.

CHILD BEHAVIOR CHECKLIST FOR AGES 4-16

For office use only
ID #

CHILD'S
NAME

PARENT'S TYPE OF WORK *(Please be specific—for example: auto mechanic, high school teacher, homemaker, laborer, lathe operator, shoe salesman, army sergeant, even if parent does not live with child.)*

SEX ☐ Boy ☐ Girl

AGE

RACE

FATHER'S
TYPE OF WORK:_____

MOTHER'S
TYPE OF WORK:_____

TODAY'S DATE

Mo. _____ Day _____ Yr. _____

CHILD'S BIRTHDATE

Mo. _____ Day _____ Yr. _____

THIS FORM FILLED OUT BY:

☐ Mother

☐ Father

☐ Other *(Specify)*:

GRADE
IN
SCHOOL

I. **Please list the sports your child most likes to take part in.** For example: swimming, baseball, skating, skate boarding, bike riding, fishing, etc.

☐ None

Compared to other children of the same age, about how much time does he/she spend in each?

	Don't Know	Less Than Average	Average	More Than Average
a. _____	☐	☐	☐	☐
b. _____	☐	☐	☐	☐
c. _____	☐	☐	☐	☐

Compared to other children of the same age, how well does he/she do each one?

Don't Know	Below Average	Average	Above Average
☐	☐	☐	☐
☐	☐	☐	☐
☐	☐	☐	☐

II. **Please list your child's favorite hobbies, activities, and games, other than sports.** For example: stamps, dolls, books, piano, crafts, singing, etc. (Do not include T.V.)

☐ None

Compared to other children of the same age, about how much time does he/she spend in each?

	Don't Know	Less Than Average	Average	More Than Average
a. _____	☐	☐	☐	☐
b. _____	☐	☐	☐	☐
c. _____	☐	☐	☐	☐

Compared to other children of the same age, how well does he/she do each one?

Don't Know	Below Average	Average	Above Average
☐	☐	☐	☐
☐	☐	☐	☐
☐	☐	☐	☐

III. **Please list any organizations, clubs, teams, or groups your child belongs to.**

☐ None

Compared to other children of the same age, how active is he/she in each?

	Don't Know	Less Active	Average	More Active
a. _____	☐	☐	☐	☐
b. _____	☐	☐	☐	☐
c. _____	☐	☐	☐	☐

IV. **Please list any jobs or chores your child has.** For example: paper route, babysitting, making bed, etc.

☐ None

Compared to other children of the same age, how well does he/she carry them out?

	Don't Know	Below Average	Average	Above Average
a. _____	☐	☐	☐	☐
b. _____	☐	☐	☐	☐
c. _____	☐	☐	☐	☐

PAGE 1

3-81 Edition

Figure 1-3. Social competence Items I–IV of the Child Behavior Checklist.

V. **1.** About how many close friends does your child have? ☐ None ☐ 1 ☐ 2 or 3 ☐ 4 or more

2. About how many times a week does your child do things with them? ☐ less than 1 ☐ 1 or 2 ☐ 3 or more

VI. Compared to other children of his/her age, how well does your child:

		Worse	About the same	Better
a.	Get along with his/her brothers & sisters?	☐	☐	☐
b.	Get along with other children?	☐	☐	☐
c.	Behave with his/her parents?	☐	☐	☐
d.	Play and work by himself/herself?	☐	☐	☐

VII. **1.** Current school performance—for children aged 6 and older:

☐ Does not go to school

	Failing	Below average	Average	Above average
a. Reading or English	☐	☐	☐	☐
b. Writing	☐	☐	☐	☐
c. Arithmetic or Math	☐	☐	☐	☐
d. Spelling	☐	☐	☐	☐
Other academic subjects—for example: history, science, foreign language, geography. e. _____	☐	☐	☐	☐
f. _____	☐	☐	☐	☐
g. _____	☐	☐	☐	☐

2. Is your child in a special class?

☐ No ☐ Yes—what kind?

3. Has your child ever repeated a grade?

☐ No ☐ Yes—grade and reason

4. Has your child had any academic or other problems in school?

☐ No ☐ Yes—please describe

When did these problems start?

Have these problems ended?

☐ No ☐ Yes—when?

Figure 1-4. Social competence Items V–VII of the Child Behavior Checklist.

Chapter 2
The Child Behavior Profile: Behavior
Problem Scales

The Child Behavior Checklist is designed to obtain parents' descriptions of their children's behavior in a standardized format. The value of the descriptions depends on their ability to distinguish between children who differ in other important ways. How should the descriptive items of the CBCL be aggregated to reflect patterns that discriminate between children whose disorders may differ with respect to etiology, outcome, or appropriate interventions? This is the problem of *taxonomy*: It is a key problem in the study and treatment of children and adolescents.

The study of adult psychopathology has been dominated by Emil Kraepelin's (1883) taxonomic model. The major categories of Kraepelin's system, such as affective disorders and schizophrenia, have molded training, theory, research, and treatment since the nineteenth century. Despite varying conceptions of these disorders, they are still mainstays of official classification systems, such as the American Psychiatric Association's *Diagnostic and Statistical Manual of Mental Disorders* (DSM-I, 1952; DSM-II, 1968; DSM-III, 1980).

Children's disorders were long neglected by Kraepelinian classifications. The first edition of the *Diagnostic and Statistical Manual* (DSM-I, 1952), for example, included only two categories of childhood disorders: *Adjustment Reaction,* which was applied to a broad range of problems thought to be transient, and *Childhood Schizophrenia,* which was reserved for seriously disturbed children.

The second edition of the DSM (DSM-II, 1968) added several behavior disorders of childhood and adolescence, but — except for the *Hyperkinetic Reaction* — most of these were seldom used. The third edition of the DSM (DSM-III, 1980) included many new categories of child and adolescent disorders, but most of them lack clear forerunners in earlier classifications. Even the hyperkinetic reaction was renamed and split into *Attention Deficit Disorder with Hyperactivity* and *Attention Deficit Disorder without Hyperactivity.* Which of the new categories will prove viable is not yet clear, but they were formulated through committee negotiations rather than empirical research or systematic trial-and-error.

The lack of a well-established taxonomy of childhood disorders has inspired numerous efforts to identify syndromes through multivariate analyses of behavior checklists. Despite the diversity of checklists, subjects, informants, and analytic methods, these studies show considerable convergence on a few global, broad-band syndromes and a larger number of more specific, narrow-band syndromes (for reviews of this work, see Achenbach & Edelbrock, 1978; Quay, 1979). However, few of the multivariate findings were translated into practical procedures for assessing children. Furthermore, by combining children of both sexes and diverse ages in the same analyses, most studies may have obscured syndromes peculiar to one sex or a particular developmental period.

PRINCIPAL COMPONENTS (FACTOR) ANALYSES OF THE CHILD BEHAVIOR CHECKLIST

To find out which of our behavior problem items occur together to form syndromes, we performed principal components analyses of CBCLs filled out by the parents of children referred for outpatient mental health services. (A principal components analysis is essentially a factor analysis in which 1.00 is used as the communality estimate.) We used clinically-referred children, because in nonclinical populations many problem behaviors are too infrequent to permit identification of syndromes. Factor analyses of nonclinical samples might therefore fail to detect syndromes that characterize deviant children. However, as detailed in Chapter 3, norms for our factor-based scales are based on nonclinical samples.

To reflect possible age and sex differences in the prevalence and patterning of behavior problems, we performed separate principal components analyses for children of each sex at ages 4 to 5, 6 to 11, and 12 to 16. These age ranges were chosen because they mark important transitions in cognitive, physical, educational, and/or social-emotional development.

Clinical Samples

The data for our principal components analyses were obtained from 42 mental health services that used the CBCL as part of their intake procedure. Located mainly in the eastern United States, the services included the following: 12 community mental health centers; 8 private psychological and psychiatric practices; 6 university child psychiatry clinics; 3 child guidance clinics; 3 clinics in general hospitals; 3 clinics for military dependents; 2 child psychiatry units of health maintenance organizations; 2 clinical services operated by religious agencies; 1 family service agency; 1 research hospital; and 1 day school for emotionally disturbed children. The large variety of settings provided a broad distribution of socioeconomic levels and other client characteristics that should minimize selective biases affecting the caseloads of individual services.

Each sample of boys and girls aged 6–11 and 12–16 numbered 450, while each sample of boys and girls aged 4–5 numbered 250, for a total of 2,300 children. The samples of younger children were limited to 250, because low referral rates for children in this age range made it difficult to obtain larger samples; 4- and 5-year old girls, in particular, make up a very small proportion of most child mental health caseloads.[1] However, a sample of 250 still provided more than twice as many subjects as variables for our principal components analyses. The sampling distribution of the Pearson correlation — on which our factor analyses were based — also becomes quite stable at Ns above 200. In addition, multiple regressions of scores on each CBCL item for each sex showed no significant differences between 4- and 5-year-olds on any of the 118 behavior problem items (see Achenbach & Edelbrock, 1981).

Socioeconomic status (SES) was scored on Hollingshead's (1957) 7-step scale of occupation, as reported by the parent on the CBCL. Hollingshead's (1975) draft revision of his occupational scale was used as a supplement to cover occupational stratification emerging since his original version. Occupations not listed on Hollingshead's scale were scored by obtaining their ratings on the dimensions listed in the *Dictionary of Occupational Titles* (U.S. Department of Labor, 1965) and scoring them like similarly-rated occupations that were listed on Hollingshead's scale. If remunerative occupations were reported for both parents, the higher-status occupation was used to score SES.

Occupation was used in preference to education or income as a measure of SES, because Hollingshead (1957) found it to be the best single index of his multidimensional socioeconomic stratification. Occupation is also more likely to be reported in a uniformly scalable manner and to be a more stable index of SES than income or education, which have been changing radically over time and from region to region. Table 2-1 shows the distribution of occupations for our clinical samples in terms of Hollingshead's seven categories. The average of the mean scores for the 6 sex/age groups was 4.1, which is almost exactly the midpoint of Hollingshead's 7-step scale.

The overall racial distribution was 81.2% white, 17.1% black, and 1.8% other. The CBCL was filled out by mothers for 83% of the children, fathers for 11.5%, and others, such as relatives and foster parents, for 5.6%.

Selection of Items for Principal Components Analyses

Within each sample, we tabulated the frequency with which parents endorsed each item (i.e., scored it 1 or 2). To exclude items too rare to contribute reliable discriminative power in the principal components analyses, we omitted any that were endorsed by less than 5% of the parents in a sample. (We would also have omitted any items endorsed by more than 95%, but none were.) The number omitted ranged from four for boys aged 4–5 and 6–11 to seven for several of the other samples. The items omitted for each sex/age group are listed in Table 2-2. Because they cover such diverse responses, Items *56h. Other physical problems* and *113. Other problems not listed* were also omitted from the principal components analyses.

---

[1]Because it took nine years to accumulate 250 4-5-year-old girls, the First Edition of the Profile was based on a sample of 171. Although the overall factor structure did not change much from the First Edition sample of 171 to the Revised Edition sample of 250, Chapter 9 details the changes in item placements that did occur.

Table 2-1
Percent of each Occupational Level for Parents of Clinically-
Referred Children Whose CBCLs were Factor-Analyzed

| | Boys | | | Girls | | | Combined |
| | 4–5 | 6–11 | 12–16 | 4–5 | 6–11 | 12–16 | Groups[b] |
Occupational Level[a]	N = 250	N = 450	N = 450	N = 250	N = 450	N = 450	N = 2300
1. Executives, large proprietors, major professionals	10	9	13	8	9	16	11
2. Managers, medium proprietors, lesser professionals	10	10	15	15	16	17	14
3. Administrative personnel, small independent proprietors, minor professionals	10	11	13	15	11	11	12
4. Clerical, sales, technicians, owners of little businesses	22	24	23	17	22	21	22
5. Skilled manual employees	23	17	15	20	14	12	17
6. Machine operators, semi-skilled employees	13	13	10	11	11	12	12
7. Unskilled employees	12	16	11	15	18	10	14
Mean	4.3	4.4	3.9	4.3	4.2	3.7	4.1
SD	1.8	1.8	1.8	1.8	1.9	1.9	1.9

Note — Because of rounding, columns may not sum to 100%.

[a]1 = highest level, 7 = lowest level scored according to Hollingshead's (1957) scale, supplemented with Hollingshead's (1975) draft revision and the Dictionary of Occupational Titles (U.S. Dept. of Labor, 1965). Where occupations were listed for both parents, the higher status occupation was used.

[b]Unweighted mean of the 6 sex/age groups.

Table 2-2
Items Deleted from Factor Analyses Because They
were Reported for <5% of Children[a]

Group	Items
Boys 4–5	55. Overweight; 78. Smears or plays with bowel movements; 101. Truancy, skips school; 105. Uses alcohol or drugs.
Girls 4–5	56d. Problems with eyes; 72. Sets fires; 78. Smears or plays with bowel movements; 91. Talks about killing self; 101. Truancy, skips school; 105. Uses alcohol or drugs; 106. Vandalism
Boys 6–11	73. Sexual problems; 78. Smears or plays with bowel movements; 105. Uses alcohol or drugs; 110. Wishes to be of opposite ssex.
Girls 6–11	6. Bowel movements outside toilet; 28. Eats or drinks things that are not food; 59. Plays with own sex parts in public; 72. Sets fires; 78. Smears or plays with bowel movements; 105. Uses alcohol or drugs; 106. Vandalism.
Boys 12–16	6. Bowel movements outside toilet; 28. Eats or drinks things that are not food; 59. Plays with own sex parts in public; 70. Sees things that are not there; 78. Smears or plays with bowel movements; 107. Wets self during the day; 110. Wishes to be of opposite sex.
Girls 12–16	6. Bowel movements outside toilet; 28. Eats or drinks things that are not food; 59. Plays with own sex parts in public; 60. Plays with own sex parts too much; 72. Sets fires; 78. Smears or plays with bowel movements; 107. Wets self during the day.

[a]Items *56h. Other physical problems* and *113. Other problems not listed above* were also excluded from all factor analyses.

Analytic Procedures

For each sample, a principal components analysis was performed on the Pearson correlations among the items that were reported for at least 5% of the sample. Because there is no unique criterion for rotation to simple structure, orthogonal (varimax) and oblique (direct quartimin) rotations were both performed on varying numbers of factors to identify the most robust. From the different rotations, we selected the one comprising the most representative versions of factors that repeatedly recurred in the rotations for that sample. In all samples, a varimax rotation was chosen. The chosen rotations ranged from an 8-factor matrix for the 4-5-year-old girls to a 13-factor matrix for the 12-16-year-old boys.

CONSTRUCTION OF BEHAVIOR PROBLEM SCALES

From the varimax rotation chosen for each sex/age sample, we retained the factors that (*a*) remained most intact throughout the various rotations for a particular sample, and (*b*) had at least six items with loadings ≥ .30. These factors represent syndromes of characteristics that tend to occur together, as reported by parents. For each sex/age sample, we found either eight or nine factors that met criteria (*a*) and (*b*).

The items with the highest loadings on each of the retained factors were used to construct behavior problem scales for each sex/age group. For each group, the largest factor was comprised mainly of aggressive behavior. Among its numerous high-loading items, several items with loadings ≥ .30 also had loadings ≥ .30 on other factors. We therefore decided to retain only items loading ≥ .40 for the behavior problem scale based on this factor in each group. For all other factors, items loading ≥ .30 were retained for the behavior problem scales.

If an item's loading met the cutoff criterion on more than one factor (≥ .40 for the aggressive factor, ≥ .30 for all others), it was assigned to all the scales for which it met the cutoff criterion. Some items were therefore assigned to two scales, and a few were assigned to as many as three scales. The behavior problem scales thus reflect the fact that certain items are associated with more than one syndrome: Like fever in organic illnesses, a particular behavior problem may belong to more than one behavioral pattern.

As an example, we found that Item *93. Talks too much* had loadings exceeding our cutoff criterion on two very different factors for boys aged 6–11. The content of one of these factors is summarized by the label *Obessive-Compulsive,* whereas the second is the large *Aggressive* factor found in all our sex/age samples. Boys who are reported to talk too much *and* show many behaviors of the Obsessive-Compulsive syndrome may be very different from those who talk too much *and* show many behaviors of the Aggressive syndrome. Retaining the item on both scales reflects the different contexts in which it occurs and recognizes that its meaning may vary with the context.

LABELS FOR THE BEHAVIOR PROBLEM SCALES

Names for behavioral scales are always somewhat arbitrary and susceptible to criticism. The use of names has become especially problematic since the emergence of the anti-labeling movement, which stresses the potentially stigmatizing effects of labels (e.g., Mercer, 1975).

We initially tried to avoid labels by using numbers to designate our behavior problem scales. However, the lack of any intrinsic relation between the numbers and the content of the scales made communication difficult. Because most people translated the numbers into their own labels, their idiosyncratic labels impeded communication still further. We therefore sought names that summarize the items comprising each scale, especially the items having the largest factor loadings. The scale names are listed in Table 2-3, while the items of each scale, their factor loadings, and eigenvalues are listed in Appendix C.

Table 2-3

Syndromes Found Through Factor Analysis of the Child Behavior Checklist

Group	Internalizing Syndromes[a]		Mixed Syndromes	Externalizing Syndromes[a]	
Boys	Social Withdrawal	.83	Sex	Delinquent	.88
aged 4–5	Depressed	.73	Problems	Aggressive	.80
	Immature	.66		Schizoid	.60
	Somatic Complaints	.50			
Boys	Schizoid or Anxious	.81	Social	Delinquent	.87
aged 6–11	Depressed	.74	Withdrawal	Aggressive	.85
	Uncommunicative	.73		Hyperactive	.63
	Obsessive-Compulsive	.68			
	Somatic Complaints	.64			
Boys	Somatic Complaints	.81	Hostile	Hyperactive	.80
aged 12–16	Schizoid	.74	Withdrawal	Aggressive	.77
	Uncommunicative	.74		Delinquent	.75
	Immature	.58			
	Obsessive-Compulsive	.54			
Girls	Somatic Complaints	.79	Obese	Hyperactive	.80
aged 4–5	Depressed	.73		Sex Problems	.75
	Schizoid or Anxious	.67		Aggressive	.66
	Social Withdrawal	.61			
Girls	Depressed	.83		Cruel	.83
aged 6–11	Social Withdrawal	.81		Aggressive	.80
	Somatic Complaints	.69		Delinquent	.77
	Schizoid-Obsessive	.56		Sex Problems	.65
				Hyperactive	.59
Girls	Anxious-Obsessive	.82	Immature	Cruel	.87
aged 12–16	Somatic Complaints	.79	Hyperactive	Aggressive	.83
	Schizoid	.76		Delinquent	.79
	Depressed Withdrawal	.68			

[a]Syndromes are listed in descending order of the loadings shown for the second-order Internalizing and Externalizing factors (explained in Chapter 4). There are some small differences between the First Edition and Revised Edition in the arrangement of syndromes for boys and girls aged 4–5, as explained in Chapter 4.

The similarity of some scales to traditional diagnostic categories suggested labels already in the vocabulary of mental health workers. For example, the terms *Depressed, Obsessive-Compulsive,* and *Hyperactive* seemed apt for our empirically-derived syndromes resembling these traditional syndromes. (Because Item *8. Can't concentrate, can't pay attention for long* had a high loading on all versions of the Hyperactive factor, the syndrome could also be called "attention deficit with hyperactivity," like the DSM-III disorder of this type.) The terms *Aggressive* and *Delinquent* seemed to summarize the content of other syndromes without the need for inferential qualifiers such as "socialized," "unsocialized," or "undersocialized" that have often been applied to syndromes of this sort. Note that even where traditional labels are used, they are intended only descriptively. The term "Delinquent," for example, refers to the specific transgressions comprising the delinquent scale, rather than implying present or future criminal activity or adjudication.

Uncommunicative, Somatic Complaints, Social Withdrawal, Sex Problems, Immature, and *Cruel* are shorthand descriptive labels for syndromes that do not have very clear counterparts in traditional nomenclature.

The Schizoid Scale

Somewhat more problematic are syndromes that connote different nosological constructs to different mental health workers. The prime example is the syndrome we called *Schizoid,* which is particularly hard to summarize in a non-controversial way. Although the precise composition of the syndrome varied among the sex/age samples, it included Item *40. Hears things that aren't there (describe)* in all six of the sex/age samples and Item *70. Sees things that aren't there (describe)* in five of the six groups. (In the 12–16-year-old boys sample, Item 70 fell below our 5% prevalence criterion for inclusion in the factor analysis.)

With young children, it may seem hard to discriminate between age-appropriate fantasies and the deviance that would be implied by hearing or seeing nonexistent things at older ages. Could it be, therefore, that parents' reports of these items merely reflect age-appropriate fantasy? If so, perhaps the factor they formed should not be considered a syndrome of problem behavior. This seems unlikely, because the CBCL asks parents to describe the behavior scored on Items 40 and 70, and the scoring rules (Appendix A) specify that only behavior that properly fits the items should be counted.

The low frequencies with which parents report these items indicate that normative behavior is not likely to account for the factors found: In our clinical samples, the highest prevalence of *Hears things that aren't there* was 18% for 4–5-year-old boys; in no other clinical samples did the rate exceed 9%. In our nonclinical samples, the rates were not above 4% for any sex/age group. For *Sees things that aren't there,* no clinical group exceeded 10%, and no nonclinical group exceeded 5%.

For most of the sex/age groups, the Schizoid factor also included Item *84. Strange behavior (describe)* and/or Item *85. Strange ideas (describe)*. Although the reported prevalence of Item 84 reached a maximum of 24% in the clinical sample of 4–5-year-old boys, neither item was reported for more than 6% of the nonclinical samples at any age. The substantial loadings of these items on the same factor as *Hears things that aren't there* and *Sees things that aren't there* suggest a syndrome of disordered thinking and behavior. Several other multivariate studies have also identified a syndrome of this sort among disturbed children (see Achenbach & Edelbrock, 1978).

Yet, few children in our samples would be considered frankly psychotic or would have enough features of schizophrenia for a long enough period to meet the DSM-III criteria for schizophrenia. DSM-III's new category of Schizotypal Personality Disorder resembles our factor more closely than DSM-III's categories of Schizophrenic Disorder, Schizoid Personality Disorder, or Schizoid Disorder of Childhood or Adolescence. However, we named our scales before Schizotypal Disorder was split off from Schizoid Personality as an official diagnostic category. Furthermore, the term "schizotypal" implies a constitutional predisposition to schizophrenia (Meehl, 1962) that seems unwarranted as a descriptive term for our empirically-derived syndrome.

Some versions of our Schizoid syndrome contained enough items of other types to suggest alternative interpretations. In the 6-11-year-old boys' syndrome having highest loadings on *Hears things* and *Sees things,* for example, the following items also had loadings high enough to be retained for the behavior problem scale: *29. Fears certain animals, situations, or places, other than school; 30. Fears going to school; 50. Too fearful or anxious.*

The presence of Items 29, 30, and 50 suggests to some mental health workers that anxiety rather than the weak reality-testing implied by "schizoid" should be the defining feature of the syndrome. However, Item *50. Too fearful or anxious* loaded ≥ .30 on this factor in only two of the six sex/age groups (girls aged 4-5; boys aged 6-11). In both groups, furthermore, Item 50 had high loadings on other factors as well. Although we have added *Anxious* as an alternative title for this syndrome for girls aged 4-5 and boys aged 6-11, it seemed better to acknowledge the similarity of this factor across sex/age groups by also retaining *Schizoid* than to omit this label from these two groups.

Nevertheless, it should be remembered that we chose labels as shorthand summaries for the descriptive content of the behavior problem scales. Each scale is operationally defined by scores on the behavior problems comprising it. Because children receive quantitative scores on the scales (as described later), the scales are not equivalent to the categorical, yes-or-no diagnoses of traditional psychiatric nosology. Furthermore, whenever parents report items such as *Hears things, See things, Strange behavior,* and *Strange ideas,* the clinician should carefully inquire to determine the precise basis for the parents' reports.

Remember: Neither the Schizoid scale nor any other scale is directly equivalent to any clinical diagnosis. A high score on a behavior problem scale should never be the sole basis for conferring a diagnostic label.

Combination Scales

In certain sex/age groups, a particular factor included items that formed separate factors in other groups. The main instances of this were among the 12-16-year-old girls: Items that defined separate factors of depression and withdrawal in other groups were combined on one factor that we named

Depressed Withdrawal; likewise, items that defined separate factors of immaturity and hyperactivity elsewhere were combined in one factor that we named *Immature Hyperactive*. Also for this group, Item *50. Too fearful or anxious* was the highest loading item on a factor that otherwise resembled the Obsessive-Compulsive factor found in other groups. Because Item *29. Fears certain animals, situations, or places,* loaded on this factor as well, we named it *Anxious-Obsessive*. For the 6–11-year-old girls, many items that were on separate Schizoid and Obsessive factors in other groups were combined on a factor we called *Schizoid-Obsessive*.

SCORING THE BEHAVIOR PROBLEM SCALES

Our factor analyses were intended to determine which items occurred together in each sex/age group, as reported by parents. If an item loaded $\geq .30$ on a factor ($\geq .40$ on the Aggressive factor), it is included in the behavior problem scale based on the factor. Each item is given equal weight in computing scale scores. For example, a 6-year-old boy's total score on the Hyperactive scale is the sum of 1s and 2s his parent circled for him on the items of that scale. His raw score is thus a linear index of the degree to which he is reported to manifest the behavior of the syndrome represented by the scale. (Appendix A gives detailed hand scoring procedures, while Appendix B provides information on computer scoring.)

In scoring the scales, we did not use traditional factor scores or otherwise preserve the factor loadings. Our rationale for not weighting items according to their factor loadings was as follows:

1. Because traditional factor scores include a weighted score for every item in the factor analysis, the many items having low or negative loadings can collectively contribute as much variance to a factor score as the relatively few high-loading items that really define the factor. To take an extreme instance, the Somatic Complaints factor for boys aged 4–5 had six items loading $\geq .30$. Traditional factor scores for this factor could therefore be influenced as much by the 108 items having loadings $< .30$ as by the six items that carried the most weight in defining the factor.

2. Another alternative is to retain only the high-loading items (called "salients"), but to weight these items according to their factor scores. However, among items that all have substantial loadings, the precise numerical differences among the loadings are likely to be unreliable and to add error variance when used to weight raw scores in new samples (Cattell, 1978; Wainer, 1976).

3. Within a sample on which the factors are derived, there is usually a high correlation between scores obtained by using factor loadings to weight all items of a factor, weighting just the salients, and using the unweighted raw scores of the salients (Cattell, 1978).

4. Increasing the complexity of scoring by weighting items would reduce

the practical utility of the behavior problem scales, especially for hand scoring, without offering any clear advantages.

THE CHILD BEHAVIOR PROFILE

Once we had constructed the behavior problem scales, we arranged them in a profile which forms a major component of the Child Behavior Profile (other components will be discussed later). By viewing a child's scores in a profile format, the user gains a more comprehensive picture of the behavior problems reported by the child's parents than if the child's standing on each scale is considered separately. Figure 2-1 illustrates a hand-scored profile.

Although profiles of quantified dimensions have long been used for scoring personality and ability tests, the profile approach differs from traditional categorical approaches to behavior disorders. Categorical approaches, such as the DSM, require a yes-or-no decision about whether an individual has a particular disorder. This can mask quantitative and qualitative variations in patterns of behavior problems. As an example, consider Johnny and Billy, two boys who both meet the DSM-III criteria for Attention Deficit Disorder with Hyperactivity:

> Johnny shows extreme forms of the behavior specified in all five of the criteria listed by the DSM for inattention, all six listed for impulsivity, and all five for hyperactivity. Johnny also meets the other DSM criteria for Attention Deficit Disorder, including onset of the behavior before the age of 7, duration of at least 6 months, and absence of schizophrenia, affective disorder, and mental retardation. Johnny is therefore diagnosed as having an Attention Deficit Disorder with Hyperactivity. He does not meet the criteria for any other DSM disorder, but does show many of the behaviors listed as criteria for the DSM's various conduct disorders.
>
> Billy shows much milder forms of three out of the five DSM criteria for inattention (e.g., Billy is judged to be "easily distracted," but much less so than Johnny). Billy also shows milder forms of three out of six of the criteria for impulsivity and two out of the five for hyperactivity. He meets the additional criteria for onset before age 7, duration of at least 6 months, and absence of schizophrenia, affective disorder, and mental retardation. Like Johnny, Billy does not meet the DSM criteria for any other disorders, but he meets four of the criteria for Avoidant Disorder of Childhood, four of the criteria for Overanxious Disorder, and five of the criteria for Schizoid Disorder of Childhood.
>
> The DSM tells us that Johnny and Billy both manifest a single disorder — Attention Deficit Disorder with Hyperactivity. Yet, profiles of their behavior would show that their differences are greater than their similarities, even in terms of behavior listed as criteria for DSM diagnoses: Johnny would obtain higher scores than Billy on the inattention, impulsivity, and hyperactivity dimensions embodied in the DSM's Attention Deficit Disorder, as well as on dimensions representing the DSM's conduct disorder categories. Billy, by contrast, would obtain higher scores on dimensions representing DSM's Avoidant, Overanxious,

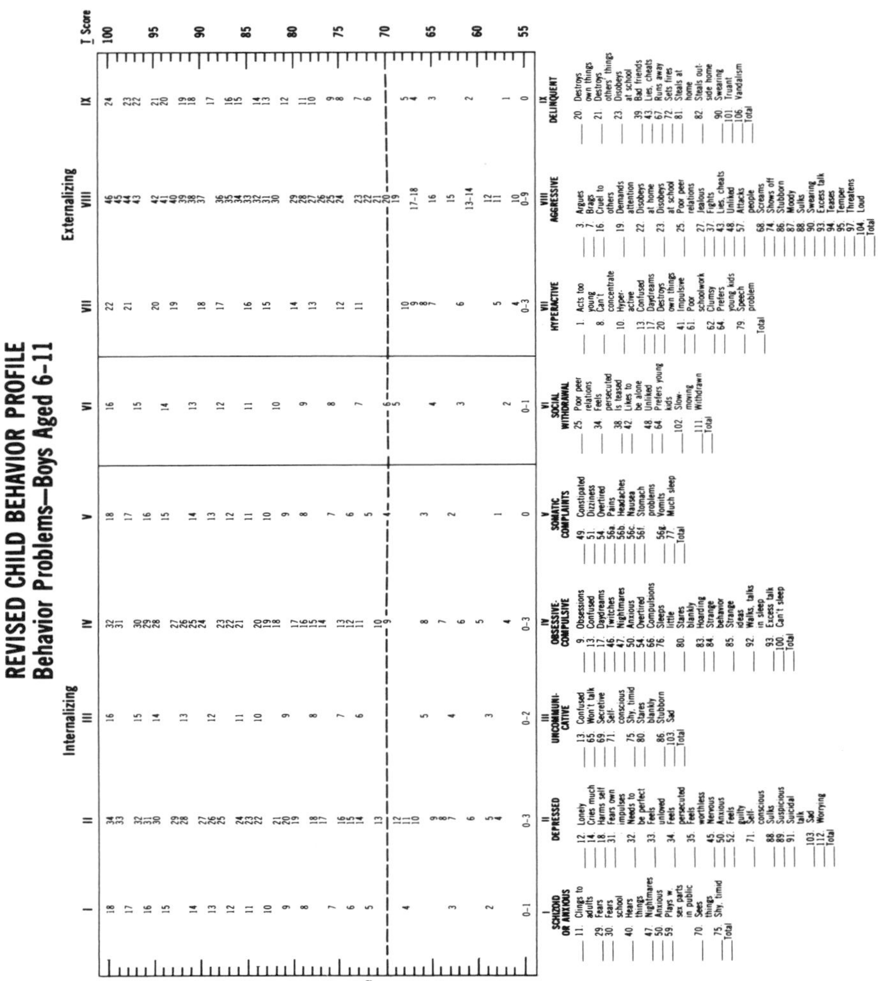

Figure 2-1. Behavior problem scales of the Revised Child Behavior Profile for boys aged 6-11.

and Schizoid disorders. In terms of overall behavior patterns, Johnny's problems mainly involve aggression, overt conflicts with other people, and a lack of self-control, whereas Billy's problems mainly involve anxiety, withdrawal, and social ineptness.

Because there is no litmus test for diagnosing most behavior disorders in a yes-or-no fashion, we considered it important to assess the *degree* to which children manifest various kinds of behavior problems. In some cases, the concentration of a child's problems exclusively in one area may argue for a categorical, yes-or-no diagnosis of the DSM type. In other cases, children's behavior problems may be distributed across several areas in a manner that is not accurately reflected by a single categorical diagnosis or even several categorical diagnoses. In either case, a profile of quantified dimensions preserves a more complete picture of the child's behavior than categorical diagnoses do. As discussed in Chapter 8, profiles can also be used as a basis for taxonomy of behavior problem patterns.

Behavior Problems Omitted from the Scales of the Profile

In each sex/age group, some items were omitted from the factor analyses because they were reported for less than 5% of the clinical sample (see Table 2-2). Other items did not have high enough loadings on any factors to be retained on a behavior problem scale. Being rare or lacking high factor loadings does not necessarily mean that an item is unimportant. It means only that the item does not help to *discriminate* statistically among the empirically derived syndromes for a particular sex/age group. Although these items are not scored on the behavior problem scales, they are listed under the heading of *Other Problems* on the Profile and are counted toward the child's total behavior problem score. The list of other problems does not receive a separate *T* score, because they have nothing in common to warrant scoring them as a scale. However, the clinician should consider each one as potentially important in its own right.

Missing Data

As indicated in the scoring instructions (Appendix A), the behavior problem portion of the Profile should *not* be scored if data are missing for more than 8 behavior problem items, not counting Items 56h and 113, unless it is clear that the respondent intended omitted items to be scored 0. If a respondent has omitted more than 8 items, information from the CBCL may be used informally, but would not be sufficiently comparable to our standardization data to warrant scoring on the Profile.

SUMMARY

To identify syndromes of behavior problems, we performed principal components analyses of CBCL behavior problems rated by parents of children referred for outpatient mental health services. Because the patterning and prevalence of behaviors may differ with the age and sex of the children, we performed separate analyses for children of each sex at ages 4 to 5, 6 to 11, and 12 to 16.

For each sex/age group, we found either eight or nine factors that remained intact through different rotations to simple structure. The items that had the highest loading on each factor were retained for behavior problem scales. The behavior problem scales were given descriptive labels to summarize the items comprising them. Although some of the descriptive labels correspond to traditional diagnostic terms, none of the scales is directly equivalent to any clinical diagnosis. A high score on a behavior problem scale should *never* be the sole basis for conferring a diagnostic label on a child.

To provide a comprehensive view of the behavior problems reported for a child, the behavior problem scales for each sex/age group are scored on the Child Behavior Profile. Items that were of low frequency or that had no high loadings on any of the factors retained for a particular sex/age group are listed under the heading of *Other Problems* on the Profile for that sex/age group.

Chapter 3
Norming the Behavior Problem Scales

We used clinical samples for our factor analyses in order to detect clinically significant syndromes. However, it is also important to compare a child with normative samples of agemates. Knowing that a 10-year-old boy has a score of 20 on the Aggressive scale, for example, does not tell us whether he is any more or less aggressive than most other 10-year-old boys. Because all children have at least some behavior problems, positive scores on the behavior problem scales do not necessarily indicate deviance.

To provide a basis for comparing children's behavior problem scores with those of normative groups of agemates, we obtained CBCL ratings from parents of randomly selected children who had not received mental health services for at least the preceding year. Some of the children in our samples might not be considered "normal" even though they were not receiving mental health services, but actual referral provided an operational criterion more feasible than individual clinical assessments, which are generally of low reliability anyway (see Achenbach & Edelbrock, 1981, pp. 56–57).

To obtain normative data, we sent interviewers to randomly selected homes in Washington, D.C., Maryland, and Northern Virginia, an area encompassing over 3,000,000 residents in urban, suburban, and semirural environments. Using census tract data on socioeconomic, race, and age distributions, we randomly selected blocks from census tracts to obtain a sample that approximated the socioeconomic and racial distribution of our clinical sample (reported in Chapter 2).

City directories were used to select residents living in the target blocks. Letters were then sent to these residents, indicating that an interviewer would visit the home to request information on the interests, skills, and behavior of one child. Residents who had *no* children between the ages of 4 and 16 living with them were asked to return an enclosed postpaid postcard indicating their address.

If no postcard was received from an address within about 10 days, an interviewer went to the home. If no parent or parent-surrogate was home, the interviewer returned later, making at least one visit on a weekend in order to avoid biasing the sample against families in which parents were absent because of work. When contact with a parent was made, the interviewer presented the letter that had been sent initially. If the parent consented to be interviewed, the interviewer began as follows:

> I would like to ask you some questions about one of your children. I will not ask your name or your child's name. No one in your family will be identified in any way, and all information will be strictly confidential. First, what are the age and sex of any children you have who are 4 through 16 years old and living here with you? Have any of them been seen at a child guidance clinic or other mental health agency during the

past year? Or for evaluation or treatment by a psychologist or psychiatrist? Okay, now I'd like to ask you about just one of your children. Let's take the ____-year-old boy/girl (selected according to a random number table as described below). Here are the questions I'd like to ask (CBCL is given to interviewee). I'll read each question, and when you give your answer, I'll code your answer onto this sheet (IBM Opscan form). Okay? Before I start the questions about your child, what is your occupation? And your (spouse's) occupation?

The interviewer then asked each question on the CBCL and recorded the responses on the IBM Opscan form. To preserve anonymity, no names or addresses were recorded. The interview was designed to approximate the general conditions under which parents fill out the CBCL in clinical settings. The interviewer answered parents' questions about the specific meaning of items but did not attempt to elicit information beyond the response choices provided on the CBCL. Where there was more than one child in a family between the ages of 4 and 16 who had not received mental health services within the preceding year, the interviewer consulted a random number table containing listings for each sex at each of the ages from 4 to 16. The choice of a child within a family was determined by the first entry in the table that corresponded to a child within that family. The relevant entry in the table was crossed off when the interview was completed, making the selection procedure a random one without replacement. When interviews had been obtained for a total of 50 children of a particular age and sex, all entries corresponding to that age and sex were crossed off the interviewers' tables.

The interviews were conducted from September through December 1976, by five female interviewers. A black interviewer visited the predominately black neighborhoods and white interviewers the predominately white neighborhoods. Of the 1,752 parents reached, interviews were completed with 1,442 (82.3%). The remaining 17.7% included refusals and some who were willing to be interviewed but could not do so when the interviewer called or at subsequent mutually convenient times. No attempt was made to persuade reluctant parents to be interviewed, since participation was purely voluntary and information from unwilling respondents would be of questionable validity.

After excluding children who had received mental health services during the previous year, we drew samples of 50 of each sex at each age having SES and race distributions like those of our clinical samples.[1]

In our normative samples, the overall racial distribution was 80.5% white, 18.2% black, and 1.3% other. Mothers provided the CBCL data for 83.1% of the children, fathers for 13.5%, and others, such as relatives and foster parents, for 3.4%. Table 3-1 shows the distribution of occupations of our narmative samples in terms of Hollingshead's seven categories.

---

[1]The nonclinical samples used to norm the scales of the Profile closely overlap the samples for which we reported item analyses in our 1981 S.R.C.D. *Monograph*. However, the samples reported in the *Monograph* excluded children of race other than white or black in order to confine analyses to those races. Because races other than white and black accounted for less than 2% of our samples, the findings reported in the *Monograph* would have been quite similar if the present samples were used.

Table 3-1
Percent of each Occupational Level for Parents of
Children in the Normative Sample

	Boys			Girls			Combined
	4-5	*6-11*	*12-16*	*4-5*	*6-11*	*12-16*	*Groups*[b]
Occupational Level[a]	*N = 100*	*N = 300*	*N = 250*	*N = 100*	*N = 300*	*N = 250*	*N = 1300*
1. Executives, large proprietors, major professionals	17	9	14	12	16	14	14
2. Managers, medium proprietors, lesser professionals	17	13	15	13	16	15	15
3. Administrative personnel, small independent proprietors, minor professionals	15	18	21	22	17	21	19
4. Clerical, sales, technicians, owners of little businesses	11	14	11	15	15	11	13
5. Skilled manual employees	22	25	22	26	22	22	23
6. Machine operators, semi-skilled employees	7	12	8	8	9	8	9
7. Unskilled employees	10	8	8	4	5	8	7
Mean	3.7	4.1	3.7	3.8	3.6	3.7	3.8
SD	1.9	1.7	1.8	1.6	1.7	1.8	1.8

Note—Because of rounding, columns may not sum to 100%.

[a]1 = highest level, 7 = lowest level scored according to Hollingshead's (1957) scale, supplemented with Hollingshead's (1975) draft revision and the Dictionary of Occupational Titles (U.S. Dept. of Labor, 1965). Where occupations were listed for both parents, the higher status occupation was used.

[b]Unweighted mean of the 6 sex/age groups.

ASSIGNING NORMALIZED *T* SCORES

To provide a common metric across scales differing in raw scores, we used the normative data to derive standard scores for our factor-based behavior problem scales. Within each sex/age sample, we first computed the cumulative frequency distribution of total scores on each behavior problem scale. For example, the scores obtained by each of the 300 6–11-year-old boys in our normative sample on all the items of the Aggressive scale were summed to obtain each boy's total score for the Aggressive scale. Using percentiles derived from the cumulative frequency distribution of these 300 scores, we assigned normalized T scores to raw scores at each percentile, as specified by Abramowitz and Stegun (1968).

Like ordinary T scores, normalized T scores have a mean of 50 and a standard deviation of 10 when derived from a normal distribution of raw scores. However, rather than being based on the standard deviation of the raw scores, they are based on the *percentiles* of the distribution of raw scores in such a way as to transform non-normal distributions into more normal ones. We used normalized T scores to provide a uniform calibration between percentiles and standard scores across the behavior problem scales. The percentiles make it easy for clinical users to compare a child's score on each scale with scores obtained by our normative samples, while the T scores are useful for statistical purposes. For reasons explained in the following sections, the mean T score exceeds 50 on all our narrow-band behavior problem scales (see Appendix D for means, standard deviations, and standard errors of measurement in demographically-matched clinical and nonclinical samples).

T Scores in the First Edition of the Profile

In the First Edition of the Profile, T scores for the behavior problem scales were based on percentiles that started with the lowest percentile for a particular scale and ranged up to the 99.9th percentile (T score = 80). The lowest percentile varied from scale to scale, because the percentage of children obtaining a score of 0 varied from one scale to another. On the most skewed scales, 50% or more of the normative sample scored 0. As a result, the lowest possible T score for these scales was 50 or higher.

On less skewed scales, small percentages of the children obtained a score of 0, 1, and each of several other low scores. This meant that T scores on a scale of this sort could range well below 50. The most extreme case was on the Aggressive scale for 4–5-year-old boys, where only about 2% of the normative sample obtained a score of 0. As a result, a raw score of 0 was equal to a T score of 30 on this scale.

Because the lowest possible T score varied from one scale to another, a child who obtained a raw score of 0 on every scale could nevertheless have T scores that differed substantially from one scale to another. For example, a 7-year-old girl who obtained a score of 0 on all scales would receive a T score of 32 on the Aggressive scale but 57 on the Delinquent scale. Because all the T scores would be well within the normal range, this would *not* imply that the girl was more deviant on the scales where a raw score of 0 equaled a T score well below 50. Yet, some users may have been misled by profile patterns that mainly reflected differences in the T scores assigned to the lowest raw scores on different scales.

T Scores in the Revised Edition of the Profile

Low Scores. To reduce differences in the lowest T scores obtainable on the various scales, the Revised Edition of the Profile assigns a T score no lower than 55 to the lowest raw score on each scale. A T score of 55 is equivalent to the 69th percentile. For scales having raw scores at or below the 69th percentile, these raw scores are all given a T score of 55.

Because more than 69% of a sample obtained a score of 0 on a few scales, the lowest possible T score for these scales is above 55. The highest of these, *Sex Problems* for the 4–5-year-old girls, starts with a T score of 59. Of the others starting from a T score above 55, two start with a T score of 57: The *Delinquent* scale for girls aged 6–11 and the *Cruel* scale for girls aged 12–16. Three scales start with a T score of 56: *Sex Problems* for boys aged 4–5; *Cruel* for girls aged 6–11; and *Somatic Complaints* for girls aged 12–16. Note that T scores of 56, 57, or 59 are the lowest possible for these scales, whereas a T score of 55 is the lowest possible for all other behavior problem scales.

On scales having several raw scores below the 69th percentile, our decision to collapse these low raw scores into a single T score of 55 reduces the differentiation among children obtaining the lowest raw scores. However, the loss of differentiation at the low end of these behavior problem scales is of little importance, since it concerns small differences among children who are all well within the normal range. If differentiation at the low end is nevertheless desired for assessing differences that are within the normal range, raw scale scores may be used in preference to T scores.

High Scores. At the upper end of the behavior problem scales, T scores for the First Edition were based as closely as possible on percentiles ranging up to a T score of 80 (99.9th percentile). However, the top percentiles represented very few subjects in the normative samples. Furthermore, some of the distributions of scores were discontinuous at these high percentiles. As a result, a difference of one point in raw scores sometimes produced large differences in T scores. Even though this does not violate the rationale for normalized T scores, the small number of subjects and the interpolations needed to derive fractional percentiles at the top of the distribution weakened the calibration of T scores and percentiles.

The tenuous relations between raw scores, T scores, and percentiles at the upper extreme produced some large gaps around the point where we wish to distinguish between the normal and clinical range. In the Revised Edition, we therefore based T scores on percentiles only up to the 98th percentile (T score = 70). Furthermore, at the top of the clinical range, we extended the T scores up to 100 (instead of 90 as on the First Edition). This permits more differentiation among the scale scores of children obtaining exceptionally high scores, such as those in inpatient settings.

On each scale of the Revised Edition, we derived the T scores from 71 to 100 by dividing raw scores above the 98th percentile into 30 intervals. T scores from 71 to 100 were then assigned to the intervals in succession. For example, for the 6–11-year-old boys, a raw score of 20 constituted the 98th percentile of the Aggressive scale, but a maximum score of 46 was possible on the 23 items of the scale. There are 26 raw scores from 21 through 46 and 30 possible T scores from 71 through 100. We therefore divided 30 by 26 to find the size of each interval. Because $30/26 = 1.15$, a T score interval of 1.15 was assigned to each raw score. Thus, a raw score of 21 was assigned a *T* score of 71.15, rounded off to 71. A raw score of 22 was assigned a *T* score of 72.30, rounded off to 72, and so on. A look at the sample Profile in Figure 2-1 should help to make this clear.

Assigning Normalized *T* Scores to Total Behavior Problem Scores

The total behavior problem score is simply the sum of the 1s and 2s circled by the parent on the behavior problems of the CBCL. There are 118 behavior problem items, plus spaces for parents to write in and score additional physical problems without known medical cause and other problems that are not listed. As specified in the scoring instructions (Appendix A), one additional physical problem and one additional nonphysical problem can be counted toward the total score. Total scores can therefore range from 0 (if a parent circles 0 on every item) to 240 (if a parent circles 2 on all 118 behavior problems listed on the CBCL and circles 2 for an additional physical problem and 2 for an additional nonphysical problem).

We derived normalized *T* scores for the total behavior problem scores in much the same way as we did for the behavior problem scales. However, there were two differences:

1. The total number of items is much greater than the number on any behavior problem scale, and nearly all parents endorse at least some of them. Consequently, few children in our normative samples obtained extremely low total behavior problem scores. It therefore seemed unnecessary to set a minimum *T* score at which to group low raw scores as we did for the behavior problem scales. Instead, we based normalized *T* scores directly on the percentiles of the distribution of total scores obtained by our normative samples, up to the 98th percentile (*T* score = 70).

2. No child in either our normative or clinical samples obtained anywhere near the highest possible score of 240. If we had assigned *T* scores above the 98th percentile by dividing all the top raw scores into the 30 intervals formed by *T* scores from 71 to 100, we would have compressed scores actually obtained by our clinical samples into a narrow range of *T* scores. We would also have assigned scores above those actually obtained to a broad range of *T* scores. For example, the highest total score obtained in our clinical sample of 12- to 16-year-old boys was 117. If we had assigned equal *T* score intervals to the raw scores from the 98th percentile (raw score = 59) to the highest possible raw score (240), only 10 *T* scores would have been allocated for the 58 raw scores that we actually found, whereas 20 would have been allocated for the 123 above that.

   To allow the upper *T* scores to reflect differences among raw scores actually apt to occur, we assigned a *T* score of 89 to the highest raw score found in our clinical sample for each sex/age group. The raw scores from the 98th percentile to the highest raw score were then assigned T scores in equal intervals from 71 to 89. The raw scores above the highest actually found in our clinical sample were assigned T scores in equal intervals from 90 through 100. (Appendix A lists the T score assigned to each total raw score for each sex/age group.)

SUMMARY

We obtained normative data by sending interviewers to randomly selected homes in Washington, D.C., Maryland, and northern Virginia. Census tract data were used to obtain a sample that approximated the socioeconomic and racial distributions of our clinical sample. From each participating family, one child who had received no mental health services during the previous year was randomly selected as the subject on whom a parent provided CBCL data.

Data on 50 children of each sex at each age from 4 to 16 were used to provide norms for the scales of the Child Behavior Profile (total $N = 1300$). Normalized T scores were derived from the distribution of raw scores on each behavior problem scale for each sex/age group. Because of the large proportion of very low scores on many of the scales, all scores falling at or below the 69th percentile in the normative samples were assigned a T score of 55. T scores from 55 to 70 were based on the percentiles of the normative samples, ranging from the 69th to the 98th percentile. T scores from 71 to 100 were derived by dividing all the remaining raw scores of a scale into 30 intervals.

For the total behavior problem score, normalized T scores were based entirely on percentiles up to a T score of 70 (98th percentile). We then assigned T scores from 71 to 89 to raw scores in intervals ranging from the 98th percentile of the normative sample to the highest score obtained in the clinical sample of each sex/age group. The remaining possible raw scores, up to the maximum of 240, were assigned T scores in intervals from 90 to 100.

Chapter 4
The Internalizing-Externalizing Dichotomy

Although our factor analyses showed that either eight or nine syndromes could be identified from CBCL ratings of each sex/age group, much of the child clinical literature has focused on two broad-band groupings of behavior problems. These groupings have been repeatedly identified in other multivariate analyses (for reviews, see Achenbach & Edelbrock, 1978; Quay, 1979). They reflect a distinction between fearful, inhibited, overcontrolled behavior, and aggressive, antisocial, undercontrolled behavior. They have been variously called Personality Problem versus Conduct Problem (Peterson, 1961), Inhibition versus Aggression (Miller, 1967), Internalizing versus Externalizing (Achenbach, 1966), and Overcontrolled versus Undercontrolled (Achenbach & Edelbrock, 1978).

DERIVING BROAD-BAND GROUPINGS

Because broad-band groupings of behavior problems may be useful for certain purposes, we performed second-order principal components analyses of our factor-based narrow-band behavior problem scales. We did this as follows:

1. Within the clinical samples on which we did our first-order factor analyses, we computed each child's raw score on the eight or nine behavior problem scales for that sex/age group.
2. We then converted each child's raw scores to the normalized T scores that had been derived from the normative samples (described in Chapter 3). Because some items were scored on more than one factor-based behavior problem scale, we counted these items only on the scale that they loaded highest on in each sex/age group.
3. We computed Pearson correlations among the T scores on the behavior problem scales for each sex/age group.
4. We performed principal components analyses of the intercorrelations among the behavior problem scales.
5. We performed varimax and direct quartimin rotations of all principal components having eigenvalues > 1.00.

For all groups, we obtained two second-order factors corresponding to the dichotomy between overcontrolled and undercontrolled behaviors found in other studies. The exact composition of the factors varied from one group to another, owing to differences in the composition of the narrow-band scales from which they were derived and differences in the alignment of the narrow-band scales on the second-order factors. However, they were similar enough to the Internalizing-Externalizing dichotomy found previously (Achenbach, 1966) to be given the same names. Table 2-3 (Chapter 2) shows the loadings of the narrow-band scales that defined the second-order Internalizing and Externalizing factors.

On the Child Behavior Profile, the narrow-band scales are arranged in the order of their loadings on the second-order factors: Starting at the left of the Profile, the scale having the highest loading on the Internalizing factor is followed by those having progressively lower loadings on the Internalizing factor; then come those having progressively higher loadings on the Externalizing factor; the Profile ends on the right with the scale having the highest loading on the Externalizing factor. For each sex/age group, the leftmost scale is thus the most extreme Internalizing scale and the rightmost scale is the most extreme Externalizing scale for that sex/age group.

For most sex/age groups, one scale had moderate loadings on both the Internalizing and Externalizing factors. It was therefore placed in the middle of the Profile, between the Internalizing and Externalizing groupings, and is not counted as part of either one.

Owing to changes in the composition of the first-order factors and the increased size of our clinical sample, the second-order factors for girls aged 4–5 changed somewhat from the First Edition to the Revised Edition. The second-order factor analysis of the revised *T* scores for boys aged 4–5 also produced a slightly different ordering of the behavior problem scales on the Internalizing factor than in our second-order factor analysis of the First Edition *T* scores. In the new order, which is reflected in the arrangement of behavior problem scales on the Revised Profile, *Somatic Complaints* is shifted from number II to number IV; *Depressed* is number II; and *Immature* is number III. However, because all these scales remained part of the second-order Internalizing factor, the items included in the Internalizing (and Externalizing) scores are the same on the First Edition and Revised Edition.

NORMING THE INTERNALIZING AND EXTERNALIZING GROUPINGS

To provide norm-referenced scores for Internalizing and Externalizing, we summed the scores obtained by members of each normative sample on all the Internalizing items and all the Externalizing items. Items belonging to more than one Internalizing scale were counted only once in the Internalizing score, and items belonging to more than one Externalizing scale were counted only once in the Externalizing score. However, items belonging to both an Internalizing and an Externalizing scale were each counted once in both the Internalizing and Externalizing scores.

Assigning Normalized *T* Scores

Within each sex/age group, the distributions of total raw scores for Internalizing and Externalizing were used to derive normalized *T* scores in the same way as for the total behavior problem scores, as explained in Chapter 3. This procedure is similar to that followed for Internalizing and Externalizing in the First Edition, except that the First Edition based T scores up to 80 on percentiles and assigned a T score of 90 to all raw scores above the highest in the clinical sample, whereas the Revised Edition bases T scores on percentiles up to a T score of 70 and assigns T scores of 90–100 to the raw scores above the highest in the clinical sample.

To assess a child's behavior problems in terms of the broad-band Internalizing-Externalizing distinction, hand-scored versions of the Profile provide a table for entering and summing all the Internalizing items and all the Externalizing items. The table also indicates the T score assigned to each total raw score for Internalizing and Externalizing (see Appendix A for detailed instructions). The computer-scored versions of the Profile automatically provide the child's raw scores and T scores for Internalizing and Externalizing (Appendix B).

RELATIONS BETWEEN INTERNALIZING AND EXTERNALIZING SCORES

Although the Internalizing and Externalizing groupings reflect contrasting types of behavior problems, they are not mutually exclusive. The degree and direction of correlation between them depends on characteristics of the sample studied. The average of the Pearson correlations between total Internalizing and total Externalizing T scores in the six clinical samples that we factor analyzed was .48. Across our six normative samples, the average correlation was .63. (In computing these correlations, we deleted the few items that are scored on both an Internalizing scale and an Externalizing scale, but Appendix E presents the correlations for all sex/age groups without deletion of redundant items.)

Even without the few overlapping items, there is clearly a positive association between behaviors that have often been viewed as opposites. This is because there is a general dimension among behavior problems that resembles the general (g) dimension among ability tests: Individuals who score very high in one area tend to be above average in other areas as well, whereas individuals who score very low in one area tend to be low in other areas.

Despite the positive association between Internalizing and Externalizing found in our samples as a whole, however, some children's behavior problems are primarily Internalizing, whereas other children's problems are primarily Externalizing. This is analogous to the relation between Verbal IQ and Performance IQ on the Wechsler intelligence tests: Across groups, there is a positive correlation between the Verbal and Performance IQ but some individuals have much lower scores in one area than the other. For these individuals, different scores in different areas form a pattern which distinguishes them from those whose scores show the opposite pattern.

How large must the difference between scores be in order to mark a child as an Internalizer or Externalizer? This depends on the user's purpose. The stringency of criteria for classifying children as Internalizers versus Externalizers will affect the proportion of children classified, the homogeneity of the resulting groups, and the strength of the association between the Internalizing-Externalizing dichotomy and other variables of interest. For example, very stringent criteria will cause a small proportion of children to be classified as Internalizers or Externalizers and a large proportion to remain unclassified. But stringent criteria will also produce relatively pure groups of Internalizers and Externalizers who are likely to differ more on other variables than would less pure Internalizing and Externalizing groups.

The trade-offs between stringency of criteria, proportion of children classified, and degree of association with other variables must be judged by users of the Profile in light of their own purposes. However, we suggest that children not be classified as Internalizers or Externalizers unless (*a*) their total behavior problem score exceeds the 90th percentile for their sex/age group *and* (*b*) there is a difference of at least 10 points between their Internalizing and Externalizing T score. Requiring the total score to exceed the 90th percentile insures that children have enough behavior problems to be in the clinical range (see Table 7-6 for 90th percentile scores). Otherwise, the discrepancy between Internalizing and Externalizing scores may be based on too few items to be meaningful.

The larger the difference between T scores, the "purer" the Internalizing and Externalizing groups will be. As discussed in Chapter 8, overall Profile patterns can also be used as a basis for classifying children as Internalizers and Externalizers.

SUMMARY

Second-order factor analyses of our behavior problem scales showed that the scales form two broad-band groupings in all sex/age groups. The broad-band groupings correspond to the distinction between fearful, inhibited, overcontrolled behavior and aggressive, antisocial, undercontrolled behavior that has long been familiar to those who work with children. We call these groupings *Internalizing* and *Externalizing,* respectively. On each version of the Child Behavior Profile, the narrow-band behavior problem scales are arranged according to their loadings on the second-order factors: Starting at the left of the Profile, the scale with the highest loading on the Internalizing factor is followed by those with progressively lower loadings on the Internalizing factor and then those with progressively higher loadings on the Externalizing factor, ending on the right with the scale having the highest loading on the Externalizing factor. For most sex/age groups, one scale had moderate loadings on both the Internalizing and Externalizing factors and is not counted as part of either one. T scores for Internalizing and Externalizing are derived from the same normative samples as the T scores for the narrow-band behavior problem scales.

Like Verbal IQ and Performance IQ on ability tests, the Internalizing and Externalizing scores are positively correlated with each other across entire samples of children. However, some children have much higher scores on one broad-band grouping than the other. The stringency of criteria for classifying children as Internalizers or Externalizers should be based on the user's objectives. We suggest that children not be classified as Internalizers or Externalizers unless their total behavior problem score exceeds the 90th percentile for their sex/age group *and* there is a difference of at least 10 points between their Internalizing and Externalizing T scores.

Chapter 5
Social Competence Scales

As discussed in Chapter 1, there had been less previous research on social competence than behavior problems. We began by testing various types of items expected to discriminate between disturbed and normal children. After discarding several other approaches, we settled on the items now included on pages 1 and 2 of the CBCL (Appendix A gives detailed scoring procedures).

Clinically-referred children scored lower than demographically-matched nonreferred children on each of these items, as detailed in our (1981) *Monograph*. Table 2 on page 45 of the *Monograph* indicates that the difference between referred and nonreferred children was not significant on two of the items (Number of sports and Participation in activities). This was because we excluded the least significant differences, up to the number that could be significant by chance, given the number of tests done. Considered by themselves without this conservative correction for the number of analyses, these two items both showed significant differences between referred and nonreferred children (F values of 7.97 and 11.73, $df = 1/2570$; both $p < .01$).

The nature of our social competence items makes them less appropriate than our behavior problem items for deriving dimensions or syndromes via multivariate analyses. This is because scores on some items are intrinsically dependent on other items. On the items pertaining to sports, nonsports activities, organizations, and jobs and chores, for example, parents can rate the amount and quality of their child's participation only if they also report that their child is actually involved in a specified activity.

We designed our scoring rules to minimize artifactual correlations between the *number* of activities of a particular type and *ratings* of quality and amount of participation. For example, a child reported to like one sport gets the same score (0) as a child reported to like no sports. However, only the child who likes at least one sport can get a score above 0 for amount and quality of participation. Thus, a score of 0 for number of sports can be accompanied either by a score of 0 or by a score above 0 for amount and quality of participation. Furthermore, because scores for amount and quality of participation are averaged over all sports reported, these scores do not automatically increase as the number of sports increases. Nevertheless, it would hardly make sense to use multivariate analyses to find out which of these intrinsically interdependent scores covary to form syndromes or dimensions as was done with the behavior problems. Instead, we grouped items into three scales designated as *Activities, Social,* and *School* on the basis of their content.

Missing Data

As indicated in the scoring instructions (Appendix A), if data are missing for one item on the Activities or Social scale, the mean of the other five items is substituted for the missing item to obtain the total score for the scale.

However, if data are missing for any of the four items of the School scale, a total score should not be calculated for this scale.

NORMING THE SOCIAL COMPETENCE SCALES

The School scale is not scored for 4–5-year-olds, but the scoring rules are otherwise the same for all sex/age groups. However, the total raw scores obtained on each scale are transformed into normalized T scores derived from our normative sample of a child's age and sex. Thus, like T scores on the behavior problem scales, T scores on the social competence scales do not represent *absolute* quantities, but show how children *compare* with a normative sample of agemates of the same sex, as reported by their parents.

Assigning Normalized T Scores

T scores for the social competence scales were derived from the same normative samples as T scores for the behavior problems. However, the distributions of raw scores for the behavior problem scales in the normative samples are *positively* skewed, whereas scores on the social competence scales are *negatively* skewed, owing to the large proportion of nonreferred children receiving high scores. Furthermore, *high* scores are clinically significant on the behavior problem scales, whereas *low* scores are clinically significant on the social competence scales. To take account of this reverse pattern and the need for finer differentiation between low scores than between high scores on the social competence scales, we reversed two of the procedures used in deriving T scores from the raw scores on the behavior problem scales.

1. At the top end of each social competence scale, we assigned a T score of 55 to all raw scores at the 69th percentile and above. We did this because about 30% of children in our normative samples obtained the highest possible score (6.0) on the School scale. This meant that a very small difference in raw scores (5.5 versus 6.0) could produce a disproportionately large difference in T scores. Furthermore, like the *low* end of the behavior problem scales, differences at the *high* end of the social competence scales are unlikely to be important, since they are well within the normal range.

2. At the low end of the scales, we based T scores on percentiles down to the second percentile (T score $= 30$). We then divided the remaining raw scores into T score intervals down to a T score of 10. Because there are fewer possible raw scores below the second percentile of the social competence scales than above the 98th percentile of the behavior problem scales, we assigned the low social competence scores a range of only 20 T scores (29 to 10), instead of 30 T scores (71 to 100) as done for the clinical range (highest scores) on the behavior problem scales.

As a result of our changes in assigning T scores, the T scores for the social competence scales of the Revised Edition of the Profile range from 10 to 55.

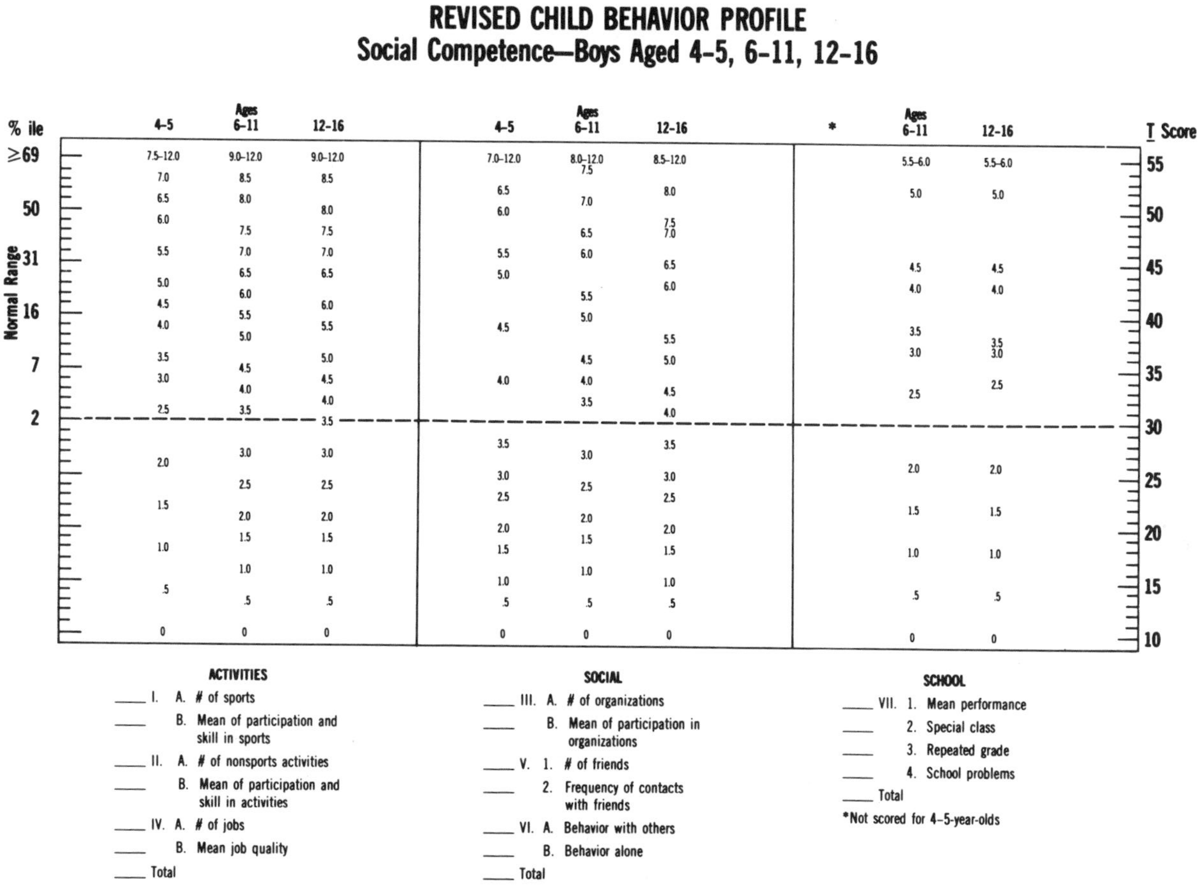

Figure 5-1. Social competence scales of the Revised Child Behavior Profile for boys.

This covers the same number of T score intervals (46) as the behavior problem scales. Owing to the greater skew of the behavior problem scores, only 16 of the T score intervals (T = 55 to 70) of the behavior problem scales are in the normal range, whereas 30 (T = 71 to 100) are in the clinical range. For the social competence scales, by contrast, 26 of the T score intervals (T = 30 to 55) are in the normal range, whereas 20 (T = 10 to 29) are in the clinical range.

A minor change in the layout of the social competence scales on the hand-scored version of the Revised Edition should be noted: As shown in Figure 5-1, the distributions of raw scores for all three age groups of boys are now printed side-by-side for each scale and likewise for all three age groups of girls. Users of the hand-scored profile should therefore be careful to use the column of scores appropriate for the age of the child being scored.

Assigning Normalized T Scores to Total Social Competence Scores

Because the School scale is not scored for 4–5-year-olds, their total social competence scores can range from 0 to 24 (i.e., sum of scores ranging from 0 to 12 on the Activities scale and 0 to 12 on the Social scale). By contrast, the total social competence scores for 6–16-year-olds can range from 0 to 30 (i.e., sum of scores ranging from 0 to 12 on the Activities and Social scales and from 0 to 6 on the School scale).

We used the distribution of raw scores in our normative samples to obtain T scores for the total social competence score (listed in Appendix A). For the Revised Edition of the Profile, we did this by basing normalized T scores on the percentiles of the distribution of raw scores in our normative samples from the second percentile (T = 30) to the highest possible raw score (T = 80). We then divided the raw scores below the second percentile into T score intervals from a T score of 29 down to a T score of 10.

SUMMARY

The social competence scales encompass parents' reports of their child's participation and performance in areas designated as Activities, Social, and School. The School scale is not scored for 4–5-year-olds, but the scoring rules are otherwise the same for all sex/age groups. The total raw scores obtained on each scale are transformed into normalized T scores derived from our normative samples of each sex and age. Unlike the behavior problem scales, *low* scores on the social competence scales are clinically significant. A total social competence score is obtained by summing the raw scores on the social competence scales. This total score can be converted to a T score based on our normative samples.

Chapter 6
Reliability, Interparent Agreement, and Stability

There are many forms of reliability and many ways to assess it. It would therefore be misleading to offer any single number as representing the overall reliability of the CBCL or Child Behavior Profile. Instead, we computed various indices of agreement to assess forms of reliability that are relevant for different purposes. The following sections deal with the reliability of individual items on the CBCL and the reliability of scores on scales of the Profile.

RELIABILITY OF ITEM SCORES ON THE CBCL

We computed the intraclass correlation coefficient (ICC) from one-way analyses of variance (Bartko, 1976) to assess various types of reliability in scoring the behavior problem and social competence items of the Child Behavior Checklist. Used in this way, the ICC reflects the proportion of total variance in item scores that is associated with differences among the items themselves, after the variance due to a specific source of unreliability has been subtracted.

It should be noted that the ICC can be affected both by differences in the *rank ordering* of the correlated scores and differences in their *magnitude*. More commonly used correlational indices of reliability — such as the Pearson correlation — reflect mainly differences in *rank ordering*. These correlations can therefore be large even when the two sets of correlated scores differ markedly in magnitude. For example, if Rater A scores every subject 10 points lower than Rater B, their ratings can nevertheless have a Pearson correlation of 1.00. This reflects the identical rank ordering of subjects by both raters, despite the numerical differences in the scores they assign each subject.

On the other hand, *tests of differences* between the *magnitudes* of two sets of scores can obscure differences in rank ordering. For example a *t* test of the difference between scores assigned by Rater C and Rater D might show no significant differences, suggesting good agreement. Yet, the Pearson correlation between their ratings may be .00, reflecting no agreement in their *ranking* of subjects.

Agreement in rank ordering is especially important for some purposes, whereas agreement in the magnitude of scores is important for other purposes. We have assessed both kinds of agreement in scores on the scales of the Profile. However, the range of possible scores for individual items is small (3 points for all behavior problems and most social competence items). Neither correlation coefficients that reflect similarities of rank order nor tests of differences between scores therefore seem as appropriate as the ICC, which is affected by both aspects of variance. Because the ICC is applicable to all the types of item reliability we assessed, it also offers a common scale for comparing the relative amount of unreliability contributed by each source of variance.

Test-Retest Reliability of Item Scores

Test-retest reliabilities were computed from CBCLs obtained by a single interviewer who visited the mothers of nonreferred children at a 1-week interval. Ratings of nonreferred children were used to assess test-retest reliability, because their scores would be less susceptible to regression toward the mean than the scores of referred children. The overall ICC was .952 for the 118 behavior problems and .996 for the 20 social competence items ($N = 72$). Longer term stability was assessed by computing ICCs for CBCLs obtained from 12 mothers of nonreferred children at 3-month intervals. These ICCs were .838 for the 118 behavior problems and .974 for the 20 social competence items (all $p < .001$).

Interparent Agreement on Item Scores

This was computed from CBCLs independently filled out by mothers and fathers of 168 children being evaluated in mental health settings. The overall ICC was .985 for the 118 behavior problems and .978 for the 20 social competence items (both $p < .001$).

Inter-interviewer Reliability of Item Scores

Although the CBCL is designed to be self-administered, there are situations in which an interviewer administers it or is at least present to aid the respondent. In order to assess the effect of interviewer differences, we compared the results obtained by three interviewers who participated in the home interview survey that provided our normative data on nonreferred children (Achenbach & Edelbrock, 1981). Rather than having each interviewer administer the CBCL to the same parents—which would have confounded test-retest and inter-interviewer reliability—we compared the data obtained by each interviewer on 241 children who were matched for age, sex, race, and socioeconomic status to 241 children whose parents were interviewed by each of the other two interviewers. We thus compared the scores obtained by three interviewers on 241 matched triads of children, for a total sample of 723 children. The overall ICC was .959 for the 118 behavior problems and .927 for the 20 social competence items (both $p < .001$).

TEST-RETEST RELIABILITY OF SCALE SCORES

In order to assess agreement in both rank ordering and magnitude of scale scores, we computed test-retest reliabilities for raw scale scores in terms of Pearson correlations and t tests of differences between the scores. Table 6-1 presents the test-retest reliability of scores obtained from CBCLs filled out by mothers of nonreferred children at 1-week intervals.

In Table 6-1, reliabilities are shown separately for each sex/age group on the behavior problem scales, Internalizing, Externalizing, total behavior prob-

Table 6-1
One-Week Test-Retest Reliabilities

Behavior Problem Scales	Boys			Girls			Combined[d] Samples
	4–5 $N=11$	6–11 $N=13$	12–16 $N=15$	4–5 $N=13$	6–11 $N=16$	12–16 $N=12$	
Aggressive	.91	.95	.87	.92	.95	.93	.92
Anxious-Obsessive					.74		
Cruel					.94	.93	.92
Delinquent	.85	.95	.97		.94	.97	.92
Depressed	.62	.91		.84	.90[a]		.78
Depressed Withdrawal						.85	
Hostile Withdrawal			.88[ac]				
Hyperactive		.92[ac]	.90[a]		.98		.96[ac]
Immature	.87		.70				.81
Immature-Hyperactive						.82	
Obese				(.42)			
Obsessive-Compulsive		.82	(-.12)				.61
Schizoid (or Anxious)	.81	.84	.82	.65		.69	.86[ac]
Schizoid-Obsessive					.79[a]		
Sex Problems	(.48)			(.52)	(.22)		.68
Social Withdrawal	.74	.90		.96	.87		.91
Somatic Complaints	.96	.88	.93	.61	.96	.79	.87
Uncommunicative		.69	.82[ac]				.70
Internalizing	.83	.93[ac]	.83	.93	.93[a]	.81	.82[a]
Externalizing	.93	.95[ac]	.90	.94[ac]	.97	.96	.91[a]
Total Score	.89	.97[a]	.89	.95	.97[a]	.87	.91[a]
Social Competence Scales							
Activities	.83	.65	.80	.95	.68	.81	.83[b]
Social	.91	.84	.89[bc]	.93	.92	.98	.86
School		.96	.95		.89	.91	.89
Total Score	.92	.76	.93[bc]	.93	.80	.91[bc]	.89

Median r for entire Table = .89

Mean difference between Time 1 and Time 2 scores = .7

Note: Figures in the body of the Table are Pearson correlations of Time 1 vs. Time 2 scores for a sample of nonreferred children. Within each sex/age group, correlations are for raw scores. Correlations in the right hand column are for T scores of combined sex/age groups on scales that are similar in two or more groups. All correlations are significant at $p = .05$ or better, except those in parentheses.

[a] Time 1 > Time 2, $p < .05$ by t test

[b] Time 2 > Time 1, $p < .05$ by t test

[c] When corrected for the number of comparisons, Time 1 – Time 2 difference is not significant.

[d] N for combined samples = sum of the Ns for samples having reliabilities indicated in the same row as the combined sample.

lem score, social competence scales, and total social competence score. For scores that encompass similar items for two or more sex/age groups, Table 6-1 also shows reliabilities computed for the *T* scores of the combined groups. Because *T* scores show how an individual compares with his/her own group, they control for the effects of differences among the sex/age groups in the magnitude of the raw scores.

Test-Retest Correlations between Scale Scores

The Pearson correlations in Table 6-1 show reliability in terms of the *rank ordering* of scores, whereas the superscripts *a* and *b* indicate statistically significant changes in the *magnitude* of scores from the first to the second ratings. As pointed out earlier, these are two different facets of reliability that may be important for different purposes.

Of the 110 Pearson correlations, 105 were statistically significant at $p = .05$ or better. The median correlation for the entire table was .89. Of the five correlations that were not statistically significant, three were on the Sex Problems scale for all three sex/age groups that had this scale; one was on the Obese scale for 4–5-year-old girls; and one was on the Obsessive-Compulsive scale for the 12–16-year-old boys. These nonsignificant correlations may be partly due to the small range and variance of scores, reflecting the lack of these particular problems in the nonclinical test-retest samples.

When all three samples having a Sex Problems scale were combined, the test-retest correlation for their *T* scores was .68. When both samples having an Obsessive-Compulsive scale were combined, the correlation was .61. Both of these were statistically significant at $p < .001$, but they were the lowest of all the test-retest correlations for combined samples. (Table 6-2 shows a significant *interparent* correlation of .63 for the Obsessive-Compulsive scale for boys 12–16 but nonsignificant correlations for the Sex Problems scales in individual clinical samples, although there was a significant correlation of .26 for Sex Problems in the Combined Samples. Table 6-4 shows a significant test-retest correlation of .64 over 6 months and .46 over 18 months for the Obsessive-Compulsive scale among clinically-referred 12–16-year-old boys. It also shows a significant correlation of .56 over 6 months and .80 over 18 months for the Sex Problems scale among clinically-referred 6–11-year-old girls.)

Test-Retest Changes in Mean Scale Scores

Over the 1-week interval, *t* tests showed significant differences between Time 1 and Time 2 scores in 21 out of the 110 comparisons at $p < .05$. Eleven out of 110 are expected to be significant by chance (using a .01 protection level; Feild & Armenakis, 1974; Sakoda, Cohen, & Beall, 1954). It would therefore be legitimate to exclude the 11 comparisons that surpass the nominal .05 level of significance by the smallest amount. These 11 are marked with the superscript *c* in Table 6-1.

Whether or not we exclude the 11 comparisons expected to be significant by chance, the trend of the differences was consistent: Where there were significant changes in ratings across the 1-week period, all of them showed either *decreases* in reported behavior problems or *increases* in reported competencies. Decreases in reported problems for nonreferred children re-rated over brief periods have also been found with other rating scales (Evans, 1975; Milich et al, 1980; Miller et al, 1972). These findings probably do not reflect regression toward the mean, because they involve nonclinical samples that were not selected for deviance in initial scores. It thus appears that there is a tendency for nonreferred children to be presented in a somewhat more favorable light when re-rated over periods too short for their behavior to actually change much. However, this tendency is of relatively small magnitude. The largest significant difference between mean Time 1 and Time 2 scores was 3.2 points (26.4 versus 23.2 for the total behavior problem score for boys aged 6–11). The mean of the 21 nominally significant differences was 1.4 points, and the mean of all differences was .7.

AGREEMENT BETWEEN MOTHERS' AND FATHERS' SCALE SCORES

Table 6-2 shows relations between raw scale scores derived from mothers' and fathers' ratings of their clinically-referred children in terms of Pearson correlations and *t* tests of differences between the scores. For scales that were similar across two or more groups, Table 6-2 shows correlations and *t* tests of differences between the *T* scores for mothers' and fathers' ratings of the combined groups.

Correlations between Mothers' and Fathers' Scale Scores

Of the 110 correlations, 94 were statistically significant at $p = .05$ or better. The median correlation for the entire table was .66. One of the 16 nonsignificant correlations was for boys, while the other 15 were for girls. This is partly because the smaller sample sizes for girls cause a correlation of a particular magnitude to achieve lower statistical significance. The magnitudes of the correlations also tended to be slightly smaller for girls than boys (mean correlation for girls = .62 versus .69 for boys, computed by z transformation), but this difference did not approach statistical significance ($z = .04$, $p > .90$).

Mother-Father Differences in Mean Scale Scores

Our *t* tests showed fathers' scores to be significantly higher than mothers' scores in 2 comparisons and mothers' scores to be significantly higher in 14. Both comparisons in which fathers' scores were higher involved social competence scales, as did 3 of the 14 comparisons in which mothers' scores were higher. The actual size of the differences between fathers' and mothers' scores was small, with the largest significant difference being 2.8 *T* score points (43.8

Table 6-2
Interparent Agreement

Behavior Problem Scales	Boys 4-5 N=33	Boys 6-11 N=78	Boys 12-16 N=40	Girls 4-5 N=11	Girls 6-11 N=21	Girls 12-16 N=24	Combined[d] Samples
Aggressive	.72	.80[ac]	.74	.68	.33	.53	.72[a]
Anxious-Obsessive						(.34)	
Cruel					.65	.82	.69
Delinquent	.61[ac]	.83	.83		.87	.80	.78[ac]
Depressed	.68	.59		(.51)	(.09)		.54
Depressed Withdrawal						(.16)	
Hostile Withdrawal			.55				
Hyperactive		.61	.62	.74	.81		.65
Immature	.79[a]		.71				.69
Immature-Hyperactive						.66	
Obese				.71			
Obsessive-Compulsive		.62	.63				.57
Schizoid (or Anxious)	.79	.54	.64	.88		(.06)	.53
Schizoid-Obsessive					.47		
Sex Problems	(.32)			(.50)	(.07)		.26
Social Withdrawal	.69	.62[ac]			.83	.51	.58
Somatic Complaints	.84	.47	.70	.73	.73	(.19)	.63[ac]
Uncommunicative		.58	.69				.63
Internalizing	.77	.61	.71	.74	(.35)	(.19)	.59[a]
Externalizing	.74	.77[ac]	.72	.70	.55	.68	.75[ac]
Total Score	.75	.65	.69	.64	(.40)	(.40)	.64[a]
Social Competence Scales							
Activities	.47[ac]	.54	.60	(.08)	.54	.64[ac]	.44[a]
Social	.68	.66	.72	(.41)	.74[bc]	.71	.66
School		.79[bc]	.84		.91	.83	.81
Total Score	.52	.67	.77	(.23)	.73	.82	.59

Median *r* for entire Table = .66
Mean difference between mothers' and fathers' scores = 1.2

Note: Figures in the body of the Table are Pearson correlations of scores from CBCLs filled out by mothers and fathers of clinically-referred children. Within each sex/age group, correlations are for raw scores. Correlations in the right hand column are for *T* scores of combined sex/age groups on scales that are similar in two or more groups. All correlations are significant at $p = .05$ or better, except those in parentheses.

[a]Mothers' scores > fathers' scores, $p < .05$

[b]Fathers' scores > mothers' scores, $p < .05$

[c]When corrected for the number of comparisons, Mother-Father difference is not significant.

[d]*N* for combined samples = sum of the *N*s for samples having reliabilities indicated in the same row as the combined sample.

versus 41.0 on the Activities scale for the combined samples). The mean of the 16 nominally significant differences was 1.5 and the mean of all differences was 1.2. The 11 significant differences that can be expected by chance in 110 comparisons are marked with the superscript c in Table 6-2.

It thus seems clear that the overall scores yielded by CBCLs filled out by mothers and fathers do not differ much, on the average. When two parents do disagree markedly, the reasons should be explored rather than being dismissed as merely due to intrinsic differences between mothers and fathers. If one parent reports many more problems than the other, it should be asked whether this reflects such factors as one parent's ignorance, lack of tolerance, greater sensitivity, poor reality testing, or more negative impact on the child. These are important considerations in planning how to help the child and family, as discussed further in Chapter 10.

STABILITY AND CHANGE IN THE SCORES OF CLINICAL SAMPLES

Changes in ratings of children receiving clinical services reflect a variety of factors, including the effects of treatment, changes that might occur without treatment, and changes in raters' judgements that are determined by their own attitudes and behavior toward the children, as well as actual changes in the children themselves. Our data on stability and change should not be viewed as direct indices of any single factor, but as multidetermined reflections of how disturbed children are seen by important adults at different points in time. If there were no consistency from one rating period to another, this would cast doubt on the ability of the ratings to capture enduring individual differences. Yet, if there were no long-term changes in ratings of treated children, this would cast doubt on the sensitivity of the ratings to changes that might actually occur. Users who wish to assess treatment effects, outcomes, or longitudinal changes can refer to our findings as guidelines for the degree of stability and change likely to be found for heterogeneous samples receiving eclectic residential or outpatient treatment.

3-Month Stability and Change for Inpatients

Table 6-3 presents Pearson correlations and significant changes in scores for 6–11-year-old boys in residential treatment whose parents and child care workers independently filled out the behavior problem portion of the CBCL at 3-month intervals. The social competence scales were not assessed, because residential treatment precludes meaningful variation in many of the social competence items. The boys had behavior disorders severe enough to warrant residential treatment averaging about 9 months, but they were not mentally retarded or significantly brain-damaged. The treatment program was eclectic, employing contingency management for the modification of specific behaviors, but also social milieu therapy, psychotherapy, medication, work with parents, and structured schooling in small classes. Because children went home for weekends, holidays, and vacations, parents remained important informants about their children's behavior.

Table 6-3
Stability and Change for Inpatient Boys
Aged 6-11 Over 3 Months

Behavior Problem Scales	Parents' Ratings	Child Care Workers' Ratings
Schizoid or Anxious	.86	(.51)
Depressed	.69[ab]	.80
Uncommunicative	.55[ab]	.81
Obsessive-Compulsive	.86	.75
Somatic Complaints	.81[a]	.63
Social Withdrawal	.56[ab]	.69
Hyperactive	.47	.78
Aggressive	.69[a]	.84
Delinquent	.83[ab]	.51
Internalizing	.85[a]	.75
Externalizing	.66[ab]	.77
Total Score	.76[a]	.78
Mean r (computed by z transformation)	.74	.73

Note—All correlations are significant at $p = .05$ or better, except the one in parentheses. $N = 14$ in both groups.
[a]Time 1 > Time 2, $p < .05$ by t test.
[b]When corrected for the number of comparisons, Time 1–Time 2 difference is not significant.

The mean of the correlations for parents' and child care workers' ratings is quite similar over the 3-month period (.74 for parents versus .73 for child care workers), and all but one of the correlations was significant. However, the parents' ratings showed significant decreases in 9 of the 12 behavior problem scores whereas the child care workers' ratings showed significant changes in none of the scores. This could indicate that the children's behavior improved more during home visits than in the treatment center. It underlines the importance of separately assessing the stability of *rank ordering* in scores, which was similar for parent and child care worker ratings, and changes in the *magnitude* of scores, which occurred in parent ratings but not child care workers' ratings.

6-Month and 18-Month Stability and Change for Outpatients

Table 6-4 presents Pearson correlations and significant changes in parents' ratings of 6–16-year-olds seen in a community guidance clinic. (There were too few 4–5-year-olds for analysis.) The first rating was obtained at intake into the clinic, while the follow-up ratings were obtained by mailing CBCLs to parents at 6- and 18-month intervals thereafter. Parents who did not respond to the mailing were telephoned, but the sample size decreased from the first to the

Table 6-4
Stability and Change for Outpatients
over 6 and 18 Months

	6 Months				18 Months			
	Boys		Girls		Boys		Girls	
Behavior	6-11	12-16	6-11	12-16	6-11	12-16	6-11	12-16
Problem Scales N=	135	66	57	37	41	20	17	27
Aggressive	.69[a]	.76	.70[a]	.79[ac]	.76[a]	.73[a]	.76[ac]	.46
Anxious-Obsessive				.72[a]				(.32)
Cruel			.66[a]	.76[a]			.81	.72
Delinquent	.71[ac]	.71[a]	.65[a]	.69	.80[a]	.61	.83	.70
Depressed	.67[a]		.67[a]		.66[a]		.63	
Depressed Withdrawal				.73[a]				.62[a]
Hostile Withdrawal		.72[a]				.58[a]		
Hyperactive	.73[a]	.76[a]	.71[a]		.72[a]	.57[a]	.55[ac]	
Immature		.68[a]				(.41[ac])		
Immature-Hyperactive				.62				.70[a]
Obsessive-Compulsive	.68[a]	.64[a]			.67[a]	.46		
Schizoid (or Anxious)	.66[a]	.44[ac]			.71[a]	.49[a]		
Schizoid-Obsessive			.50[a]	.54			.50[ac]	(.36[ac])
Sex Problems			.56[a]				.80[a]	
Social Withdrawal	.65[a]		.66[a]		.69[a]		.73[a]	
Somatic Complaints	.57	.62	.53[ac]	.57[ac]	.69[a]	.53[a]	(.35)	.40
Uncommunicative	.70[a]	.53[a]			.66[a]	(.36[a])		
Internalizing	.72[a]	.59[a]	.62[a]	.68[a]	.75[a]	(.34[a])	.59[ac]	.39[a]
Externalizing	.73[a]	.74[a]	.72[a]	.75[a]	.81[a]	.67[a]	.77[a]	.59
Total Score	.74[a]	.71[a]	.71[ac]	.73[a]	.77[a]	(.44[a])	.89[a]	.51[a]
Mean r (computed by z transformation)	.69	.67	.65	.69	.74	.53	.71	.53
Social Competence Scales								
Activities	.60[b]	.62	.65	.70	.55[b]	(.14)	(.49)	.70
Social	.59[b]	.61	.47[b]	.54	.56[bc]	.51	.51[b]	.85
School	.56	.70	.68	.70	.63	.87	(.56)	(.46)
Total Score	.71[b]	.58	.70[b]	.58	.70[b]	.59	(.28)	.87
Mean r (computed by z transformation)	.62	.63	.64	.63	.62	.59	.47	.76

Note—Not enough 4–5-year-olds were available for analysis; all correlations are significant at $p = .05$ or better except those in parentheses; Ns vary within groups because of missing data for some scales.

[a]Time 1 > Time 2 or Time 3 significant by t test at $p < .05$.

[b]Time 2 or Time 3 > Time 1 significant by t test at $p < .05$.

[c]When corrected for the number of comparisons, difference in means is not significant.

second follow-up, owing to moves, loss of cooperation, and, in some cases, parents' loss of contact with their children. The clinic was eclectic in orientation. Many children received some form of one-to-one psychotherapy, but behavior modification, family therapy, medication, and group therapy were also used.

The mean correlations for the behavior problem scales are in the .60s for all sex/age groups over the 6-month follow-up period. There is more variation over the 18-month period, however, with mean correlations ranging from .47 for the 6–11-year-old girls' competence scores to .76 for the 12–16-year-old girls' competence scores. Most of the behavior problem scores showed significant *decreases* from intake to both follow-up periods, while 9 of the 32 competence scores showed significant *increases*. Although behavior problem scores improved in all groups, the competence scores improved significantly only among 6–11-year-olds. The lack of improvement in the competence scores of 12–16-year-olds does not reflect a ceiling effect imposed by the CBCL, because most of the initial scores for 12–16-year-olds were *lower* than those for 6–11-year-olds. Instead, the lack of improvement may reflect the greater difficulty of changing the types of behavior tapped by the CBCL competence items among adolescents than among younger children.

SUMMARY

Because there are many forms of reliability and many ways to assess it, it would be misleading to express the overall reliability of the CBCL and Profile in terms of any single number. We therefore assessed test-retest reliability, inter-rater agreement, and longer-term stability.

For individual *items*, we computed intraclass correlations (ICCs) between item scores obtained from mothers filling out the CBCL at 1-week intervals, mothers and fathers filling out the CBCL on their clinically-referred children, and three different interviewers obtaining CBCLs from parents of demographically matched triads of children. All these ICCs were in the .90's. The ICC for 3-month stability of mothers' ratings of individual items was .838 for behavior problems and .974 for social competence items.

For *scale scores* and *total problem* and *competence scores*, the median Pearson correlation for 1-week test-retest reliability of mothers' ratings was .89. Nominally significant changes in scores from the first to the second rating occurred in 21 out of 110 comparisons, although 11 would be expected by chance. The significant changes reflected a small tendency to report fewer problems and more competencies from the first to the second ratings.

The median Pearson correlation between mothers' and fathers' ratings was .66. Nominally significant differences between mothers' and fathers' ratings occurred in 16 out of 110 comparisons, although 11 would be expected by chance and all the differences were small. Two of the differences reflected higher scores by fathers, while 14 reflected higher scores by mothers. Because the scores obtained from mothers' and fathers' ratings do not differ much on the average, major disagreements found between ratings by the mother and father of a child are likely to be clinically important and should be explored further.

Test-retest correlations for inpatients' scores over a 3-month period averaged .74 for parents' ratings and .73 for child care workers' ratings of behavior problems. The parents' ratings showed significant decreases in problem scores on most scales, but the child care workers' ratings showed no significant changes.

Test-retest correlations for outpatients' scores over a 6-month period were in the .60s for both behavior problem and competence scores. Over an 18-month period, mean correlations ranged from .46 to .76 for problem and competence scores in the various sex/age groups. Most behavior problem scores improved (decreased) significantly over the 6- and 18-month periods. Competence scores improved (increased) significantly only for 6–11-year-olds.

Chapter 7
Validity

The concept of validity pertains to the accuracy with which a procedure measures what it is supposed to measure. Like reliability, the question of validity has multiple answers.

CONTENT VALIDITY

The most elementary form of validity is *content validity*—i.e., whether a measure's content includes what it is intended to measure. Chapter 1 presented our procedures for assembling CBCL items that tap a broad range of problems and competencies of clinical concern to parents and mental health workers. As documented in detail by Achenbach and Edelbrock (1981), clinically-referred children received significantly higher scores ($p < .005$) than demographically similar nonreferred children on 116 of the 118 behavior problem items. The only two items showing nonsignificant differences were Item *2. Allergy* and *4. Asthma*. On all 20 social competence items, the clinically-referred children received significantly *lower* scores ($p < .01$) than the nonreferred children. These findings indicate that the items of the CBCL indeed relate to independently established mental health concerns. However, prospective users should judge whether the content of the CBCL is appropriate for their particular purposes.

CONSTRUCT VALIDITY

Construct validity is perhaps the most discussed but elusive form of validity. For variables that lack a standard operational criterion, construct validity involves a "nomological network" of interrelated procedures intended to reflect the hypothesized variables in different ways (Cronbach & Meehl, 1955). It was the *lack* of satisfactory constructs and operational definitions for childhood behavior disorders that prompted us to develop the CBCL in order to assess parents' perceptions of their children's behavioral problems and competencies. A key index of the validity of the resulting measures is their ability to identify children whose behavior problems arouse enough concern to warrant referral for professional help. This will be discussed in the section on criterion-related validity.

The total behavior problem score can be viewed as representing a dimension of behavioral problems analogous to the construct of general ability represented by total scores on intelligence tests. Similarly, the behavior problem scales of the Child Behavior Profile can be viewed as subgroupings of problems somewhat analogous to the subtests included in many general ability tests, such as the WISC-R. However, most ability subtests consist of items chosen to redundantly measure the hypothetical construct of a specific ability.

Our syndromes, by contrast, were empirically derived from covariation among items intended to be nonredundant.

The value of the empirically derived syndromes lies largely in their ability to use parents' reports to assess behavioral phenotypes, rather than to operationalize pre-existing taxonomic constructs. These phenotypes can guide inferences about relations between childhood behavior disorders and other variables and can be used to group children in order to test differences in etiology, prognosis, response to treatment, and outcomes (discussed further in Chapter 11). It remains to be seen, however, whether the phenotypic distinctions provided by the Profile will evolve into more formal constructs or whether they will function primarily as descriptive conveniences.

Relations between scores derived from the Child Behavior Checklist and roughly analogous scores from other instruments have been tested in several studies. Tables 7-1 and 7-2 show the Pearson correlations between raw scores on our Profile scales and raw scores on the Conners (1973) Parent Questionnaire and the Quay-Peterson (1983) Revised Behavior Problem Checklist scales whose content appeared most similar to our Profile scales. The data were obtained by having parents of 51 clinically-referred 6–11-year-olds fill out the three instruments in sequences that were counterbalanced across the sample. The children were being seen in 51 clinical settings distributed widely across the United States and Canada. Profile scales that lacked a counterpart among the Conners or Quay-Peterson scales are not listed in the tables.

In some cases, the correspondence between the actual items of the scales is minimal. For example, the Conners Learning Problem scale is comprised of the following items: *Has no friends*; *is not learning*; *does not like to go to school*; *will not obey school rules*. We paired this with our School scale, which is scored in the opposite direction and is comprised of ratings for academic performance, special class placement, repetition of grades, and an open-ended item for other school problems. Despite marked differences in many items, however, the correlations between all the narrow-band scales in Tables 7-1 and 7-2 are significant, except for the correlation of .26 between our Schizoid-Obsessive scale for 6–11-year-old girls and the Quay-Peterson Psychotic scale (Table 7-2).

Tables 7-1 and 7-2 also include correlations of our Internalizing and Externalizing scores with Conners and Quay-Peterson scales that seemed aligned with one of our broad-band groupings or the other. As the tables show, the correlations between our total behavior problem score and the total scores of the other instruments ranged from .71 to .92.

In another study, T scores on our narrow-band Profile scales showed the following significant correlations with Conners Parent Questionnaire ratings by 34 mothers of 6–11-year-old boys referred for evaluation of hyperactivity (Achenbach & Edelbrock, 1978): Conners Learning Problem with School, $r = -.59$; Conners Anxiety with Schizoid (or Anxious), $r = .64$, and with Depressed, $r = .54$; Conners Psychosomatic with Somatic Complaints, $r = .60$; Conners Impulsive-Hyperactive with Hyperactive, $r = .39$; Conners Conduct Problem with Aggressive, $r = .78$; Conners Antisocial with Delinquent, $r = .61$.

Table 7-1
Pearson Correlations Between Child Behavior Profile
and Conners Parent Questionnaire

Child Behavior Profile	Conners Parents Questionnaire Scale							
	Learning Problem	Anxiety	Perfectionism	Psychosomatic	Impulsive-Hyperactive	Conduct Problem	Antisocial	Total
Boys 6–11 (N=35)								
School	−.48[a]							
Schizoid or Anxious		.58						
Depressed		.73						
Obsessive-Compulsive			.58					
Somatic				.85				
Hyperactive					.46			
Aggressive						.84		
Delinquent							.77	
Internalizing		.58	.52	.62				
Externalizing					.45	.77	.65	
Total Problems								.77
Girls 6–11 (N=16)								
School	−.45[a]							
Depressed		.70						
Somatic Complaints				.44				
Hyperactive					.85			
Delinquent							.75	
Aggressive						.88		
Cruel						.76		
Internalizing		.59	.55	(.42)				
Externalizing					.91	.85	(.33)	
Total Problems								.91

Note — Correlations are between Child Behavior Profile and Conners scales that are most similar in content. All correlations are significant at $p = .05$ or better, except those in parentheses.

[a]Negative correlation because Profile scale and Conners scale are scored in opposite directions.

Table 7-2

**Pearson Correlations Between Child Behavior Profile
and Quay-Peterson Revised Behavior Problem Checklist**

Child Behavior Profile	Quay-Peterson Revised Behavior Problem Checklist						
	Psychotic	Anxiety-Withdrawal	Attention Problems-Immaturity	Motor Excess	Conduct Disorder	Socialized Aggression	Total
Boys 6–11 (N=35)							
Schizoid or Anxious	.40	.44					
Depressed		.78					
Uncommunicative		.62					
Obsessive-Compulsive	.61						
Social Withdrawal		.34					
Hyperactive			.65	.42			
Aggressive					.88		
Delinquent					.77	.52	
Internalizing	.51	.65					
Externalizing			.43	(.13)	.84	.43	
Total Problems							.71
Girls 6–11 (N=16)							
Depressed		.89					
Social Withdrawal		.78					
Schizoid-Obsessive	(.26)						
Hyperactive			.88	.88			
Delinquent						.80	
Aggressive					.82		
Cruel					.68	.72	
Internalizing	.45	.84					
Externalizing			.88	.92	.77	.75	
Total Problems							.92

Note—Correlations are between Child Behavior Profile and Quay-Peterson scales that are most similar in content. All correlations are significant at $p = .05$ or better, except those in parentheses.

In a study by Weissman, Orvaschel, and Padian (1980), total scores on the Conners Parent Questionnaire correlated .91 with T scores for total behavior problems on the CBCL filled out by mothers of 28 children aged 6 to 17. The CBCL total behavior problem score was significantly higher for children who had psychiatric disorders, according to Research Diagnostic Criteria, than for children who did not, whether the diagnosis was based on the children's self-reports or mothers' reports about their children ($p < .01$ in both cases). Mothers' and fathers' ratings on the Conners Abbreviated Rating Scale and the Werry–Weiss–Peters Activity Scale also correlated significantly with T scores for Externalizing ($r = .82$ to .87) and Internalizing ($r = .62$ to .72) in a sample of 91 hyperactive and normal children (Mash & Johnston, 1983).

These findings indicate reasonable agreement with measures that are rough counterparts of ours. The correlations between total scores on the CBCL and the Conners and Quay-Peterson are as high as found between intelligence tests. Similarly, the correlations between our Profile scales and Conners and Quay scale scores are as high as those often found between different scales designed to test the same specific abilities (e.g., Wechsler, 1974). Additional data on relations between Profile scores and other measures can be obtained from sources listed in Appendix F and from research currently under way.

CRITERION-RELATED VALIDITY

Because there were no well-substantiated diagnostic criteria corresponding to the scales of our Profile, we used referral for mental health services as a criterion against which to test the validity of the scales. We did this by comparing the scores obtained by children referred for outpatient mental health services with the scores obtained by demographically similar children who had not had contacts with mental health services for at least the preceding year. (Chapters 2 and 3 present details of the overall clinical and nonclinical samples.)

Referral status is not an infallible criterion of children's need for help. Some children in our clinical samples may have been referred because of custody disputes, parents' desire for help with their own problems, or excessive concern about behavior that is in the normal range. On the other hand, some children in our nonclinical samples may have been candidates for imminent referral. If we were able to exclude (a) referred children who should not be referred and (b) nonreferred children who should be referred, this could increase the differences between the scores of our clinical and nonclinical samples. Since we could not exclude such children, our findings may underestimate the power of the scores to identify children whose behavior warrants professional help. Yet, because mental health services were readily available in the localities that provided our data, actual referral seemed an ecologically more valid criterion than other alternatives, such as ad hoc clinical assessment (see Achenbach & Edelbrock, 1981, pp. 56–58 for further discussion of alternative criteria).

Our sampling procedure for obtaining data on nonreferred children was designed to approximate the socioeconomic (SES) and racial distributions found in our clinical sample, as reported in Chapters 2 and 3. To make the comparisons reported in this chapter, we drew CBCLs from both samples in such a way as to form groups matched for SES and race within each of the six sex/age groups. Because race was to be assessed as an independent variable, we selected only blacks and whites, since our samples did not include enough children of other races (< 2%) to be analyzed separately. Within each sex/age group, we then performed regressions of each scale score on the independent variables of clinical status (50% referred vs. 50% nonreferred); age (equal Ns at each age); race (approximately 20% black vs. 80% white); and SES (distribution on Hollingshead's 1957 7-step scale of parents' occupation shown in Chapter 3). The contribution of each independent variable was assessed with the other three held constant. Thus, any significant differences between CBCLs for referred and nonreferred children are not confounded with differences associated with age, race, or SES.

As mentioned at the beginning of this chapter, 116 of the 118 behavior problem items and all 20 of the social competence items discriminated significantly between the referred and nonreferred children, with the effects of age, race, sex, and SES controlled. To indicate the magnitude of the association of item scores with clinical status, Achenbach and Edelbrock (1981) reported the percent of variance in each item accounted for by each significant effect. For example, Item *103. Unhappy, sad, or depressed* showed larger effects of clinical status than any other single item, across all sex/age groups. We have followed the same general procedure here in analyzing the association of scale scores with clinical status for each of the six sex/age groups.

To provide a common index of effect sizes across all scales, Table 7-3 presents the percent of variance in each scale score that was accounted for by significant ($p < .05$) associations with clinical status, age, race, and SES. To take account of possible chance effects occurring in such a large number of statistical analyses, we have marked (superscript *e*) the nominally significant effects that could be excluded as chance findings, using a .01 protection level for the .05 *alpha* level (Feild & Armenakis, 1974; Sakoda et al, 1954). The effect size indicated for each independent variable is what remained after partialling out the other three variables. According to Cohen's (1977) standards for effect size when other independent variables are partialled out, regression coefficients accounting for 2 to 13% of the variance in a dependent variable represent *small* effects; coefficients accounting for 13 to 26% of the variance represent *medium* effects; and those accounting for 26% or more of the variance represent *large* effects.

Effects of Demographic Variables

Although collinearity between variables such as SES and race can reduce the independent contributions of each of them, our samples were selected to minimize collinearity by including a broad SES distribution for both races. For

Table 7-3
Percent of Variance Accounted for by Significant Effects of Clinical Status, Age, Race, and SES

Boys 4-5 N=200	Clinical Status[a]	Age[b]	Race[c]	SES[d]
Social Withdrawal	26	--	--	--
Depressed	22	--	--	--
Immature	32	--	--	--
Somatic Complaints	14	3[O]	--	--
Sex Problems	5	--	<1[eB]	3[eU]
Schizoid	16	--	--	--
Aggressive	35	--	--	2[eL]
Delinquent	23	--	--	4[L]
Internalizing	31	--	--	--
Externalizing	36	--	--	1[eL]
Total Problems	39	--	--	--
Activities	12	4[eO]	--	2[eU]
Social	25	--	1[eB]	--
Total Competence	22	--	--	2[eU]

Girls 4-5 N=200	Clinical Status[a]	Age[b]	Race[c]	SES[d]
Somatic	22	--	--	--
Depressed	20	--	--	--
Schizoid or Anxious	31	--	--	--
Social Withdrawal	26	--	--	3[eL]
Obese	13	--	--	2[eL]
Aggressive	22	--	--	6[L]
Sex Problems	11	--	--	--
Hyperactive	18	--	--	6[L]
Internalizing	37	--	--	2[eL]
Externalizing	26	--	--	7[L]
Total Problems	34	--	--	4[eL]
Activities	9	2[eO]	--	4[eU]
Social	24	3[eO]	--	6[U]
Total Competence	21	3[eO]	--	6[U]

Note—Percent of variance is listed for all effects significant at $p = .05$ or better.

[a] Referred children had significantly lower scores on all competence scales and significantly higher scores on all problem scales than nonreferred children at $p < .001$.

[b] O = higher scores for older children; Y = higher scores for younger children.

[c] B = higher scores for blacks; W = higher scores for whites.

[d] L = higher scores for lower SES; U = higher scores for upper SES.

[e] Not significant when corrected for the number of analyses.

Table 7-3 (cont'd)

Boys 6–11 N= 600	Clinical Status[a]	Age[b]	Race[c]	SES[d]
Schizoid or Anxious	21	1^{eY}	--	--
Depressed	31	--	--	--
Uncommunicative	28	--	--	--
Obsessive-Compulsive	26	--	--	--
Somatic Complaints	8	--	--	--
Social Withdrawal	29	--	1^{eW}	--
Hyperactive	35	--	--	--
Aggressive	33	--	--	--
Delinquent	38	--	--	1^{eL}
Internalizing	39	--	--	--
Externalizing	48	--	--	--
Total Problems	49	$< 1^{eY}$	--	--
Activities	11	--	--	4^{a}
Social	29	1^{eO}	--	1^{eU}
School	28	--	--	1^{eU}
Total Competence	35	1^{eO}	--	5^{U}

Girls 6–11 N= 600	Clinical Status[a]	Age[b]	Race[c]	SES[d]
Depressed	36	$< 1^{eO}$	1^{eW}	--
Social Withdrawal	34	--	--	--
Somatic Complaints	16	$< 1^{eO}$	--	--
Schizoid-Obsessive	22	--	--	--
Hyperactive	40	$< 1^{eO}$	--	--
Sex Problems	12	--	--	--
Delinquent	22	--	1^{eB}	1^{L}
Aggressive	35	--	--	$< 1^{eL}$
Cruel	22	--	--	1^{L}
Internalizing	43	--	--	--
Externalizing	45	--	--	$< 1^{L}$
Total Problems	48	--	--	$< 1^{L}$
Activities	11	1^{eO}	--	5^{U}
Social	28	--	--	1^{U}
School	34	--	--	1^{eU}
Total Competence	35	1^{O}	--	5^{U}

[a]Referred children had significantly lower scores on all competence scales and significantly higher scores on all problem scales than nonreferred children at $p < .001$.

[b]O = higher scores for older children; Y = higher scores for younger children.

[c]B = higher scores for blacks; W = higher scores for whites.

[d]L = higher scores for lower SES; U = higher scores for upper SES.

[e]Not significant when corrected for the number of analyses.

Table 7-3 (cont'd)

Boys 12-16 N=500	Clinical Status[a]	Age[b]	Race[c]	SES[d]
Somatic Complaints	18	--	--	--
Schizoid	16	--	--	--
Uncommunicative	26	--	< 1[eW]	--
Immature	23	2[Y]	--	--
Obsessive-Compulsive	20	--	--	< 1[eL]
Hostile Withdrawal	37	1[eY]	< 1[eW]	--
Delinquent	39	--	--	--
Aggressive	27	--	1[eW]	--
Hyperactive	38	--	--	< 1[eL]
Internalizing	37	--	--	--
Externalizing	43	--	--	--
Total Problems	44	< 1[eY]	--	--
Activities	13	3[Y]	--	4[U]
Social	32	--	--	--
School	33	--	--	2[U]
Total Competence	39	< 1[eY]	--	3[U]

Girls 12-16 N=500	Clinical Status[a]	Age[b]	Race[c]	SES[d]
Anxious-Obsessive	35	< 1[eY]	< 1[eW]	--
Somatic Complaints	27	--	--	--
Schizoid	19	--	--	--
Depressed Withdr.	36	--	--	--
Immature-Hyper.	29	1[eY]	--	--
Delinquent	45	--	--	--
Aggressive	29	1[eY]	--	--
Cruel	33	1[eY]	--	--
Internalizing	44	--	--	--
Externalizing	45	--	--	--
Total Problems	47	1[eY]	--	--
Activities	13	--	--	3[U]
Social	26	< 1[eO]	--	< 1[eU]
School	33	--	--	--
Total Competence	33	--	--	2[U]

[a]Referred children had significantly lower scores on all competence scales and significantly higher scores on all problem scales than nonreferred children at $p < .001$.

[b]O = higher scores for older children; Y = higher scores for younger children.

[c]B = higher scores for blacks; W = higher scores for whites.

[d]L = higher scores for lower SES; U = higher scores for upper SES.

[e]Not significant when corrected for the number of analyses.

the six sex/age groups taken separately, the point-biserial correlation between SES and race was .12 for girls aged 4–5; .22 for girls aged 6–11; .26 for boys aged 12–16; and .31 for the three remaining groups. Race and SES thus share from about 1 to 9% of variance in our samples.

Because both race and SES were partialled out of the regression coefficients for clinical status, their collinearity would not distort the percent of variance obtained for clinical status. The collinearity of race and SES could reduce the percent of variance credited to each of them, but, as Table 7-3 shows, all the effects of race and SES are small. In the few instances where both of them accounted for significant variance, the sum of their effects still constitutes only a small effect, and much less than the effect of clinical status. Most of the SES effects reflect a tendency for lower SES parents to report fewer competencies and more problems than upper SES parents, which is consistent with higher rates of diagnosed psychopathology in lower SES children (Davie, Butler, & Goldstein, 1972; Rutter et al, 1974). However, the effects are small enough to prevent most nonreferred low SES children from scoring in the clinical range. Mean scale scores are presented separately for lower, middle, and upper SES children in Appendix D.

Race had very few effects on scale scores, and none accounted for more than 1% of the variance.

Age effects on the social competence scales reflected slightly higher scores for older than younger children in some groups. On the behavior problem scales, scores on three scales increased with age among 6–11-year-old girls, but scores on five scales decreased with age among 12–16-year-old girls. None of these effects exceeded 1% of the variance.

As Table 7-3 shows, deletion of the nominally significant effects expectable by chance would eliminate most of the effects of the demographic variables. Those that remain are all quite small according to Cohen's (1977) criteria. Most are so much smaller than the effects of clinical status that they are not likely to affect the power of the scale scores to discriminate between children like those in our clinical and nonclinical samples.

Effects of Clinical Status

The effect of clinical status was significant at $p < .001$ for all scores in all sex/age groups, accounting for a large percent of variance ($\geq 26\%$) in most cases. The mean scores, standard deviations, and standard errors of measurement for the clinical and nonclinical groups are presented in Appendix D.

Among the behavior problem scales, the only small effects of clinical status were for Somatic Complaints among boys aged 6–11 (8%) and Sex Problems for all three groups having this scale (5% for boys aged 4–5; 11% for girls aged 4–5; 12% for girls aged 6–11). The low raw scores on these scales restrict the magnitude of group differences, but even the smallest difference was significant at $p < .001$. The Activities Scale also showed small effects of clinical status (9 to 12%) for 4- to 11-year-olds of both sexes.

The total behavior problem score showed the largest effect of clinical status in all groups except girls aged 4–5, for whom it was second only to Internalizing. The percent of variance in total score accounted for by clinical status ranged from 34% for 4–5-year-old girls to 49% for 6–11-year-old boys (Table 7-3). These effects represent differences in mean T scores ranging from 16 to 18 points and differences in mean raw scores ranging from 34 to 39 points (Appendix D).

The stronger association of clinical status with total behavior problem score than with the other scale scores is understandable in light of the much greater breadth and number of problem behaviors represented by the total score than by the scores on specific scales. Because most clinically-referred children are not equally deviant in all areas, each specific scale reflects differences between only some of the clinically-referred and nonreferred children, whereas the total behavior problem score includes all the problems of all the scales, plus problems that are not included on the specific scales. As a global index of need for help, then, the total behavior problem score is likely to be superior to any of the more specific scales.

To delineate the relation of total problem scores to clinical status, Table 7-4 shows the probability of particular scores being from our clinical sample of each sex and age. This was determined by tabulating the number of children from our clinical and nonclinical samples who had each total behavior problem score. The probabilities shown in Table 7-4 represent the proportion of children within each range of scores who were from the clinical sample. The proportion from the clinical sample generally increases as the scores increase. The few exceptions are relatively minor: Once a .50 probability is reached, all the succeeding scores have probabilities > .50 of being from the clinical sample. Users can refer to this table to estimate the likelihood that a total score of a particular magnitude represents deviance severe enough to warrant concern.

Table 7-4
Probability of Total Behavior Problem Score
Being from Clinical Sample

	Boys			*Girls*		
Total Score	*4–5*	*6–11*	*12–16*	*4–5*	*6–11*	*12–16*
0–4	.00	.00	.02	.00	.03	.05
5–9	.27	.02	.04	.14	.06	.10
10–14	.11	.06	.15	.20	.08	.10
15–19	.11	.13	.22	.17	.17	.27
20–24	.11	.15	.28	.35	.20	.38
25–29	.37	.31	.48	.17	.25	.41
30–34	.36	.42	.64	.18	.47	.26
35–39	.44	.54	.63	.33	.64	.75
40–44	.43	.72	.91	.67	.62	.74
45–49	.77	.76	.80	.73	.81	.78
50–54	.78	.77	.83	.67	.94	.75
55–240	.95	.94	.91	.92	.93	.96

Note—Clinical plus nonclinical N of each sex = 200 age 4–5; 600 age 6–11; 500 age 12–16.

The total social competence scores also showed substantial effects of clinical status, ranging from 22% for boys aged 4–5 to 39% for boys aged 12–16, as shown in Table 7-3. As with the total behavior problem score, we tabulated the number of children from the clinical and nonclinical samples who had each total social competence score. The probabilities shown in Table 7-5 represent the proportion of children within each range of scores who were from the clinical sample. The relation between clinical status and social competence scores is, of course, *opposite* to that for behavior problem scores: The proportion from the clinical sample *decreases* as the competence scores increase.

Table 7-5
Probability of Total Social Competence Score
Being from Clinical Sample

	Boys			Girls		
Total Score	*4–5[a]*	*6–11*	*12–16*	*4–5[a]*	*6–11*	*12–16*
0.0–4.5	1.00	1.00	1.00	1.00	1.00	1.00
5.0–7.0	.94	1.00	1.00	.92	1.00	1.00
7.5–9.5	.58	.95	1.00	.61	1.00	1.00
10.0–12.0	.42	.95	.97	.49	1.00	.95
12.5–14.5	.29	.83	.80	.42	.75	.85
15.0–17.0	.28	.65	.71	.21	.67	.66
17.5–19.5	.20	.41	.43	.09	.44	.43
20.0–22.0	--	.25	.21	--	.16	.26
22.5–24.5	--	.09	.11	--	.15	.16
25.0–30.0	--	.00	.00	--	.04	.09

Note — Clinical plus nonclinical N of each sex = 200 age 4–5; 600 age 6–11; 500 age 12–16.
[a]Maximum possible score = 24 for 4–5-year-olds vs. 30 for other age groups.

Cutoff Scores

Beside viewing criterion-related validity in terms of associations between clinical status and linear scale scores, users may wish to discriminate in a more categorical fashion between children likely to resemble our clinical sample and those more likely to resemble our nonclinical sample. Because the total behavior problem score generally showed stronger associations with clinical status than did any other scores, and because the total score includes all the items of the other behavior problem scales, it is a good index of differences between children whose reported behavior problems are in the "clinical" versus "normal" range. Similarly, the total social competence score is the most comprehensive summary of the CBCL's social competence items and is strongly associated with clinical status in all groups.

After comparing several approaches, we concluded that the 90th percentile of the behavior problem scores and the 10th percentile of the social competence scores in the nonclinical sample were desirable cutoff points for the following reasons (see Achenbach & Edelbrock, 1981, pp. 58–62, for further details):

1. The distributions of scores in our nonclinical samples were much more continuous on the "normal" side of cutoffs than on the "clinical" side, where scores were scattered at irregular intervals.

2. The sum of false negatives and false positives arising from overlaps between the scores of referred and nonreferred children was at a fairly constant minimum between about the 80th and 90th percentiles of the behavior problem distributions and the 10th and 20th percentiles of the social competence distributions of nonreferred children.

3. The 90th and 10th percentiles are intuitively appealing, because not more than about 10% of the nonreferred children in the localities sampled are likely to have behavior disorders of clinical proportions at any one time.

4. The raw scores approximating the 90th and 10th percentiles were fairly similar for all sex/age groups, except for the 4–5-year-olds' social competence scores, which were reduced by the exclusion of the School scale. (Because the behavior problem score at the 90th percentile for 4–5-year-old girls was an outlier, it was preferable to use the behavior problem score at the 88th percentile as the cutoff for this group.)

Table 7-6 presents the cutoff scores marking the limits of the "normal range" for each sex/age group: Behavior problem scores *above* those in Table 7-6 are considered to be in the clinical range, while social competence scores *below* those in Table 7-6 are considered to be in the clinical range.

Table 7-6
Cutoff Points for Total Behavior Problem
and Social Competence Scores

	Total Behavior Problem Scores Greater than These are in "Clinical Range"		*Total Social Competence Scores Less than These are in "Clinical Range"*[a]	
Age	*Girls*	*Boys*	*Girls*	*Boys*
4–5	42	42	10.0	9.5
6–11	37	40	16.5	16.0
12–16	37	38	16.5	16.0

[a]In Table 3 of Achenbach & Edelbrock (1981), the social competence scores are each .5 lower than those listed here. This is because the 1981 scores are exactly at the 10th percentile, which should be counted in the clinical range to include 10% of children from our nonreferred sample. The difference between using the 1981 scores and those shown above is extremely small.

Table 7-7

Percent of Children from Clinical and Nonclinical Samples Who Scored in the "Clinical Range" on Each Scale[a]

Behavior Problem Scales	Boys						Girls					
	4–5		6–11		12–16		4–5		6–11		12–16	
	Clin	Non-Clin	Clin	Non-Clin	Clin	Non-Clin	Clin	Non-Clin	Clin	Non-Clin	Clin	Non-Clin
Aggressive	61	6	43	2	26	4	32	2	46	3	27	2
Anxious Obsessive									35	2		
Cruel									21	2	35	1
Delinquent	29	2	40	4	35	3			23	2	41	2
Depressed	37	4	31	2			23	2	50	3		
Depressed Withdrawal											43	2
Hostile Withdrawal					33	2						
Hyperactive			34	3	46	4	27	2	44	2		
Immature	42	3		3	23	3						
Immature Hyperactive											37	2
Obese							18	2				
Obsessive-Compulsive			30	2	22	2						
Schizoid (or Anxious)	14	2	31	3	16	2	31	3			21	2
Schizoid Obsessive									19	1		
Sex Problems	14	0					13	3	21	2		
Social Withdrawal	37	3	28	2			29	2	45	3		
Somatic Complaints	25	3	14	2	20	2	25	2	19	2	36	3
Uncommunicative			44	6	20	2						

[a]Clinical Range: Narrow band behavior problem scale $T > 70$
Internalizing and Externalizing $T > 63$
Total behavior problem score > 90th %ile
Social competence scales $T < 30$
Total social competence $\leq$ 10th %ile

Table 7-7 (cont'd)

Behavior Problem Scales	Boys 4-5		6-11		12-16		Girls 4-5		6-11		12-16	
	Clin	Non-Clin	Clin	Non-Clin	Clin	Non-Clin	Clin	Non-Clin	Clin	Non-Clin	Clin	Non-Clin
≥1 Scale in Clinical Range	76	11	79	16	75	10	65	9	78	12	76	11
Internalizing	59	11	68	10	62	10	68	9	69	9	58	5
Externalizing	62	10	70	8	66	9	42	6	72	9	52	4
Int. and/or Ext.	74	14	83	14	76	12	69	12	82	14	68	7
Total Score	72	10	77	9	71	10	73	12	75	10	74	10
Social Competence Scales												
Activities	19	2	8	2	12	1	15	0	8	0	7	2
Social	43	4	18	1	22	1	18	1	25	1	10	1
School			14	1	24	3			31	2	18	1
≥1 Scale in Clinical Range	46	6	35	3	45	6	28	1	49	3	29	3
Total Score	48	9	62	10	58	10	39	10	58	10	60	9
Total Behavior Problem and/or Social Comp.	84	15	88	17	83	16	78	20	86	18	85	17

[a]Clinical Range: Narrow band behavior problem scale $T > 70$
Internalizing and Externalizing $T > 63$
Total behavior problem score > 90th %ile
Social competence scales $T < 30$
Total social competence ≤ 10th %ile

The behavior problem cutoff scores in Table 7-6 classified an average of 90.2% of the six nonreferred samples and 25.9% of the six referred samples as in the normal range. Using referral as a criterion and the 50-50 split of referred versus nonreferred in our samples, the total misclassification rate was 17.85% (9.8% of nonreferred children scoring in the clinical range and 25.9% of referred children scoring in the normal range). Table 7-7 shows the percent of referred and nonreferred children scoring in the clinical range for each sex/age group. Users can employ these figures to estimate the misclassifications likely to occur for each sex/age group in their own base rate situations.

The social competence cutoff scores classified 90.1% of the nonreferred and 42.9% of the referred children as being in the normal range, for a total misclassification rate of 26.4% (9.9% of nonreferred children scoring in the clinical range and 42.9% of the referred children scoring in the normal range). It is probably inevitable that more clinically-referred children will be misclassified by the social competence than the behavior problem score, because the social competence score has a more limited clinical range than the behavior problem score. Furthermore, the presence of behavior problems is more often a reason for clinical referral than is the absence of social competencies.

Combined Behavior Problem and Social Competence Cutoffs

Despite the superiority of the behavior problem cutoff, the social competence score may add discriminative power if the two are used together, because the two do not reflect exactly the same variance. Omitting 4-5-year-olds, whose social competence scores exclude the School scale, the Pearson correlation between the total social competence and behavior problem scores was $-.56$ for the referred and nonreferred samples combined. *Within* the refered and nonreferred samples, the more restricted range of the scores reduced the correlations to $-.29$ and $-.24$, respectively. To assess the discriminative power of the combined social competence and behavior problem cutoffs, we divided our samples into three categories:

1. Children who were in the *clinical range on both scores* (above the behavior problem cutoff and below the social competence cutoff).
2. Children falling in the normal range on one score but not the other.
3. Children who were in the *normal range on both scores* (at or below the behavior problem cutoff and at or above the social competence cutoff).

Considering only the children whose scores were consistently in the clinical range (category 1) or the normal range (category 3), 2% of the nonreferred children were classified in the clinical range and 16% of referred children were classified in the normal range, for a total misclassification rate of 9%. However, 26.8% of the children were in the normal range on one score but in the clinical range on the other (category 2).

An intermediate category may be useful for many purposes, such as screening and outcome studies, where gradations of status from consistently deviant to consistently nondeviant are desired. Alternatively, the intermediate category can be combined with either category 1 or category 3. Combining the intermediate category with category 1 left the misclassification of referred children at 16% but raised the misclassification of nonreferred children to 15%, for a total misclassification rate of 15.5%. (Table 7-7 shows the rates for each sex/age group.) By contrast, combining the intermediate category with category 3 left the misclassification of nonreferred children at 2%, but raised the misclassification of referred children to 57.4%, for a total misclassification rate of 29.7%.

In summary, use of an intermediate category produced the lowest overall rate of misclassification (9%). Categorizing cases having one deviant score as outside the normal range was second (15.5%); use of the behavior problem cutoff score alone was third (17.85%); the social competence cutoff score alone was fourth (26.4%); and categorizing intermediate cases in the normal range was the poorest (29.7%) in terms of overall misclassification.

Choices among these procedures should be based on the user's aims rather than on the total misclassification rate alone. When false positives are much more undesirable than false negatives, the procedures that minimize the proportion of normal children categorized as deviant would be preferred. When false negatives are much more undesirable than false positives, the procedures that minimize the proportion of deviant children categorized as normal would be preferred. Where the degree or type of deviance is important, as in outcome assessments, use of an intermediate category or separate groupings according to behavior problems and social competence may be preferable to a dichotomy.

Discriminant Analysis

Discriminant analysis offers another way to categorize people according to their similarity to particular criterion groups. Because discriminant analysis *weights* predictors to maximize their collective correlation with the predefined groupings in a particular sample, the classification yielded by the predictors must be cross-validated by testing their empirically-derived weights in new samples. To form separate samples for derivation and cross-validation of the discriminant functions, we divided our referred and non-referred samples of each sex/age group in half by alternating the assignment of cases to the derivation and cross-validation sample. A stepwise discriminant function was then computed for each derivation sample by entering behavior problems in the order of their reduction of Wilk's *lambda* in relation to the criterion of referral versus nonreferral. We stopped adding predictors when they ceased reducing Wilk's *lambda* significantly ($p < .01$).

The number of items that significantly reduced *lambda* ranged from three among the 4-5-year-olds of both sexes to seven for the 6-11-year-old boys. The particular items having significant weights differed among the six sex/age groups. However, within a particular sex/age group, the discriminant function's choice of the most significant predictors reflects each item's distribution and correlation with other items. For example, if Items A and B have similar frequencies and correlate highly with each other in a particular sample, the discriminant function may select only Item A to represent the predictive power they have in common. If the two items have slightly different correlations in another sample, Item B may be selected instead of Item A. In yet another sample, their correlations with other items may cause them both to be excluded in favor of Item C that represents much the same predictive variance. Discriminant functions derived from a larger item pool thus tell us little about the importance or intrinsic discriminative power of individual items. The detailed presentation of prevalence rates and variance associated with clinical status for each item in the Achenbach and Edelbrock (1981) monograph would be more informative in this respect.

When we used the discriminant functions derived for each sex/age group to categorize children in their respective cross-validation samples, 10.9% of the nonreferred cases were incorrectly classified as resembling referred children, while 23.9% of the referred children were incorrectly classified as resembling nonreferred children. The misclassification of nonreferred children is thus slightly higher (10.9% vs. 9.8%) and the misclassification of referred children is slightly lower (23.9% vs. 25.9%) than achieved using the 90th percentile as a cutoff point. However, the overall misclassification rate of 17.4% for the discriminant functions is similar to the overall misclassification rate of 17.85% for the 90th percentile cutoff.

The combination of social competence items with behavior problems in discriminant functions reduced overall misclassification slightly to 16.5%. The combination of total behavior problem and social competence scores in the discriminant functions produced a slight additional improvement, to a misclassification rate of 15.4%, compared with 15.5% using the criterion of behavior problem and/or social competence cutoff score.

The weighting of items in discriminant functions thus seems to offer little advantage over the cutoff scores for identifying children who resemble our referred versus nonreferred samples. Although the discriminant functions employ fewer items than the cutoff scores, the items vary among the sex/age groups. Because most users will want more data than provided by the few items required for discrimination into two categories, the more complete information obtained with the entire CBCL than with the few items required for each discriminant function would seem to outweigh the potential advantage of brevity offered by using the discriminant function items alone. Because the CBCL can be self-administered, use of the entire instrument need not increase the time required of the practitioner or researcher. If administration or scoring time is at a premium, however, a possible compromise is to omit the social competence portion of the CBCL, which appears to add little to the overall discriminative power of the behavior problems. Nevertheless, for prediction or assessment of outcomes, the social competence items may tap important adaptive characteristics not fully reflected in the behavior problem scores.

Scale Scores in the Clinical Range

Table 7-7 shows the percent of our normal and clinical samples who obtained T scores above 70 on each narrow band behavior problem scale and T scores below 30 on each social competence scale. The T score of 70 represents approximately the 98th percentile, while the T score of 30 represents approximately the 2nd percentile of our normative samples. In contrast to the cutoffs demarcating the most extreme 10% of our normative samples on the total behavior problem and social competence scores, we chose to demarcate the most extreme 2% on the narrow band scales for the following reasons:

1. The smaller number of items comprising each scale than the total scores argues for a more conservative standard for judging deviance.

2. A child could be deviant on at least one scale without being generally deviant enough to warrant clinical concern, either because the child had few problems in other areas or had enough competencies to offset concern about a narrow range of problems.

3. T scores of 70 are conventionally used to distinguish between the "normal" and "clinical" range on the narrow-band scales of other instruments for assessing psychopathology, such as the MMPI.

An additional feature of the T scores of 70 on the behavior problem scales and 30 on the social competence scales is that they are the most extreme T scores derived from percentiles of our normative samples. As described in Chapter 3, the raw scores beyond these points were assigned to T scores in regular intervals.

Because each narrow-band scale represents a limited range of behavior, the cutoffs on the total behavior problem and social competence score are preferable for discriminating between children who are most like our referred and nonreferred samples. Nevertheless, Table 7-7 shows that the percent of referred and nonreferred children who have at least one behavior problem T score greater than 70 is fairly similar to the percent exceeding the 90th percentile of the total behavior problem score in each sex/age group. Although no single narrow-band scale discriminates between referred and nonreferred children as well as the total score, deviance on one or more scales approximates the total score cutoff as a discriminator between the two groups. The general agreement between deviance in total score and at least one scale score is further indicated by the fact that an average of 96.3% of clinically-referred children having a total score above the 90th percentile also have at least one behavior problem score above a T score of 70.

Internalizing and Externalizing

Although the Internalizing and Externalizing scores are intended to indicate the primary concentration of a child's problems rather than to discriminate between deviant and nondeviant children, they are included in Table 7-7 for the sake of comparison. Because of the large number of items on these scales, their global nature, and the use of the same procedure in assigning T scores as done with the total score, we selected a T score of 63 (approximately the 90th percentile) as the limit of the normal range. Table 7-7 shows that the percent of referred children in the clinical range on the Internalizing and Externalizing scores taken separately is somewhat lower than that for the total score. However, the percent of referred children who score in the clinical range on at least one of the broad-band scores is generally similar to the percent who score in the clinical range on the total behavior problem score.

SUMMARY

The *content validity* of the CBCL is viewed in terms of whether its items are related to the clinical concerns of parents and mental health workers. We found that 116 of the 118 behavior problem items and all 20 of the social competence items were significantly ($p < .01$) associated with clinical status, as established independently of the CBCL. However, prospective users should judge whether the content of the CBCL is appropriate for their purposes.

Empirically-derived syndromes are intended to provide an operational basis for assessing behavioral phenotypes, rather than to operationalize pre-existing taxonomic constructs. However, the total behavior problem score can be viewed as representing a dimension of behavior problems analogous to the construct of general ability represented by total scores on intelligence tests. Similarly, the behavior problem scales of the Profile can be viewed as subgroupings of problems analogous to the subtests of general ability tests. When the scales are viewed in this way, significant correlations with other behavior rating scales and empirically-derived syndromes provide evidence of *construct validity*. Correlations between the total CBCL behavior problem score and total scores on other widely used parent rating forms are as high as those typically found between tests of general intelligence, while correlations between Profile scales and the scales of the other rating forms are in the range often found among the subtests of different intelligence tests.

Using referral for mental health services as a criterion, we presented evidence for *criterion-related validity* in terms of significant differences ($p < .001$) between demographically-matched referred and nonreferred children on all Profile scores for all sex/age groups. Most of the effects associated with clinical status accounted for a large percentage of variance in the scores, with the effects of SES, race, and age within sex/age group partialled out. SES had more significant effects than race or age within sex/age groups, but all demographic effects were small. Procedures for discriminating between scores in the normal versus clinical range are presented.

Chapter 8
A Taxonomy of Profile Patterns

Earlier chapters dealt with the Child Behavior Checklist and Profile as instruments for describing and quantifying children's behavioral problems and competencies and for comparing them with normative groups. Children referred for mental health services differ significantly from nonreferred children on most of the behavioral problem and competence items, scale scores, and total scores.

In addition to assessment in terms of individual items and scale scores, the Profile reflects overall behavioral *patterns*. By summarizing a child's standing on a variety of scales, the Profile provides a basis for descriptive taxonomy that is more comprehensive than classification according to individual syndromes or scores on individual scales. How should we use the Profile to group children according to the behavioral patterns reported by their parents? No classification of disorders had shown sufficient reliability or validity to serve as a criterion against which to validate Profile patterns (see Achenbach, 1982, Chapter 15). We therefore chose an empirical approach to identifying groups of children with similar Profile patterns.

This chapter explains our approach and the resulting taxonomy. The discussion is necessarily somewhat technical and may be skipped by readers who are not interested in the taxonomic function of the Child Behavior Profile.

DIMENSIONAL AND CATEGORICAL APPROACHES
TO EMPIRICALLY-BASED TAXONOMY

Recall from Chapter 2 that we factor analyzed behavior problem ratings in order to identify syndromes of behavior problems that covary. Our general strategy was to construct syndromes on the basis of empirically-derived correlations among reported behaviors rather than imposing preconceived categories. We adopted the same general strategy for identifying *groups* of children. However, factor analytic methods are not as appropriate for identifying *groups of individuals* as for identifying covariation among *items*.

Although it is feasible to factor analyze correlations between profiles of scores, the result is a set of factors in which each individual has a loading on each factor. This is called "Q factor analysis" or "inverse factor analysis." The fact that individuals can have high loadings on several factors is undesirable for taxonomic purposes, which require assignment of each individual to a *particular* group.

Yet, categorical taxonomies may sacrifice information that the quantitative-dimensional approach of factor analysis preserves. Because individuals vary in the *degree* to which they fit categories, grouping individuals into categories masks variations in the degree to which they meet the defining criteria of the categories. Furthermore, some individuals assigned to a particular category may meet the criteria for one or more *other* categories almost as well as they meet the criteria for the category to which they are assigned.

Because we sought a taxonomy based on empirically identified similarities among behavioral patterns, we wished to preserve quantitative variations in the degree of resemblance to particular categories. This would make it possible to determine how closely children must match a particular category before they will differ significantly on other important variables as well. Sensitivity to quantitative variations seemed especially crucial in the initial construction of a taxonomy to avoid imposing rigid categorical boundaries that might miss the most effective cutting points among behavioral patterns. We also wished to help others judge quantitative variations for their own purposes in clinical and research applications of the taxonomy.

CLUSTER ANALYSIS OF PROFILES

In order to construct a taxonomy of profile patterns sensitive to quantitative gradations in similarity, we experimented with various approaches to the cluster analysis of profiles. Parametric comparisons of different approaches with real and artificial data indicated that the one-way intraclass correlation (ICC) was the best measure of similarity between behavioral profiles. These comparisons also indicated that the centroid clustering algorithm was an effective way to group behavioral profiles into types (Edelbrock, 1979; Edelbrock & Achenbach, 1980; Edelbrock & McLaughlin, 1980).

Intraclass Correlation (ICC)

As discussed in Chapter 6, the ICC reflects similarities in both the *magnitude* and the *rank ordering* of two sets of scores. When applied to profiles, the ICC between two children's profiles provides a quantitative index of how similar the profiles are, taking account of both the *elevation* of scores and the *shape* of the profile pattern. Like the Pearson correlation, the ICC can range from -1.00 (perfect negative correlation) to $+1.00$ (perfect positive correlation). However, as will be graphically illustrated later (Figure 8-14), the ICC between two profiles is numerically lower than the Pearson correlation between the same two profiles. This is partly because their metric differs, in that the numerical size of the ICC is less than the square of the Pearson correlation for the same profile data. But they also reflect different aspects of the relations between two sets of scores: The Pearson correlation reflects primarily similarities between rank orders of scores that are paired in the two sets, whereas the ICC is affected by both the rank orders and the magnitudes of the scores in the two sets.

Centroid Cluster Analysis

In centroid cluster analysis, the clustering program first identifies the two subjects in a sample who have the most similar profiles. (In our analyses, this meant the two children in a sample whose Child Behavior Profiles had the highest ICCs with each other.) When the two most similar subjects are found, the program computes the mean of Subject A's score and Subject B's score on the first scale of the profile. The mean of the two subjects' scores is then computed for each of the remaining scales in turn. The resulting set of mean scores forms a new profile that is halfway between the two subjects' profiles. This new profile is called the *centroid* of the miniature cluster comprised of the two subjects. The centroid serves as the operational definition of the profile type represented by the cluster.

After the first cluster consisting of two subjects has been formed, the program determines whether any subject remaining in the sample has a profile that is more similar to the centroid of the first cluster than to any other subject. This is done by computing ICCs between the centroid and the profiles of all subjects not already included in the cluster. If a subject is found whose profile correlates higher with the centroid than with the profile of any other subject, this subject is added to the cluster. The program then averages the profiles of the two original members and the new member to form a new centroid for the cluster.

In the next step, ICCs are computed between the new centroid and the remaining unclustered subjects to determine whether any subject is more similar to the centroid than to another subject, and the process continues as before.

Whenever two subjects are found who are more similar to each other than to the centroid of an existing cluster, they are joined to form a new cluster whose centroid is computed as the mean of their profiles. As clusters are formed, ICCs are computed between their centroids, as well as between the profiles of individual subjects. Whenever the centroids of two clusters are found to be more highly correlated than the profiles of any unclustered individuals, the two clusters are joined to form a new cluster whose centroid is computed as the mean of all profiles in both clusters.

As illustrated in Figure 8-1, the clustering follows a hierarchical sequence: The bottom level in Figure 8-1 represents a sample of unclustered individuals, each of whom has a profile of scores. At the next higher level, miniature clusters of two or three individuals are formed. These are eventually joined together in larger clusters, which themselves become joined in still larger clusters, as shown at the top of Figure 8-1. Clusters at intermediate levels in the hierarchy are likely to be the most useful, because they form groups of moderate size and greater homogeneity than the larger groups formed in the final stages, shown at the top of the hierarchy.

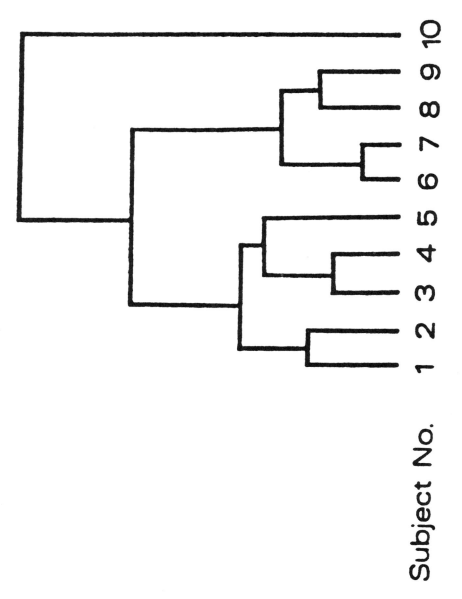

8-1. Illustration of hierarchical clustering sequence.

Subject No.

Clustering of Behavior Problem Scales

When we analyzed profiles including both the social competence scales and the behavior problem scales, we found that the social competence scales contributed little to the identification of distinctive profile types. One reason for this is that the social competence scales are *negatively* correlated with the behavior problem scales. That is, children who have many behavior problems tend to have low social competence scores and vice versa. When the social competence scales are combined with the behavior problem scales into a single profile, the profiles of clinically-referred children have a built-in pattern of high behavior problem scores with low competence scores. This pattern interferes with the detection of other differences among profile patterns. To avoid the effect of the negative correlation between the competence and problem scales, we used only the behavior problem portion of the Child Behavior Profile in our cluster analyses. However, as detailed later in this chapter, we also assessed relations between scores on the social competence scales and the profile types identified through cluster analyses of the behavior problem scales.

Standardization of Scores. Because the behavior problem scales have different numbers of items, different mean scores, and different variances, most profiles tend to be lower on some scales than on others. As a consequence of the general tendency for profiles to be lower on certain scales than on others, clusters may reflect this type of built-in patterning more than they reflect the way in which particular groups of children differ from other groups of children. To give each scale the same mean and variance within the sample to be cluster analyzed, we converted raw scores on the behavior problem scales to z scores (mean = 0, standard deviation = 1). These z scores were based on distributions of raw scores in *clinical samples*, as discussed next.

Use of Clinical Samples. Because the goal of our taxonomy is to discriminate among children who differ in their behavior disorders, we performed our cluster analyses on children considered to have severe enough disorders to warrant referral for mental health services. From our files of CBCLs that had been filled out by parents of clinically-referred children, we drew two random samples of each sex/age group. The children were from the same 42 clinical settings that supplied cases for our factor analyses. For each sex at ages 6–11 and 12–16, each of the two samples numbered 250, but the low referral rates for 4- and 5-year-olds limited our samples for these groups to 125 each. The total number of children included in the cluster analyses was 2,500.

Converting the raw scores of children within each clinical sample to z scores means that the scores show how a child differs from other *clinically-referred* children on each scale. Thus, the profile patterns identified through the cluster analysis reflect differences in behavior problem patterns for children who are regarded as having significant behavior disorders. This is important, because a taxonomy of behavior disorders should primarily reflect differences among the patterns of *disorders*, rather than variations within the normal range or gross differences between deviant and nondeviant children.

Reliability of Profile Types

Because a cluster analysis merely groups together individuals who have similar profile patterns, it is possible to obtain clusters that are peculiar to a particular sample. Although these clusters represent groups that actually exist in the sample, they may reflect a chance combination of profiles that would not be found in other samples. To control for this possibility, we performed separate cluster analyses in each of the two samples of each sex/age group. We then computed the ICC between the centroids of clusters obtained in one sample for a particular sex/age group and the centroids of the clusters obtained in the other sample for that sex/age group. Each cluster whose centroid was found to correlate significantly ($p < .05$) with a centroid in the other sample was considered to be reliable. The centroids of the two samples for a particular sex/age group were averaged to yield the final operational definition of each cluster.

RESULTS OF OUR CLUSTER ANALYSES

We found either six or seven reliable clusters for each sex/age group. The profile types are shown in Figures 8-2 through 8-7, with summary labels that reflect their distinguishing high points.

It is important to note that each profile type is defined by its entire pattern of scores and *not* just by the high points of the profile (unlike MMPI "high point" codes). It is also important to note that these profile types are based on *z* scores for our samples of clinically-referred children. Thus, the 0 point to the left of each profile in Figures 8-2 through 8-7 represents the mean of the *clinical* samples; − 1 represents one standard deviation below this mean; and + 1 represents one standard deviation above this mean. As a consequence, these profile types cannot be precisely compared to a child's pattern as seen on the Child Behavior Profile, which is scored in terms of *T* scores derived from *nonreferred normative* samples. Procedures for determining a child's profile type will be discussed later in the chapter.

Relations to Traditional Diagnostic Categories

Some of the profile patterns shown in Figures 8-2 through 8-7 correspond to traditional diagnostic categories. For example, Profile Type E for the 6- to 11-year-old boys has a high peak on the Hyperactive scale but is relatively low on the other scales. This resembles the Hyperkinetic Reaction specified in DSM-II and the Attention Deficit Disorder with Hyperactivity specified in DSM-III. Yet, even where a traditional diagnostic category happens to resemble a profile pattern such as Profile Type E, the profile preserves a more comprehensive picture of the child's reported behavior than unidimensional scales

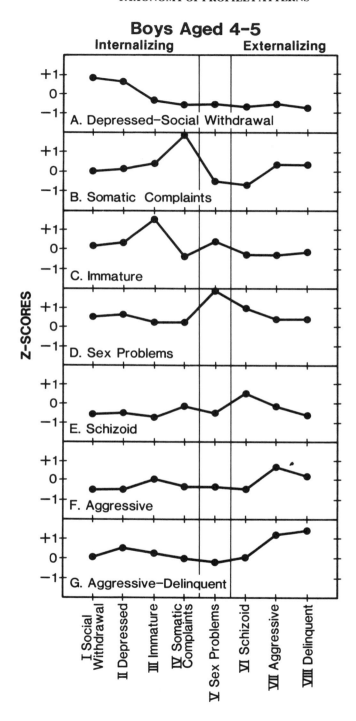

Boys Aged 4-5

8-2.   Child Behavior Profile types found for boys aged 4-5.

Boys Aged 6-11

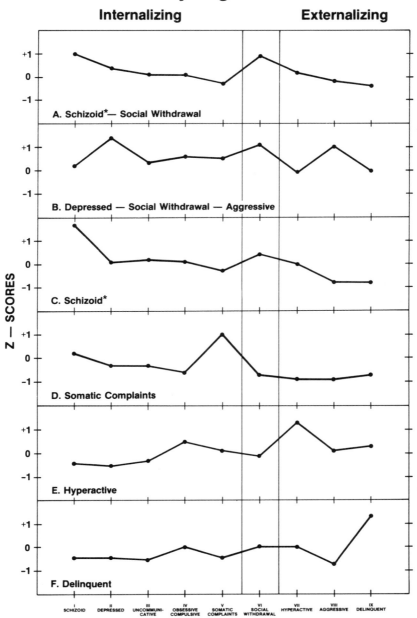

8-3. Child Behavior Profile types found for boys aged 6–11.
    * Schizoid or Anxious

Boys Aged 12-16

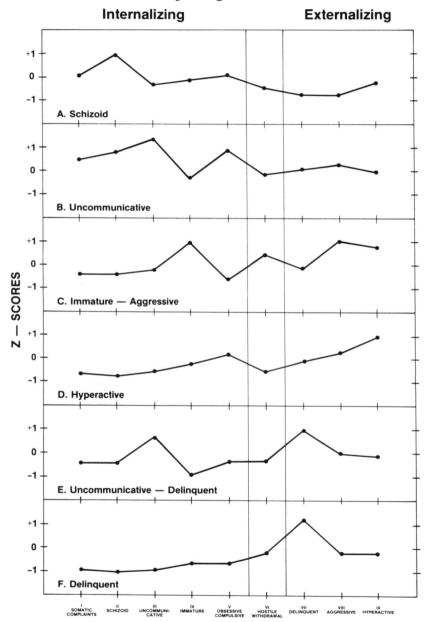

8-4. Child Behavior Profile types found for boys aged 12-16.

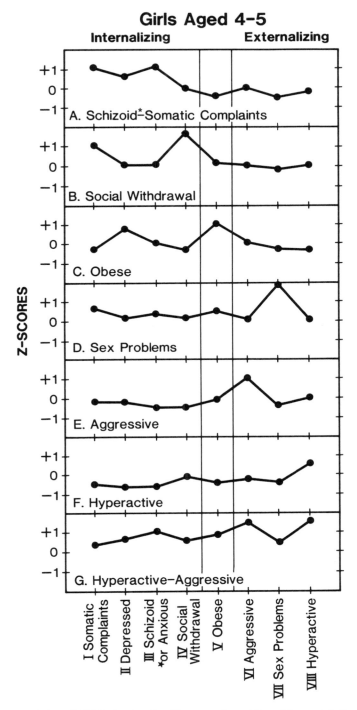

8-5. Child Behavior Profile types found for girls aged 4–5.
* Schizoid or Anxious

Girls Aged 6-11

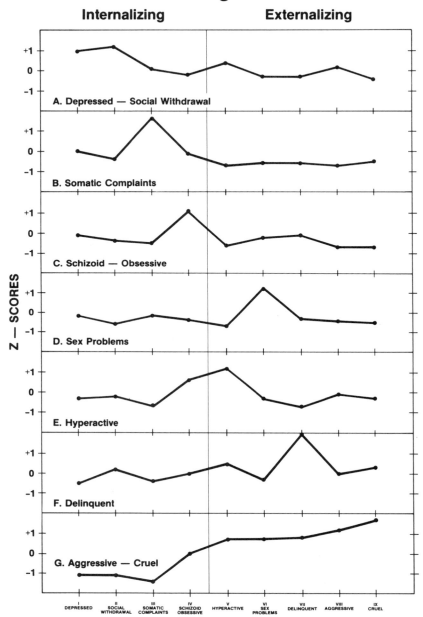

8-6.   Child Behavior Profile types found for girls aged 6–11.

Girls Aged 12-16

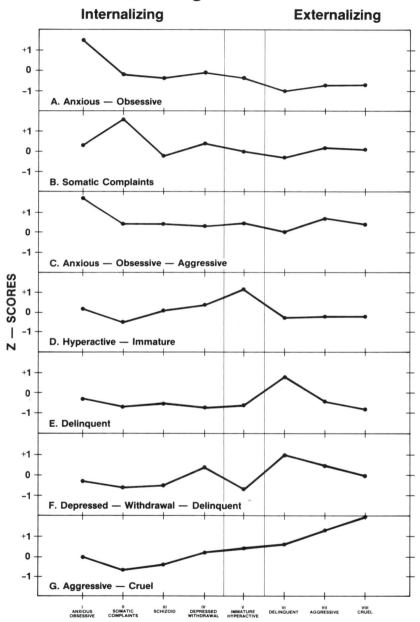

8-7. Child Behavoir Profile types found for girls aged 12-16.

or nosological constructs do. For example, many boys who are labeled hyperactive by teachers or clinicians may indeed show more hyperactive behaviors than their normal peers, yet not have Profile Type E, because they are even more deviant in other ways. For these boys, hyperactivity may be but a minor facet of an overall pattern very different from that of boys whose main problem really is hyperactivity.

Profile Type B for the 6- to 11-year-old boys exemplifies a pattern that does not have a clear counterpart in traditional nosological categories. It has peaks on the Depressed, Social Withdrawal, and Aggressive scales. If this pattern exists among clinically-referred boys, why wasn't it recognized in traditional nosological approaches?

Boys having the *Depressed-Social Withdrawal-Aggressive* pattern display an exceptional amount of aggressive behavior. Even nonreferred boys in our normative sample are reported to display a lot of aggressive behavior. Clinically-referred boys display considerably more than nonreferred boys. And the Aggressive scale of Profile Type B is more than one standard deviation above the mean for clinically-referred boys. Perhaps the sheer volume of these boys' aggressive behavior prevented diagnosticians from noting that they also show far more depressive and withdrawing behaviors than other clinically-referred boys. If a boy is outstandingly aggressive, his aggressive behavior is apt to dominate the referring complaints and the attention of mental health workers. Without a standardized assessment of his other behaviors, such a boy may be labeled as "undersocialized aggressive" or "acting-out aggressive," instead of being distinguished from other aggressive boys who lack the depressive and withdrawn behaviors.

The profile types provide a broader view of children's behavior problem patterns than do the nosological categories of DSM-II or DSM-III. In general, the DSM's categories are more analogous to factor-analytically derived behavior problem scales than to profile types (see Achenbach, 1980, for a comparison between DSM-III categories and syndromes derived through factor analysis). Although profile types that are elevated on only one scale, such as the Hyperactive type, may resemble a particular DSM syndrome, profile patterns that are elevated on multiple scales would be analogous to several DSM syndromes occurring together.

Hierarchical Relations Among Profile Types

As illustrated in Figure 8-1, the clustering procedure started with a sample of individual profiles and then formed ever-larger clusters in a hierarchical sequence. The profile types shown in Figures 8-2 through 8-7 represent clusters at an intermediate level in the hierarchy.

As the clustering proceeded, the differentiated profile types were eventually joined into broad-band Internalizing and Externalizing clusters. An additional broad-band cluster (labeled as "Mixed") was found for girls of all three age groups and boys aged 4-5. In some groups, some pairs of the profile types shown in Figures 8-2 through 8-7 also joined together before culminating in

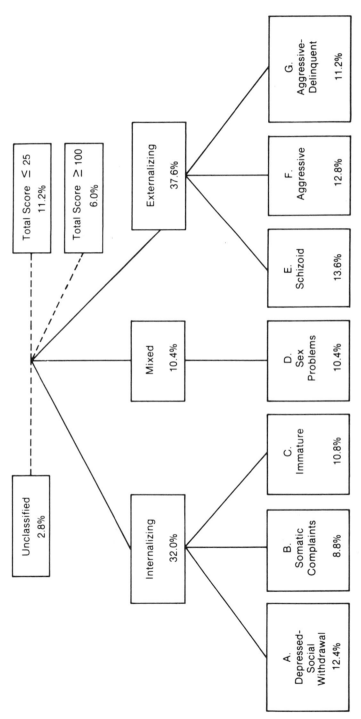

BOYS 4-5
n=250

8-8. Distribution of profile types found for clinically-referred boys aged 4-5.

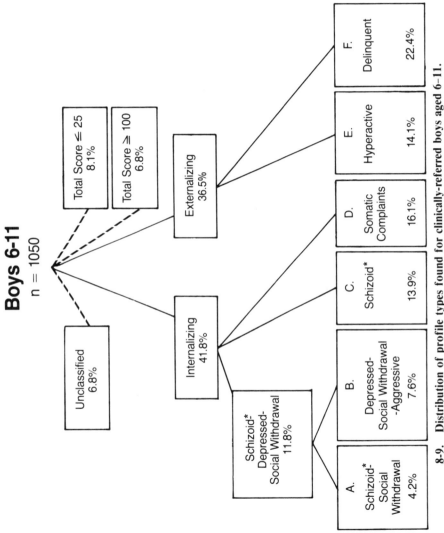

8-9.   Distribution of profile types found for clinically-referred boys aged 6–11.
*Schizoid or Anxious

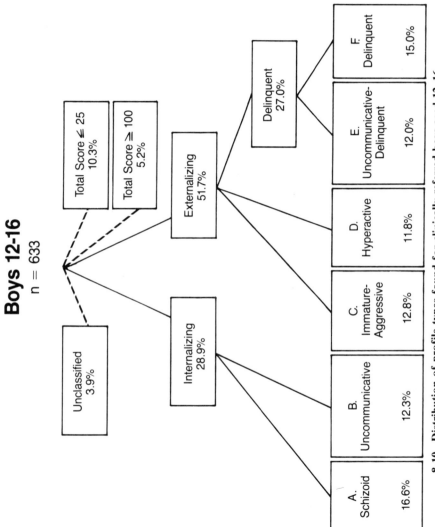

8-10. Distribution of profile types found for clinically-referred boys aged 12-16.

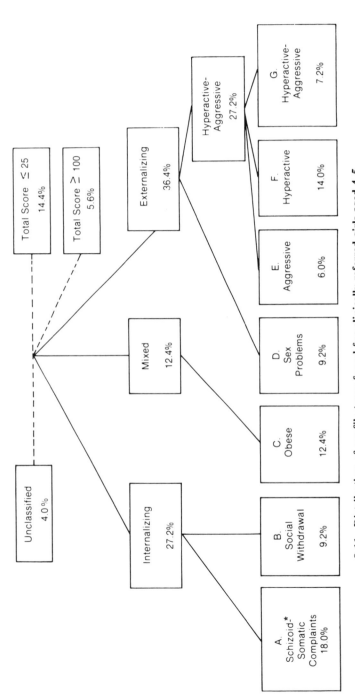

8-11. Distribution of profile types found for clinically-referred girls aged 4–5.
*Schizoid or Anxious

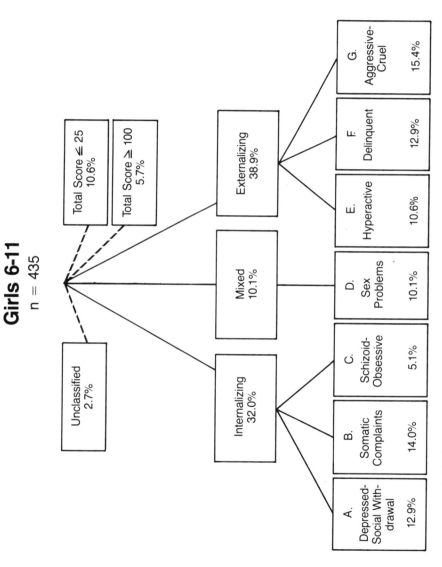

8-12. Distribution of profile types found for clinically-referred girls aged 6–11.

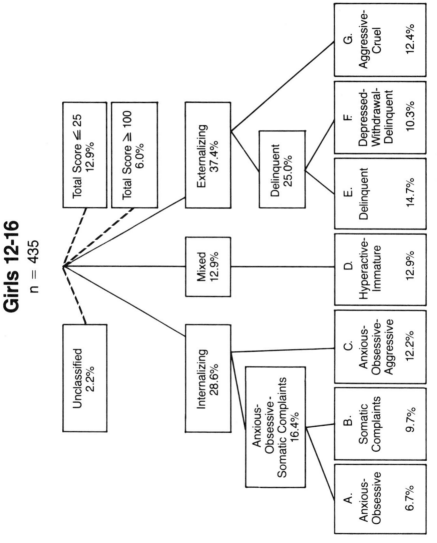

8-13. Distribution of profile types found for clinically-referred girls aged 12-16.

the broad-band clusters. Figures 8-8 through 8-13 depict these hierarchical relations for each sex/age group. The percent of clinically-referred children whose profiles correlated highest with each type is shown in the boxes representing the profile types. Children whose total behavior problem scores were ≤25 or ≥100 were excluded, because the overall magnitude of these scores places them at the limits of the scales, thereby reducing the possibilities for distinctive patterning of scale scores. The percent of children whose profiles did not correlate positively with any type is indicated in the box designated as unclassified.

For some purposes, classification according to the global clusters may afford adequate differentiation among behavior disorders, whereas classification according to the more differentiated clusters may be better for other purposes. Because the same children can be classified at both levels of the hierarchy, users can compare the relative utility of broad-band and narrow-band classification for their own purposes.

CLASSIFICATION OF INDIVIDUAL CHILDREN

Recall that the clustering program computes the intraclass correlation (ICC) between the profile of individual children and the *centroid* (average profile) of each cluster. Once the profile types have been identified, the same procedure can be used to determine which type a particular child resembles most, even if the child was not included in the sample that was cluster analyzed. This is done by computing an ICC between the child's profile and the centroids of each of the clusters (shown in Figures 8-2 through 8-7). The child is then considered to belong to the profile type with which his/her profile correlates most highly.

Users of the taxonomy can stipulate the correlation required for a child to be considered a member of the category defined by a particular profile type. If a user wishes to create very homogeneous groups, then only children whose profiles correlate very highly with a profile type would be included. However, the more stringent the criterion for classification, the fewer the children who will be classified.

On the other hand, if a user wishes to insure that large proportions of children are classified, then children having a low ICC with a profile type can be included. In this case, each group will be less homogeneous than if a high ICC is required for classification.

By using the ICC to assess the *degree* of similarity between individual children and the profile types, the user can test the effects of varying the stringency of the criterion for classification. Figure 8-14 illustrates relations between:

1. various cutoff points;
2. the percentage of children that each cutoff classifies ("coverage" of the samples);
3. the homogeneity of the resulting groups (measured by the average of the ICCs among all the members of each group).

These relations are averages across our samples, as reported in detail by Edelbrock and Achenbach (1980). Figure 8-14 also shows the relations between the ICC and Pearson correlation for these data. Where the ICC is about .40, for example, the Pearson correlation among the profiles is about .75.

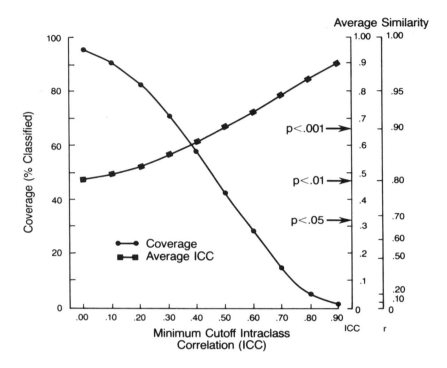

8-14. Effects of different ICC cutoff points on the coverage and homogeneity of the resulting groups. Right-hand columns indicate the average correlations among the profiles of group members in terms of ICC and Pearson *r*.

Note in Figure 8-14 that using an ICC as low as .00 as a cutoff point produces an average correlation among group members that is statistically significant at $p < .01$ (ICC = .47, Pearson $r = .80$). Using a cutoff of .00 means that some children correlate only .01 with the centroid of the group to which they are assigned. Of course, when a very low cutoff point such as .00 is used, most of the children's correlations substantially exceed this cutoff. Furthermore, those having correlations as low as .01 have null or *negative* correlations with the other profile types. Thus, the discriminative power achieved by using a particular ICC as a cutoff reflects not just the similarity to a type represented by the ICC just above the cutoff, but the cases having ICCs well above the cutoff. The cutoff also separates cases from types that they are most *unlike*, as indexed by negative ICCs with these types.

As presented in detail by Edelbrock and Achenbach (1980), the statistical power to detect differences in demographic and social competence correlates of the profile types remained at a high plateau between cutoff points of about .30 and .70 (equivalent to Pearson correlations of about .65 and .93, respectively). As Figure 8-14 shows, however, the percentage of children who can be classified declines rather sharply as the cutoff point is raised.

Reduced coverage usually reduces the practical utility of a taxonomy. It may also reduce the statistical power of a particular total sample size to reveal differences between the correlates of different profile types. This is because the decline in the size of the groups classified eventually outweighs increases in discriminative power conferred by their increasing homogeneity. We found, for example, that statistical power declined above cutoffs of .70 — any further increases in the "purity" of the groups was more than offset by shrinkage in the number of children who qualified as such pure types (Edelbrock & Achenbach, 1980).

To enable users to select their own criteria for classification, the computer program for scoring profiles prints the ICC between a child's profile and each of the profile types for his/her sex/age group. In computing the ICC between the child's profile and each profile type, the program converts the child's behavior problem scores to standard scores derived from our clinical samples. These appear at the bottom of each behavior problem scale as "CLINC T." They enable the user to compare the child's standing on each scale with that of our clinical sample, as well as with our normative sample, for which a T score is also printed.

As reported by Edelbrock and Achenbach (1980), we computed agreement between the classification of 6- to 16-year-olds' profiles scored from ratings by their mothers and a clinician. The mothers' ratings were derived from CBCLs they filled out during the intake evaluation of their children at a community mental health center. The clinician's ratings were derived from CBCLs she completed on the basis of interviews with the parents, observation and interview of the child, and information from teachers. Children with total behavior problem scores ≤ 25 or ≥ 100 on either the mother's or the clinician's CBCL were excluded.

Profiles were classified according to the type that they correlated highest with, using a lower cutoff of .00. Table 8-1 shows the agreement between classifications derived from the mother's and the clinician's ratings for Profile types and the Internalizing versus Externalizing groupings of Profile types. Because there is no entirely satisfactory index of agreement between categorical classifications, three indices of agreement are displayed in Table 8-1: (*a*) Percent agreement, which is the simplest but does not correct for chance agreements arising from differences in the proportion of cases assigned to each category; (*b*) the statistic *kappa* (Cohen, 1960), which corrects for chance agreements and can range from .00 (chance agreement) to 1.00 (perfect agreement), but cannot reach 1.00 if the distribution of types differs between the raters; and (*c*) a ratio of *kappa* to the maximum *kappa* obtainable, given the distributions of types yielded by the raters.

Table 8-1

**Agreement Between Profile Classifications Derived from Mothers' and
Clinician's Ratings**

Group	N	Profile types[a]			Internalizing/Externalizing		
		Agreement	K	K/Kmax	Agreement	K	K/Kmax
Boys 6–11	20	70%	.583	.811	95%	.900	1.00
Boys 12–16	23	70%	.555	.897	74%	.303	1.00
Girls 6–11	4	75%	.667	1.00	75%	.500	1.00
Girls 12–16	20	80%	.746	1.00	90%	.759	1.00
Average of all groups		74%	.638	.927	83%	.616	1.00

[a]K = kappa (Cohen, 1960). K/Kmax = ratio of kappa to maximum possible kappa.

The *kappas* in Table 8-1 all indicate agreement well above chance, and the ratio of *kappa/kappa max* indicates that the maximum possible *kappa* was obtained in 6 of the 8 analyses. In terms of percentage, the average agreement was 74% for assignment to specific Profile types and 83% for assignment to the Internalizing/Externalizing dichotomy.

CORRELATES OF PROFILE TYPES

Identification of profile types is a starting point but should not be the end point of empirically-based taxonomy. The profile types enable us to discriminate between children whose contrasting behavior problem patterns may mark differences in etiology, course, prognosis, and responsiveness to particular interventions. How can the descriptive taxonomy help to elucidate such differences?

The most general strategy is to group children according to their profile types and then to compare them on other important variables. The hierarchical relations among profiles and the distribution of profile types within clinical samples can also suggest hypotheses and variables to study. Because the profile types shown in Figures 8-2 through 8-7 are subsumed by the broad-band Internalizing and Externalizing clusters (as shown in Figures 8-8 through 8-13), children can be simultaneously classified according to both the differentiated profile types and the Internalizing versus Externalizing dichotomy. We can then compare the power of these two levels of classification to discriminate between children who differ on other variables.

We will summarize here only our findings on relations between profile types, social competence scores, and demographic variables, as detailed by Edelbrock and Achenbach (1980). Research presently under way is assessing other correlates of profile types, including behavior problems rated by teachers and direct observers, patterns of cognitive functioning, self-image disparity, outcomes of mental health services, and DSM-III diagnoses.

Demographic Correlates

To assess demographic correlates of the profile types, we compared the distributions of age, SES (Hollingshead scores for parental occupation), and race (black versus white) for children classified by the various profile types within each sex/age group. We did similar analyses comparing children classified by the Internalizing/Externalizing dichotomy.

One-way analyses of variance (ANOVAs) showed some significant age differences among profile types within three sex/age groups, but the magnitude of these effects was small in terms of variance accounted for, using Cohen's (1977) criteria. Among the three sex/age groups in which age effects were found, these differences were not consistently associated with a particular profile pattern or the Internalizing/Externalizing dichotomy. For example, among girls aged 6-11, those having the Depressed Social Withdrawal profile were significantly older than those having other profile types. Among girls aged 12-16, by contrast, girls having the Delinquent profile were significantly older than those having other profile types.

Significant SES differences were found between profile types only for 4-5-year-old boys, but children left unclassified because they had behavior problem scores ≥ 100 were of significantly lower SES than any of the profile types among three sex/age groups.

Chi squares showed significant racial differences among profile types for boys aged 4-5 and both sexes aged 6-11. Among 6-11-year-old boys, for example, blacks were significantly overrepresented in the Hyperactive group and underrepresented in the Delinquent group. Results of these analyses are shown in Tables 8-2 through 8-7.

Social Competence Correlates

Because we have found significant relations between demographic and social competence variables in some groups (see Chapter 7 and Achenbach & Edelbrock, 1981), our analyses of the social competence correlates of profiles were designed to control for demographic differences. For each sex/age group in which significant age, race, or SES effects were found, we used analysis of covariance (ANCOVA) to compare the social competence scores of children grouped by profile type while controlling for the demographic variable that had been found significant for that group. Differences among the profile types on the social competence scales were thus adjusted for differences in relevant demographic characteristics.

The profile types generally differed more on social competence scores than on demographic characteristics (see Tables 8-2 through 8-7). On the School scale, for example, highly significant differences among profile types were found within all 6-11 and 12-16-year-old groups. Among boys and girls aged 6-11, the Hyperactive groups obtained significantly lower School scores than

Table 8-2
Demographic and Social Competence Correlates
of the Profile Types for 459 Boys Aged 4-5[a]

Dependent variables	Comparisons among profile types			Profile types[b]							Internalizing vs. Externalizing[d]	Unclassified groups[e]		
				Internalizing			Mixed	Externalizing				ICC	Score Score	
	Significance	Effect size	LSD[c]	A	B	C	D	E	F	G		≤0	≥100	≤25
N	—	—	—	63	43	41	31	58	57	54	—	15	44	53
Demographic characteristics														
Age	n.s.	—	—	4.6	4.7	4.7	4.5	4.6	4.5	4.6	n.s.	4.5	4.7	4.6
Race[f]	$p<.01$	.22	—	95.2+	80.0	81.3	67.9+	86.3	90.4	92.2	n.s.	100+	84.2	90.2
SES	$p<.05$	.06	1.3	4.1	5.3	4.1	4.6	4.2	4.3	5.0	n.s.	3.6	4.3	3.8
Social competence														
Activities	$p<.05$	.10	1.8	5.7	5.9	3.2	5.6	6.2	4.4	6.0	n.s.	4.1	5.3	5.0
Social	$p<.01$	.14	1.6	4.6	4.5	4.1	5.5	4.9	3.4	3.0	n.s.	3.8	3.6	5.2

[a]Age (years), race (% white), SES (Hollingshead's 7-step scale). Mean values for social competence scales based on raw scale sums—range: Activities (0–12), Social (0–12).

[b]Profile types are (A) Depressed-Social Withdrawal, (B) Somatic Complaints, (C) Immature, (D) Sex Problems, (E) Schizoid, (F) Aggressive, (G) Aggressive Delinquent.

[c]Modified least significant difference (Winer, 1971) for comparisons among profile types. Not applicable to differences in race. Mean differences that meet or exceed the LSD are significant ($p<.05$).

[d]For comparisons between Internalizing and Externalizing groups, $*p<.05$, $**p<.01$, $***p<.001$.

[e]Asterisk indicates groups that differ significantly ($p<.05$) from children classified according to profile types (pooled).

[f]For race, + indicates the profile types in which the proportion of whites differed significantly ($p<.05$) from the proportion expected on the basis of the pooled sample.

Table 8-3
Demographic and Social Competence Correlates
of the Profile Types for 1,050 Boys Aged 6–11[a]

	Comparisons among profile types			Profile types[b]						Internalizing vs.	Unclassified groups[e]		
		Effect		Internalizing				Externalizing		Externalizing[d]	ICC <0	Score ≥100	Score ≤25
Dependent variables	Significance	size	LSD[c]	A	B	C	D	E	F				
N	—	—	—	44	80	146	169	148	235	—	72	71	85
Demographic characteristics													
Age	n.s.	—	—	8.5	8.9	8.3	8.6	8.4	8.5	n.s.	8.5	8.2	8.6
Race[f]	p<.001	.13	—	75.6	93.2+	82.1	74.5	68.7+	74.6	Int > Ext**	78.1	85.4	75.0
SES	n.s.	—	—	3.5	3.8	3.8	4.0	3.9	3.9	n.s.	3.6	4.0	3.9
Social Competence													
Activities	n.s.	—	—	5.7	6.7	6.3	6.6	6.0	6.3	n.s.	6.6	6.4	6.3
Social	p<.001	.24	.6	4.0	4.5	4.7	5.5	4.6	4.6	Int>Ext*	5.4*	3.9*	6.4*
School	p<.001	.26	.4	3.3	3.6	3.6	3.9	2.9	3.4	Int>Ext***	3.9	3.2	4.0*

[a]Age (years), race (% white), SES (Hollingshead's 7-step scale). Mean values for social competence scales based on raw scale sums—range: Activities (0–6), Social (0–12), School (0–12).
[b]Profile types are (A) Schizoid or Anxious-Social Withdrawal, (B) Depressed-Social Withdrawal-Aggressive, (C) Schizoid or Anxious, (D) Somatic Complaints, (E) Hyperactive, (F) Delinquent.
[c-f]See notes for Table 8-2.

Table 8-4
Demographic and Social Competence Correlates
of the Profile Types for 633 Boys Aged 12–16[a]

Dependent variables	Comparisons among profile types			Profile types[b]						Internalizing vs. Externalizing[d]	Unclassified groups[e]		
				Internalizing			Externalizing						
	Significance	Effect size	LSD[c]	A	B	C	D	E	F		ICC <0	Score ≥100	Score ≤25
N	—	—	—	105	78	81	75	76	95	—	25	33	65
Demographic characteristics													
Age	$p<.001$	.28	.6	13.2	13.8	13.0	13.6	14.1	13.8	n.s.	13.7	13.5	13.7
Race	n.s.	—	—	72.0	81.4	87.8	71.9	83.1	80.0	n.s.	88.0	71.0	81.5
SES	n.s.	—	—	3.6	3.5	3.2	3.5	3.5	3.5	n.s.	2.8	4.6*	3.5
Social Competence													
Activities	$p<.05$	.16	.8	6.8	5.8	6.3	6.7	6.2	6.3	n.s.	7.5*	5.6	6.4
Social	$p<.001$	.26	.9	5.5	4.4	4.3	5.5	5.2	5.3	n.s.	5.2	4.5	6.2*
School	$p<.01$	.19	.4	3.5	3.2	2.8	3.0	3.0	3.1	Int > Ext***	4.0*	3.0	4.0

[a]Age (years), race (% white), SES (Hollingshead's 7-step scale). Mean values for social competence scales based on raw scale sums – range: Activities (0–12), Social (0–12), School (0–6).
[b]Profile types are (A) Schizoid, (B) Uncommunicative, (C) Immature-Aggressive, (D) Hyperactive, (E) Uncommunicative-Delinquent, and (F) Delinquent.
[c-e]See notes for Table 8-2.

Table 8-5
Demographic and Social Competence Correlates
of the Profile Types for 272 Girls Aged 4–5[a]

Dependent variables	Comparisons among profile types Effect Significance	size	LSD[c]	Profile types[b] Internalizing A	B	Mixed C	Externalizing D	E	F	G	Internalizing vs. Externalizing[d]	Unclassified groups[e] ICC Score ≤0	Score ≥100	≤25
N	—	—	—	44	22	31	23	17	36	19	—	13	29	38
Demographic characteristics														
Age	n.s.	—	—	4.6	4.6	4.7	4.5	4.5	4.6	4.7	n.s.	4.5	4.5	4.6
Race	n.s.	—	—	94.6	90.0	85.7	90.5	80.0	79.4	94.4	n.s.	100	76.9	84.4
SES	n.s.	—	—	4.2	4.0	4.0	4.4	4.3	4.2	4.8	n.s.	4.0	5.0	4.3
Social competence														
Activities	n.s.	—	—	5.7	6.8	6.8	5.1	6.0	6.0	5.6	n.s.	5.9	5.2	6.0
Social	n.s.	—	—	4.2	5.1	4.6	3.6	4.7	5.0	3.5	n.s.	5.3	2.8*	5.4

[a]Age (years), race (% white), SES (Hollingshead's 7-step scale). Mean values for social competence scales based on raw scale sums—range: Activities (0–12), Social (0–12).
[b]Profile types are (A) Schizoid or Anxious-Somatic Complaints, (B) Social Withdrawal, (C) Obese, (D) Sex Problems, (E) Aggressive, (F) Hyperactive, (G) Hyperactive-Aggressive.
[c-e]See notes for Table 8-2.

Table 8-6

Demographic and Social Competence Correlates of the Profile Types for 435 Girls Aged 6–11[a]

	Comparisons among profile types			Profile types[b]							Internalizing vs. Externalizing[d]	Unclassified groups[e]		
				Internalizing			Mixed	Externalizing				ICC	Score	Score
Dependent variables	Significance	Effect size	LSD[c]	A	B	C	D	E	F	G		<0	≥100	≤25
N	—	—	—	56	61	22	44	46	56	67	—	12	25	46
Demographic characteristics														
Age	$p<.05$	.21	.8	9.1	8.5	8.5	8.5	8.3	8.5	8.0	Int > Ext**	8.2	8.3	9.1
Race[f]	$p<.05$	.22	—	78.8	79.2	94.7	76.7	95.0+	64.7+	70.7	n.s.	90.9	69.6	80.6
SES	n.s.	.12	—	4.0	3.8	4.2	3.8	4.0	4.2	4.4	n.s.	3.2	5.2*	4.1
Social competence														
Activities	$p<.05$	.16	.8	6.0	6.7	6.4	7.0	6.2	5.9	6.2	n.s.	8.0*	5.9	7.3
Social	$p<.001$	.26	.9	4.3	5.1	5.4	5.3	4.5	4.4	4.0	Int > Ext*	5.4	4.3	6.1*
School	$p<.001$	.35	.5	3.7	4.1	4.6	4.3	3.1	3.7	3.5	Int > Ext**	3.8	3.4	4.5*

[a] Age (years), race (% white), SES (Hollingshead's 7-step scale). Mean values for social competence scales based on raw scale sums–range: Activities (0–12), Social (0–12), School (0–6).

[b] Profile types are (A) Depressed-Social Withdrawal, (B) Somatic Complaints, (C) Schizoid-Obsessive, (D) Sex Problems, (E) Hyperactive, (F) Delinquent, (G) Aggressive-Cruel.

[c] See notes for Table 8-2.

Table 8-7
Demographic and Social Competence Correlates
of the Profile Types for 435 Girls Aged 12–16[a]

Dependent variables	Comparisons among profile types			Profile types[b]							Internalizing vs. Externalizing[d]	Unclassified groups[e]		
		Effect		Internalizing			Mixed	Externalizing				ICC	Score	Score
	Significance	size	LSD	A	B	C	D	E	F	G		<0	≥100	≤25
N	—	—	—	29	42	56	56	69	45	54	—	22	26	36
Demographic characteristics														
Age	p<.05	.24	.7	13.6	14.3	14.1	13.8	14.6	14.3	13.8	n.s.	14.3	14.1	14.0
Race	n.s.	—	—	82.8	79.5	92.0	73.6	79.7	79.5	79.6	n.s.	80.9	76.9	69.4
SES	n.s.	—	—	3.4	3.8	3.7	3.5	2.9	3.2	3.6	n.s.	4.1	4.6*	3.8
Social competence														
Activities	n.s.	—	—	6.5	6.1	6.1	6.4	6.1	6.1	5.4	n.s.	5.2*	5.8	7.4
Social	p<.001	.30	1.0	4.9	5.2	5.5	4.7	5.8	5.1	4.1	n.s.	5.6	3.8*	6.6*
School	p<.001	.25	.6	4.0	3.7	4.3	3.8	3.7	3.5	3.3	Int >Ext**	4.3	3.3	4.8*

[a]Age (years), race (% white), SES (Hollingshead's 7-step scale). Mean values for social competence scales based on raw scale sums – range: Activities (0–12), Social (0–12), School (0–6).
[b]Profile types are (A) Anxious-Obsessive, (B) Somatic Complaints, (C) Anxious-Obsessive-Aggressive, (D) Hyperactive-Immature, (E) Delinquent, (F) Depressed-Withdrawal-Delinquent, (G) Aggressive-Cruel.
[c–e]See notes for Table 8-2.

nearly all other groups. Among 6–11- and 12–16-year-old girls, the Aggressive-Cruel groups scored significantly lower than several other groups on the School scale.

Significant differences were likewise found within all sex/age groups on the Social scale. Among 6–11- and 12–16-year-old girls, the Aggressive-Cruel groups scored significantly lower than other groups, as did girls aged 6–11 in the Delinquent and Depressed-Social Withdrawal groups. Internalizers and Externalizers did not differ significantly on the Activities scale in any of the samples. Tables 8-2 through 8-7 include findings for children not classified because they had no positive correlations with profile types or had total behavior problem scores ≤ 25 or ≥ 100.

SUMMARY

By incorporating children's standing on all the scales for their sex and age, the Child Behavior Profile offers a more comprehensive basis for taxonomy than does classification according to individual syndromes or scores on individual scales. Because no diagnostic classification demonstrated sufficient reliability or validity to serve as a validity criterion for profile patterns, we derived a taxonomy empirically by cluster analyzing the profiles of clinically referred children.

For each sex/age group, we found either six or seven profile types that replicated across two randomly selected clinical samples. Some of the profiles are elevated mainly on a single behavior problem scale and resemble diagnostic categories of nosologies such as the DSM. Others are elevated on multiple scales and reflect patterns that have not been recognized in nosological approaches.

Individual children can be classified by computing an intraclass correlation between their profile and each of the profile types. Each type was found to classify from 4 to 22% of the clinically-referred children in a particular sex/age sample. Hierarchical relations among profile types showed that most can be grouped into global Internalizing and Externalizing patterns. Children classified by different profile types were found to differ significantly on demographic variables and social competence scores.

Chapter 9
Relations Between the First Edition and the Revised Edition of the Child Behavior Profile

Preceding chapters have dealt in detail with the Revised Child Behavior Profile. This chapter summarizes relations between the First Edition and the Revised Edition of the Profile.

SCALES OF THE PROFILE

The names of all the social competence and behavior problem scales are the same on the First Edition and the Revised Edition, except that we have added "Anxious" as an alternative title for the Schizoid scale for 4–5 year-old girls and 6–11-year-old boys. The items comprising the scales are also the same, except that a few items differ on each of the behavior problem scales for girls aged 4–5. As mentioned in Chapter 2, the very low referral rate for 4–5-year-old girls restricted our sample for the First Edition to 171 cases. After nine years of collecting data with the Child Behavior Checklist (1973–1982), we accumulated 250 cases on which to repeat our factor analyses. The new factor analyses produced the same eight factors that we used for the First Edition of the Profile, but changes in item loadings dictated changes in the composition of each scale. Table 9-1 shows these changes.

Table 9-1
Changes in Behavior Problem Scales from
First Edition to Revised Edition
for Girls Aged 4–5

Internalizing Scales[a]	First Edition Items Deleted		Items Added to Revised Edition	
I. (II.) Somatic complaints	6.	Encopresis	24.	Doesn't eat well
	19.	Demands attention	56e.	Rashes
	36.	Accident prone	71.	Self-conscious
	107.	Wets self	75.	Shy, timid
			77.	Much sleep
			92.	Talks, walks in sleep
			102.	Slow-moving
II. (I.) Depressed	30.	Fears school	9.	Obsessions
	75.	Shy, timid	25.	Poor peer relations
	111.	Withdrawn	38.	Teased

[a]Scale number on First Edition is in parentheses

Table 9-1(cont'd)

Internalizing Scales[a]	First Edition Items Deleted	Items Added to Revised Edition
III. Schizoid (or Anxious)	10. Hyperactive 47. Nightmares 85. Strange ideas 89. Suspicious 92. Talks, walks in sleep	9. Obsessions
IV. Social Withdrawal	27. Jealous 56d. Eye problems 61. Poor school work 89. Suspicious	18. Harms self 36. Accident prone

Mixed Scale[a]		
V. (VI.) Obese	66. Compulsions 82. Steals outside home 84. Strange behavior 92. Talks, walks in sleep	

Externalizing Scales[a]		
VI. (VII.) Aggressive	10. Hyperactive 19. Demands attention 23. Disobeys at school 93. Excess talk	67. Runs away 104. Loud
VII. (V.) Sex Problems	83. Hoarding	
VIII. Hyperactive	36. Accident prone 39. Bad friends 56e. Rashes	
Other Problems	9. Obsessions 18. Harms self 24. Doesn't eat well 67. Runs away 77. Much sleep	6. Encopresis 27. Jealous 30. Fears school 56d. Eye problems 82. Steals outside home 83. Hoarding 89. Suspicious 107. Wets self

[a]Scale number on First Edition is in parentheses

Because of the changes in items, raw scores on the behavior problem scales of the First Edition for the girls aged 4–5 cannot be directly translated into the T scores of the Revised Edition. Instead, to obtain Revised Edition T scores for the 4–5-year-old girls, you must use the raw scores computed from the behavior problem scales of the Revised Edition.

INTERNALIZING AND EXTERNALIZING

The shifting of items among scales of the Profile for girls aged 4–5 caused some changes in the alignment of scales on the second-order Internalizing and Externalizing factors and some changes of items that are counted toward the total Internalizing and Externalizing scores. Table 9-1 shows the ordering of the behavior problem scales on the Internalizing and Externalizing factors of the Revised Edition, along with the numbers the scales had on the First Edition.

Although there were no changes in the items of the behavior problem scales for the other sex/age groups, we repeated all the second-order factor analyses after converting the clinical samples' raw scores to the Revised Edition T scores. For 6- to 11-year-olds and 12- to 16-year olds of both sexes, the second-order factor analyses of the Revised T scores produced the same ordering of behavior problem scales as on the First Edition. For the 4- to 5-year-old boys, however, the second-order factor analysis of the Revised T scores produced a slightly different ordering of scales on the Internalizing factor: The Somatic Complaints scale now had the fourth highest loading on the Internalizing factor, whereas it had the second highest loading on the First Edition version of the Internalizing factor. Consequently, the Somatic Complaints scale is number IV on the Revised Profile. The Depressed scale replaces the Somatic Complaints scale as number II, and the Immature scale replaces the Depressed scale as number III. However, because the same scales still comprise the Internalizing score, there is no change in the computation of either the Internalizing or Externalizing score. The First Edition raw scores for Internalizing and Externalizing can therefore be converted directly to Revised Edition T scores for all groups except the 4–5-year-old girls.

CHANGES IN T SCORES

Behavior Problem Scales

On the First Edition, normalized T scores were assigned to raw scores on the basis of percentiles, starting with the lowest percentile for a particular scale and ranging up to the 99.9th percentile ($T = 80$). As discussed in Chapter 3, this had two undesirable consequences:

1. Because the percentage of children having the lowest possible score varied considerably from scale to scale, the lowest T score was as low as 30 on some scales and as high as 57 on other scales.

2. The top percentiles, especially from the 98th to the 99.9 percentile ($T = 70$ to 80), were based on very few subjects, and some T scores were derived by interpolation, because not every raw score was actually obtained by subjects in the normative samples.

Changes in the Lowest *T* Scores. To make the lowest *T* scores more uniform among the scales, the Revised Edition assigns a *T* score *no lower than 55* to the lowest raw score on each scale (equivalent to the 69th percentile of the normative sample). For scales on which the lowest raw scores were obtained by 69% or less of the normative sample, these raw scores all get a *T* score of 55. On the few scales where more than 69% of the normative sample obtained a score of zero (the lowest possible raw score), the lowest *T* scores are 56, 57, or 59, depending on the percent who obtained a zero.

Changes in the Highest *T* Scores. To avoid large gaps between *T* scores that represent small changes in raw scores between the 98th and 99.9th percentiles, the Revised Edition bases *T* scores on percentiles only up to the 98th percentile ($T = 70$). Raw scores above the 98th percentile are assigned *T* scores in regular intervals from 71 to 100. (On the First Edition, the maximum *T* score was 90 on each scale, whereas it has been extended to 100 on the Revised Edition to provide greater differentiation among children obtaining extremely high scores.) By assigning scores above the 98th percentile in regular intervals, we have reduced the large gaps that arose in the calibration between some raw scores and *T* scores of 70 to 80 on the First Edition.

Social Competence Scales

On the first Edition, *T* scores were based on percentiles from a *T* score of 20 (.1 of the first percentile) to 80 (99.9th percentile). As with the behavior problem scales, this had undesirable consequences at the extremes of the scales, but these consequences were the reverse of those on the behavior problem scales: Because *low* scores on the social competence scales represent the clinical range and few children in the normative samples had very low scores, the *T* scores from 20 to 30 (percentiles from .1 to 2) had irregular gaps. Furthermore, many children in the normative samples had high scores on the competence scales. On the School scale, in particular, the large proportion of children obtaining top scores produced a large gap between the *T* scores assigned to the highest and second highest raw scores.

Changes in the Lowest *T* Scores. To minimize the irregular gaps in *T* scores between the .1 and 2nd percentiles, the Revised Edition bases *T* scores on percentiles starting at the 2nd percentile (*T* score = 30). Raw scores below the 2nd percentile are now assigned *T* scores in regular intervals from 10 to 29. Note that the clinical range of the social competence scales spans only 20 *T* scores (10 to 29). This contrasts with the 30 *T* scores (71 to 100) spanned by the clinical range of the behavior problem scales. The smaller span of *T* scores in the clinical range on the social competence scales reflects the smaller range of possible raw scores: The raw scores below the 2nd percentile range from 0 to 2 or 3 in intervals of .5 on most of the social competence scales.

Changes in the Highest *T* Scores. To reduce large gaps in *T* scores resulting where a large proportion of children in the normative sample obtained a high score, we set 55 as the maximum *T* score on the social competence scales. All raw scores falling at the 69th percentile or *higher* in the normative sample were therefore assigned a *T* score of 55. Note that both the social competence scales and the behavior problem scales span 46 *T* scores, although the range is from 10 to 55 for the social competence scales and from 55 to 100 for the behavior problem scales.

Change in Hand-Scored Layout. One more change in the Revised Edition is that the social competence scale scores for all age groups of a particular sex are now displayed side-by-side on the hand-scored Profile. Be careful to use the columns designated for the age of the child being scored.

Internalizing, Externalizing, and Total Behavior Problem Scores

Because so many items are included in the Internalizing, Externalizing, and total behavior problem scores, and these scores had fairly normal distributions in the normative samples, we based *T* scores on percentiles from the lowest percentile to the 98th percentile (*T*=70) in each sex/age group. We then assigned *T* scores from 71 to 89 in regular intervals to the raw scores that ranged from the 98th percentile of the *normative* sample to the highest raw score found in the *clinical* sample for a particular sex/age group. *T* scores from 90 through 100 were assigned in regular intervals to the remaining raw scores. This differed in two ways from the First Edition procedure:

1. The First Edition based *T* scores on percentiles up to the 99.9th percentile (*T*=80), whereas the Revised Edition bases *T* scores on percentiles up to the 98th percentile (*T*=70).

2. On the First Edition, scores above the highest actually found in our clinical sample were all given a *T* score of 90; on the Revised Edition, these scores are assigned *T* scores from 90 to 100 in regular intervals.

Total Social Competence Scores

The Revised Edition bases total social competence *T* scores on percentiles from the 2nd percentile (*T*=30) to the highest possible raw score (*T*=80). Scores below the 2nd percentile are divided into regular intervals from a *T* score of 29 down to a *T* score of 10. This differs from the First Edition procedure of basing *T* scores on percentiles from .1 of the first percentile (*T*=20) up to the highest raw score (*T*=80).

STATISTICAL RELATIONS BETWEEN THE TWO EDITIONS

Table 9-2 presents Pearson correlations and statistically significant changes in mean scores between the First Edition and Revised Edition *T* scores for all scales, as computed for nonreferred children. Table 9-3 presents the same information for clinically-referred children who are demographically matched to the nonreferred children.

Table 9-2
Correlations between First Edition and Revised Edition *T*
Scores for Nonclinical Sample

	Boys			Girls		
Behavior Problem	*4-5*	*6-11*	*12-16*	*4-5*	*6-11*	*12-16*
Scales	*N = 100*	*N = 300*	*N = 250*	*N = 100*	*N = 300*	*N = 250*
Aggressive	.82[b]	.78[b]	.82[b]	.82[b]	.82[b]	.83[b]
Anxious Obsessive						.83[b]
Cruel					.99	1.00
Delinquent	.94[b]	.97[b]	.99[b]		1.00[b]	.85[b]
Depressed	.84[b]	.82[b]		.81[b]	.84[b]	
Depressed Withdrawal						.86[b]
Hostile Withdrawal			.92[b]			
Hyperactive		.85[b]	.86[b]	.81[b]	.85[b]	
Immature	.84[b]		.99[b]			
Immature Hyperactive						.88[b]
Obese				.85[b]		
Obsessive Compulsive		.85[b]	.86[b]			
Schizoid (or Anxious)	1.00[b]	.89[b]	.95[b]	.82[b]		.96[b]
Schizoid Obsessive					1.00[b]	
Sex Problems	.98[bc]			.72[b]	.92[b]	
Social Withdrawal	.88[b]	.88[b]		.82[b]	.89[b]	
Somatic Complaints	1.00[b]	.99[b]	.95[b]	.66[b]	.93[b]	1.00
Uncommunicative		.87[b]	.85[b]			
Internalizing	1.00	1.00[ac]	1.00[ac]	.95[a]	1.00[ac]	1.00
Externalizing	1.00	1.00	1.00[a]	.98[a]	1.00[ac]	1.00
Total Score	1.00[bc]	1.00	1.00[a]	1.00	1.00[a]	1.00[bc]
Social Competence Scales						
Activities	.91[a]	.91[a]	.91[a]	.91[a]	.90[a]	.91[a]
Social	.92[a]	.91[a]	.90[a]	.90[a]	.91[a]	.92[a]
School		.79[a]	.81[a]		.83[a]	.83[a]
Total Score	1.00	1.00	1.00[a]	1.00[ac]	1.00[ac]	1.00[a]

Median correlation = .92

Note—All correlations are significant at $p < .001$

[a]First Edition > Revised Edition at $p < .05$

[b]Revised Edition > First Edition at $p < .05$

[c]When corrected for the number of comparisons, the difference between the First Edition and Revised Edition is not significant.

Table 9-3
Correlations between First Edition and Revised Edition *T* Scores for Clinical Sample

Behavior Problem Scales	Boys			Girls		
	4-5 $N=100$	*6-11* $N=300$	*12-16* $N=250$	*4-5* $N=100$	*6-11* $N=300$	*12-16* $N=250$
Aggressive	.95	.97[b]	.96[b]	.92	.96	.96[bc]
Anxious Obsessive						.95[b]
Cruel					.99[ac]	.96[a]
Delinquent	.98	.99[b]	.97[a]		1.00[b]	.96[b]
Depressed	.93	.96[b]		.88[ac]	.96[ac]	
Depressed Withdrawal						.98[b]
Hostile Withdrawal			.98			
Hyperactive		.97[b]	.98[b]	.91[bc]	.97	
Immature	.96[b]		.99[b]			
Immature Hyperactive						.96[b]
Obese				.90		
Obsessive Compulsive		.97[b]	.95[b]			
Schizoid (or Anxious)	.94[b]	.97[b]	.98[b]	.88[ac]		.98[b]
Schizoid Obsessive					.99[a]	
Sex Problems	.98[a]			.92[b]	.97[b]	
Social Withdrawal	.97[b]	.95[b]		.91	.97	
Somatic Complaints	.99[b]	1.00[b]	.98[b]	.83[a]	.97[b]	1.00[b]
Uncommunicative		.98[b]	.97[b]			
Internalizing	1.00	.99[a]	1.00[a]	.96[a]	.98[a]	1.00[a]
Externalizing	1.00[a]	1.00[a]	1.00[a]	.93[a]	1.00[a]	1.00[a]
Total Score	.99[b]	1.00	1.00[a]	1.00	1.00[b]	1.00[b]
Social Competence Scales						
Activities	.98[ac]	.98[a]	.98[a]	.98[ac]	.95[a]	.97[a]
Social	.98[bc]	.98	.99[b]	.99	.99[a]	.99
School		.91[a]	.95		.93[a]	.93
Total Score	1.00[a]	1.00[a]	.99[a]	1.00[a]	1.00[a]	1.00[a]

Median correlation = .98

Note—All correlations are significant at $p<.001$

[a]First Edition > Revised Edition at $p<.05$

[b]Revised Edition > First Edition at $p<.05$

[c]When corrected for the number of comparisons, the difference between the two editions is not significant.

Correlations Between Scores in the Two Editions

As shown in Tables 9-2 and 9-3, the correlations between the two editions range from .99 to 1.00 for total behavior problem and social competence scores. Children's rank ordering on these scores is thus virtually identical on the two editions. For Internalizing and Externalizing, the correlations range from .93 to 1.00. The only correlations below .98 are for 4–5-year-old girls, for whom changes in a few items assigned to the Internalizing and Externalizing groupings altered the rank ordering of individual scores slightly.

The correlations for narrow-band behavior problem scales reflect some-what larger changes in rank ordering, especially in the nonclinical sample of 4–5-year-old girls, whose correlations range from .66 for Somatic Complaints to .85 for Obese. For this group, the changes in scores are caused partly by changes in the items assigned to the scales. For all the other groups, however, the only changes are in the assignment of T scores, causing some children who differed from each other in T scores on the First Edition to share the same T score on the Revised Edition, and vice versa. The generally lower correlations for the nonclinical sample than the clinical sample reflect the impact of grouping low behavior problem scores at $T = 55$ and high social competence scores also at $T = 55$. Both these changes affect the nonclinical sample more than the clinical sample.

Differences Between Mean Scores in the Two Editions

In Tables 9-2 and 9-3, the superscript *a* marks significant *decreases* in mean scores, while the superscript *b* marks significant *increases* in mean scores from the First to the Revised Edition.

On the narrow-band behavior problem scales, all 48 significant differences for the nonclinical sample and 32 of the 41 significant differences for the clinical sample involved *increases* in mean scores from the First to the Revised Edition. This tendency for Revised Edition scores to be higher is caused mainly by raising the lowest T score on each scale to a minimum of 55, which raises scores of the nonclinical sample more than those of the clinical sample.

On the Internalizing, Externalizing, total behavior problem score, social competence scales, and total social competence score, most of the significant differences in both samples involve *decreases* from the First Edition to the Revised Edition. On the narrow band social competence scales, this largely reflects the compression of the top scores to a maximum $T = 55$, while on the other scales it reflects the adjustment of T scores outside the 98% constituting the normal range.

Despite the many significant differences between the First and Revised Edition, most were very small, owing their significance mainly to the large sample sizes and small variance of changes between the editions. Most large differences occurred in the nonclinical sample, where the following scales showed *increases* exceeding 5 T scores: Aggressive scale for all groups; Depressed scale for boys aged 4–5 and girls aged 6–11; Hyperactive scale for girls aged 4–5; Anxious-Obsessive scale for girls aged 12–16. The School scale showed the largest changes of all, with *decreases* ranging from 6.2 to 9.7 in the four sex/age groups for whom it is scored. In the clinical sample, the only difference > 5 was a decrease of 6.2 in the mean Externalizing score for girls aged 4–5, owing more to the change of item assignments than to recalibration of T scores.

The smaller changes in the scores of the clinical sample than the nonclinical sample reduce the difference between their T scores, although as Chapter 7 shows, the differences remain highly significant on all scales. If more separation is desired for statistical purposes, raw scores can be substituted for T scores. Nevertheless, by reducing unimportant variance at the "healthy" end of each scale, the T scores of the Revised Edition may offer greater statistical power for discriminating between deviant and nondeviant children, even if the magnitude of differences is less than with raw scores or the T scores of the First Edition.

TRANSFORMING FIRST EDITION DATA INTO REVISED EDITION T SCORES

The precise relations between specific raw scores and specific T scores differ from scale to scale, because the scales differ in number of items and in raw score distributions. Consequently, there is no simple formula for transforming First Edition T scores directly into Revised Edition T scores. Instead, the easiest way to obtain Revised Edition T scores is to use either the hand-scoring profile forms or the computer-scoring program for the Revised Edition. Note that, because the CBCL has not been changed, the same raw data from parents are used for both editions of the Profile.

If raw scores have already been computed for the scales of the First Edition, these raw scores are the same as would be obtained on the Revised Edition, except for the behavior problem scales and Internalizing and Externalizing scores of the 4- to 5-year-old girls. As explained earlier, changes in the items of these scales for the 4- to 5-year-old girls require that raw scale scores be computed using the Revised Profile. (Note also that the location and numbering of three Internalizing scales have changed for boys aged 4–5, but the content and scoring of these scales have not changed.)

Users who purchased a computer tape of the First Edition scoring program from us can have the new program copied onto the tape by returning the tape to us with a payment of $25. The new program makes more efficient use of computer facilities and is much more compatible with IBM systems than the First Edition program was.

CLINICAL CUTOFF POINTS ON TOTAL SCORES

As discussed in Chapter 7, the 90th percentile on the distribution of total behavior problem scores for our normative samples discriminates effectively between clinically-referred and nonreferred children (see Achenbach &

Edelbrock, 1981, for details of the statistical analyses). The 10th percentile on the total social competence score adds further discriminative power when used in combination with the 90th percentile on the total behavior problem score. The computation of total behavior problem and social competence scores is the same on both editions of the Profile, and changes in the assignment of *T* scores do not affect the cutoff points.

PROFILE TYPES

In Chapter 8, we discussed the use of the Child Behavior Profile as a basis for taxonomy—a way of forming groups of children whose parents report similar patterns of behavior problems. By cluster analyzing the profiles of clinically-referred children, we constructed typologies of profile patterns for each sex/age group. Each typology includes either six or seven patterns that classify most of the profiles actually found in our clinical samples.

We also developed procedures for computing correlations between an individual child's profile pattern and each of the types found for his/her age and sex. These correlations are automatically computed and printed on profiles produced by our computer-scoring program. A look at the correlations printed across the bottom of the profile enables the user to determine which profile type the child's pattern resembles most closely and whether the child's pattern is a relatively pure example of any type. Because the intraclass correlation is used, relatively small coefficients can indicate relatively strong resemblance to a type. For example, an intraclass correlation of .40 between a child's profile and a particular type corresponds to a Pearson correlation of about .75. Groups of children whose profiles correlate $\geq .40$ with a type are quite homogeneous with respect to their profile patterns.

As explained in Chapter 8, it was preferable to perform our cluster analyses on behavior problem scale scores that were standardized within our clinical sample, instead of using *T* scores derived from the normative sample. In order to compute a child's correlation with the types, his/her raw scores must first be converted to *T* scores based on our clinical sample. (Our computer-scoring program does this automatically in the process of computing the intraclass correlations and prints the clinical *T* score, as well as the normative *T* score, for each scale.)

It is the correlation between the child's clinical *T* scores and the *T* scores of each profile type that reflects the child's resemblance to each type. As a consequence, the pattern evident when the child's scores are displayed on the profile in terms of normative *T* scores may not visually correspond to the *T* score pattern whose correlation with the profile type is computed. This is because the normative *T* scores show how a child compares with *normative* groups of agemates, whereas the clinical *T* scores show how the child compares with *clinically-referred* agemates.

The lack of direct correspondence between the pattern evident on a scored profile and the pattern used to compute resemblance to profile types may be confusing to some users of the Revised Edition, just as it was on the First Edition. The Revised Edition may reduce confusion somewhat, however, because the extension of the normative T scores to 100 and the compression of the low end of these T scores make some patterns of T scores derived from clinical and normative samples appear more similar to each other on the Revised Edition than the First Edition. Nevertheless, the profile typology and the intraclass correlations of individual profiles with profile types remain the same as on the First Edition. It is therefore still necessary to determine a child's resemblance to each type in terms of intraclass correlations, rather than visually.

SUMMARY

Relations between the First Edition and Revised Edition of the Child Behavior Profile can be summarized as follows:

1. Names of all the behavior problem and social competence scales are the same on the two editions.

2. Composition of the scales is the same except for the behavior problem scales for the 4–5-year-old girls, which are based on factor analyses of a larger sample for the Revised Edition.

3. Internalizing and Externalizing raw scores are computed in the same way on the two editions for all groups except girls aged 4–5, where changes in scale composition affect the items contributing to the Internalizing and Externalizing scores. (A slight change in the ordering of the Internalizing scales for boys aged 4–5 does not affect the composition of the Internalizing and Externalizing scores).

4. Although some raw scores get the same T scores on both editions, there are changes in the assignment of some T scores on all scales, Internalizing and Externalizing, total behavior problem score, and total social competence score. The easiest way to obtain Revised Edition T scores is to use either the hand-scoring profile forms or computer-scoring program for the revised Edition, rather than trying to convert First Edition T scores to Revised Edition T scores.

5. Tables 9-2 and 9-3 show correlations and changes in mean T scores between the two editions.

6. Raw scores for clinical cutoffs are the same on both editions for total behavior problem and social competence scores.

7. Profile types and the correlations of individual profiles with each type are computed in the same way for both editions.

Chapter 10
Clinical Use of the Child Behavior
Checklist and Profile

We feel that good clinical practice should be firmly grounded in research. Conversely, good research requires close links with clinical practice and should improve services to children. We have therefore designed the CBCL and Profile for both clinical and research purposes.

This chapter illustrates clinical applications, while Chapter 11 deals with research applications. In presenting clinical applications, we will not provide an exhaustive set of rules or "interpretations." Instead, we offer illustrations and guidelines in relation to the following topics: Intake and evaluation; clinical interviewing; comparison of mothers' and fathers' views; diagnosis; intervention; program accountability and planning; clinical training; and differing service settings.

We wish to emphasize that practitioners should adapt our materials to their own situations and integrate them with other types of data. Diagnostic formulations and management decisions should *never* be based on a single type or source of data. The essence of clinical creativity is to synthesize diverse and imperfect tools and data into practical solutions suited for each individual case.

Responsible clinical practice also requires that clinical judgment be tested against various kinds of evidence. The Profile can facilitate this process by enabling the clinician to *compare* a parent's description of his or her child with what other parents report about their children. The Profile also provides ways of comparing parents' reports about their child at different points in time, such as before and after an intervention, a mother's report with a father's report about their child, and parents' reports with those of other important adults, such as the child's teacher.

In short, our materials provide a standardized, normative framework for linking parents' observations of a particular child with other people's observations of that child and other parents' observations of their own children. However, there should be a complementary relation between individualized clinical services and standardized procedures. Standardized procedures enable the clinician to assess the individual from the perspective of data systematically aggregated across many cases and to obtain numerical scores as a baseline from which to measure change in reported behavior. Yet, standardized procedures cannot replace the detailed study of the individual case, which inevitably involves much nonstandardized, idiosyncratic information. Data from standardized procedures must be integrated into the mosaic of the case; such a picture necessarily includes totally unique features, as well as features assessable on the same dimensions as other cases.

INTAKE AND EVALUATION

A key application of the CBCL and Profile is in the intake and evaluation of children referred for mental health services. The CBCL is designed to be self-explanatory for parents with reading skills as low as the fifth grade level. Because most parents (and parent surrogates) involved in a referral expect to report on their child's behavior, the CBCL is a natural part of the intake routine. If intake materials are sent to parents before their first appointment, the CBCL can be enclosed to be filled out at home and returned by mail or brought to the first appointment.

If intake materials are not routinely mailed in advance, parents can be asked to come about 20 minutes before their first interview to fill out the CBCL in the waiting room. It is helpful for parents to have access to someone who can answer questions about the CBCL, such as a receptionist or intake worker who is familiar with the CBCL. However, answers to parents' questions about filling out the CBCL should focus only on the meaning of the items, with examples of relevant behaviors where necessary. The person answering the questions should *not* try to probe the parent's personality or encourage the parent to make inferences about the child's psychodynamics, but should merely help the parent fill out the CBCL to describe the child's behavior as the parent sees it.

If a parent cannot read or has other problems in filling out the CBCL, it can be read to the parent. If the parent can read a little, it may be helpful to give the parent the CBCL, but have an interviewer read each item and fill out the responses. However, the focus should always be on the parent's *description* of the child's behavior, rather than on either the parent's or the child's psychodynamics.

CLINICAL INTERVIEWING

When the clinician first interviews a parent, it is helpful to have the completed CBCL (and, if possible, the scored Profile) as a take-off point for interviewing. Parents may spontaneously wish to discuss some of their responses. The clinician may wish to ask for clarification of certain items that the parent reports, especially such items as *9. Can't get mind off certain thoughts, obsessions; 40. Hears things that aren't there; 70. Sees things that aren't there; 84. Strange behavior;* and *85. Strange ideas.*

After obtaining clarification of the parent's responses, the clinician can use the items of greatest concern and the Profile scales showing the most deviance as foci for interviewing about the history and context of the problems. The social competence portion of the Profile can also be used to identify a child's current strengths and needs for improvement.

As other data become available, such as reports by teachers and observers, psychological and laboratory tests, etc., the clinician can compare them with the picture presented by the parents via the CBCL and the Profile. Disagreements with other types of data do not necessarily mean that parents' reports are wrong — they may accurately reflect the behavior the parents see, but their child may behave differently in other contexts. On the other hand, if the clinician concludes that parents' perceptions are indeed distorted, then interventions can focus on changing the misperceptions revealed by their responses to the CBCL.

HAVING BOTH PARENTS FILL OUT CBCLS

Whenever feasible, it is valuable to have both parents independently fill out CBCLs. If both parents are not available, it is also useful to have CBCLs filled out by one parent and another adult who knows the child well, such as a grandparent, or by parent surrogates if no parent is available. The purpose can be explained in words such as the following:

> "We would like each of you to fill out this form to describe your child's behavior. Parents usually differ somewhat in the way they see their children, so don't worry if your spouse does not report exactly the same behavior as you do. Just fill it out to describe the way *you* see your child."

The specific behaviors reported and the Profiles scored from both CBCLs can then be compared to reveal areas of agreement and disagreement. Small semantic disagreements are not uncommon. For example, one parent may score item *37. Gets in many fights* for approximately the same behavior as another parent scores item *57. Physically attacks people.* However, most such semantic differences do not result in different scores on the Profile, because the items are closely enough related to be scored on the same scales.

Furthermore, interparent concordance data (Chapter 6) show that mothers' CBCLs do not yield significantly higher or lower scores than fathers' CBCLs on most scales of the Profile. Consequently, when major disagreements *do* occur between a particular mother and father, they are clinically informative and should be explored to answer questions such as the following:

1. Do a parent's own problems or biases toward the child make that parent a poor informant?
2. Does lack of contact with the child make one parent a poor informant?
3. Does one parent evoke particular problem behaviors from the child?
4. Is one parent absent when the problems occur?
5. Do differences in values cause one parent to judge particular behavior more harshly than the other parent?
6. Is one parent less tolerant of difficult behavior than the other?
7. Is one parent prone to deny problems for reasons of social desirability?

Disagreements between parents' CBCL responses can be explored in interviews with the parents. The reasons for the disagreements are often important in formulating plans for interventions. In some cases, for example, the clinical goal may be to change one parent's perceptions of the child or behavior toward the child, rather than to change the child's behavior. In such cases, reassessment with the CBCL after the intervention can show whether a parent's perceptions have indeed changed.

Clinical Example

As an example, Figure 10-1 shows Profiles of an 8-year-old girl drawn from CBCLs filled out by her mother and father. Even though they did not give exactly the same scores on every item, their total scores are quite similar on all scales except the Aggressive scale. On the Aggressive scale, the mother reported problems that earned a total raw score of 25, which is in the clinical range. The father, by contrast, reported problems that earned a total raw score of 15, which falls at about the 90th percentile of the normal range.

Examination of scores for each item of the Aggressive scale reveals that both parents agreed on certain problems, but the mother scored them 2, whereas the father scored them 1. On only one item, *97. Threatens people,* did the mother score a 2, while the father scored a 0. There was thus fairly good agreement on the presence of aggressive behaviors, but the father saw them as less intense than the mother. When this discrepancy was pursued in interviews with the parents, they agreed that it was because most of the aggressive behaviors occurred in interactions between mother and daughter. The father was aware of them, but not present when the most intense aggression took place in the course of mother-daughter battles. It was during these battles that the daughter often threatened her mother, leading the mother to score *97. Threatens people* as 2, whereas the father had been unaware of this particular behavior.

Although the mother's picture of her daughter was somewhat more negative than the father's, the behavior of both the mother and daughter seemed to need changing, rather than just the mother's perceptions of her daughter. The high scores on the Depressed scale obtained from both parents' CBCLs also indicate that depressive feelings were of concern in their own right. It would be especially important to determine whether the aggression toward mother led to depressive feelings or vice versa, or whether problems in both areas were byproducts of something else. A low score on the Social scale of the Profile (not shown) suggests that a lack of positive social involvement with others was another facet of the problems. Strengthening social involvement outside the home might be one avenue to improving the girl's feelings about herself and relieving conflict with her mother.

DIAGNOSIS

"To diagnose" literally means "to distinguish" or "to know apart." (The Greek roots of the word are *dia* = "apart" and *gignoskein* = "to know.") Confusion often arises because the term *diagnosis* is used in both a narrow sense and a broad sense.

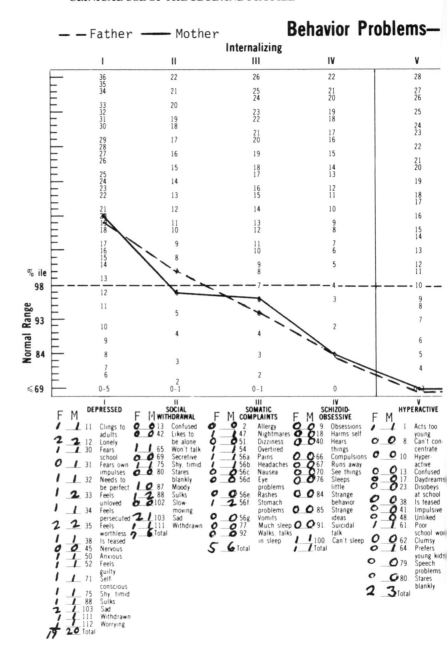

Figure 10-1. Profiles scored from CBCLs filled out by the mother and father of an 8-year-old girl.

Girls Aged 6-11

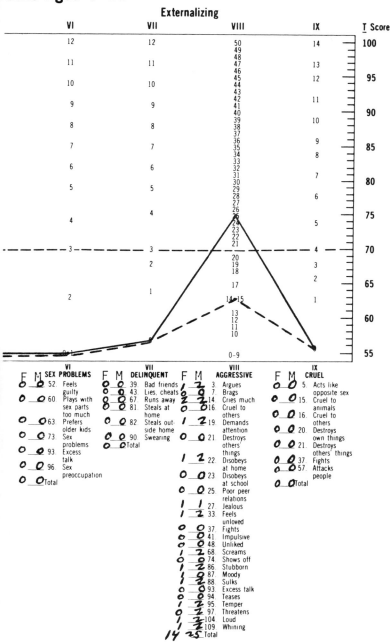

Externalizing

| | VI | VII | VIII | IX | T Score |

In its narrow sense, *diagnosis* is almost synonymous with *classification*. For example, a leading psychiatric diagnostician calls diagnosis "the medical term for classification" (Guzé, 1978, p. 53). A dictionary definition of diagnosis in the narrow sense is: "the art or act of identifying a disease from its signs or symptoms" (Woolf, 1977, p. 313). Diagnosis in the narrow sense is also called *formal diagnosis.*

In its broader sense, *diagnosis* is defined as: (*a*) "investigation or analysis of the cause or nature of a condition, situation or problem;" and (*b*) "a statement or conclusion concerning the nature or cause of some phenomenon" (Woolf, 1977, p. 313). This concept of diagnosis pertains to *diagnostic formulations.* How do the CBCL and Profile relate to diagnosis in the narrow sense and diagnosis in the broad sense?

Diagnosis in the Narrow Sense: Formal Diagnosis

Many mental health services require formal diagnoses for purposes of record keeping and third party payments. The DSM-III is currently the dominant diagnostic system for these purposes in the United States. It provides the names and criteria for specific disorders thought to characterize children. In deciding that a girl meets the DSM criteria for an Undersocialized Nonaggressive Conduct Disorder, for example, we make a *formal* diagnosis of this disorder.

The quasi-medical nature of mental health services and the mechanisms of third party payments have fostered the use of the DSM as a system for formal diagnosis. Many of the major adult categories, such as schizophrenia and affective disorders, have a long history predating the DSM and have been progressively revised through research and clinical experience. This is not true of most child and adolescent categories, however, which were formulated largely by the DSM-III committee. It remains to be seen how validly they correspond to children's disorders. Furthermore, the reliability of the DSM diagnosis of children's disorders is poor (for reliability figures, see DSM-III, Appendix F; Achenbach, 1982, Chapter 15, provides a more detailed critique). Although a key purpose of diagnostic categories is to improve the care of new cases by capitalizing on experience with similar cases, there is as yet little evidence that DSM diagnoses serve this purpose.

Because the DSM is the prevailing system for formal diagnosis, clinicians often need to relate the diagnostic data they obtain to the DSM's categories. Yet, many of the behaviors specified by the DSM criteria for childhood disorders are unlikely to be reported by the child or directly observed by the clinician. In order to make a DSM diagnosis, the clinician must therefore obtain reports from adults who have opportunities to observe the relevant behavior. For example, in its criteria for Attention Deficit Disorder with Hyperactivity, DSM-III states:

> "The signs must be reported by adults in the child's environment, such as parents and teachers" (p. 43).

Yet the DSM does not specify what data from parents and teachers determine whether a child meets the criteria. Similarly, the criteria for conduct disorders require information on physical violence, stealing, friendships, lying, violation of rules, running away, and remorse for misdeeds. Clinicians seldom have opportunities to directly observe the criterial behavior. Instead, information must be obtained from other people, although the DSM does not specify how or from whom. Nor does the DSM say how clinicians are to use other people's reports to infer the *degree* of deviance.

Because diagnostic decisions inevitably depend on the reports of nonclinicians, we have sought to make this aspect of assessment more systematic and reliable. The behavior problem scales of the Profile were derived empirically through factor analysis, whereas the DSM child categories were developed through committee negotiations. It should not be surprising, therefore, that the DSM categories do not correspond directly to the empirically derived scales. Nevertheless, a number of the behavior problem scales are highly relevant to DSM diagnoses.

As an example, if a child scores in the clinical range (above the 98th percentile or a *T* score of 70) only on the Hyperactive scale of the Profile, this suggests a DSM diagnosis of Attention Deficit Disorder with Hyperactivity. Indeed, our cluster analyses (Chapter 8) have identified a Profile pattern within most sex/age groups that is deviant mainly on the Hyperactive scale. Because the computer-scored version of the Profile prints out the correlation between a child's Profile pattern and each of the types for that sex/age group, clinicians having access to computer scoring can readily see how closely the child's Profile resembles the Hyperactive type. (An intraclass correlation $\geq .40$ indicates that a child's profile corresponds quite closely to a particular type, as explained in Chapter 8.) Similarly, a high score on the Aggressive scale would be evidence for DSM's Undersocialized Aggressive Conduct Disorder, and a high score on the Delinquent scale would be evidence for DSM's Socialized Conduct Disorder. Relations between all the Profile scales and DSM diagnoses are shown in Table 10-1.

Although the behaviors encompassed by some Profile scales approximate the behaviors specified for some DSM diagnoses, the relations between other scales and diagnoses are more tenuous. For example, the only behavior problem specified for the DSM diagnosis of Elective Mutism is "Continuous refusal to talk in almost all social situations, including at school" (p. 63). The CBCL includes "Refuses to talk" as an item, but its behavior problem scales comprise groups of behavior problems that tend to occur together. For boys aged 6–11 and 12–16, we found a group that included the item "Refuses to talk," but also a number of other items indicative of general uncommunicativeness. Because our Uncommunicative scale includes more than just refusal to talk, and the refusal to talk may not always be as extreme as required for the diagnosis of Elective Mutism, the relation of Profile scores to the diagnosis of Elective Mutism will probably be weaker than to the diagnosis of Attention Deficit Disorder with Hyperactivity.

Table 10-1
Approximate Relations Between DSM-III Diagnoses and Scales of the Child Behavior Profile

DSM-III Diagnosis	Profile Scale	Sex/Age Groups
Attention Deficit Disorders:		
314.01 With hyperactivity	Hyperactive	B 6–11, 12–16; G 4–5, 6–11
	Immature Hyperactive	G 12–16
314.00 Without hyperactivity	_____ [a]	
314.80 Residual type	_____	
Conduct Disorders:		
312.00 Undersocialized, aggressive	Aggressive	All groups
312.10 Undersocialized, nonaggressive	_____	
312.23 Socialized, aggressive	Delinquent	B 4–5, 6–11, 12–16
312.21 Socialized nonaggressive	Delinquent	G 6–11, 12–16
312.90 Atypical	_____	
Anxiety Disorders of Childhood or Adolescence:		
309.21 Separation anxiety, disorder	_____	
313.21 Avoidant disorder	_____	
313.00 Overanxious disorder	Anxious-Obsessive[b]	G 12–16
	Schizoid or Anxious	B 6–11; G 4–5
Other Disorders of Childhood or Adolescence:		
313.22 Schizoid disorder	Social Withdrawal	B, G 4–5, 6–11
	Hostile Withdrawal	B 12–16
	Depressed Withdrawal	G 12–16
313.23 Elective mutism	(Uncommunicative)[c]	B 6–11, 12–16
313.81 Oppositional disorder	_____	
313.82 Identity disorder	_____	
Pervasive Developmental Disorders:		
299.8 Childhood onset pervasive developmental	_____	
299.9 Atypical	_____	
302.60 Gender identity disorder of childhood	Sex Problems	B, G 4–5
V62.30 Academic problems	School	B, G 6–11, 12–16
Disorders not Specific to Childhood or Adolescence:		
300.30 Obsessive-compulsive disorder	Obsessive-Compulsive	B 6–11, 12–16
	Anxious-Obsessive	G 12–16
	Schizoid-Obsessive	G 6–11

300.81 Somatization disorder	Somatic Complaints	All groups
301.22 Schizotypal personality disorder	(Schizoid)[c]	B 4-5, 6-11, 12-16; G 4-5, 12-16
	(Schizoid-Obsessive)[c]	G 6-11
300.40 Dysthymic disorder	(Depressed)[c]	B, G 4-5, 6-11
	(Depressed Withdrawal)[c]	G 12-16
_____	Cruel	G 6-11, 12-16
_____	Immature	B 4-5, 12-16
_____	Obese	G 4-5
_____	Sex Problems	G 6-11

[a]The Profile for our Teacher's Report Form (Chapter 12) includes a scale entitled Inattentive that resembles the DSM's Attention Deficit Disorder Without Hyperactivity.

[b]The Teacher Profile includes a scale entitled Anxious that resembles the DSM's Overanxious Disorder.

[c]Parentheses indicate tenuous relation between DSM diagnosis and Profile Scale.

Scales that are still more weakly related to DSM diagnoses are enclosed in parentheses in Table 10-1. And, as Table 10-1 shows, some DSM diagnoses have no counterparts among the empirically derived Profile scales, while some Profile scales have no counterparts among the DSM diagnoses.

Categorical Diagnoses and Quantitative Scale Scores. In considering relations between a child's Profile and DSM diagnoses, it is important to note that the Profile makes it possible to compare the *degree* of deviance on each scale with the *degree* of deviance on each other scale. DSM diagnoses, by contrast, are made largely in terms of yes-or-no judgments of whether the child meets the criteria for a particular diagnosis. In many cases, therefore, a child having several kinds of behavior problems may meet the criteria for more than one DSM diagnosis. For example, consider the Profile shown in Figure 10-2 for a 12-year-old boy. The high score on the Hyperactive scale reflects behavior that would qualify the boy for a DSM diagnosis of Attention Deficit Disorder with Hyperactivity. Yet, his high score on the Aggressive scale reflects behavior that would also qualify him for a DSM diagnosis of Undersocialized Aggressive Conduct Disorder. These separate categorical diagnoses imply that the boy is suffering from two distinct "illnesses," whereas the main basis for the diagnoses is a *pattern* of behavior that includes overactivity and aggression (as well as behaviors encompassed by the Hostile Withdrawal and Delinquent scales).

Profile patterns offer a broader perspective that can help prevent prematurely pigeon-holing children in terms of categorical "disease entities" such as Attention Deficit Disorders, even if such categorical labels are required for record-keeping and third party payments, and may ultimately be justified in some cases. When a child's Profile pattern does correspond closely to a DSM diagnosis, other types of data — such as developmental history, school data, and family dynamics — should also be used in making the diagnosis.

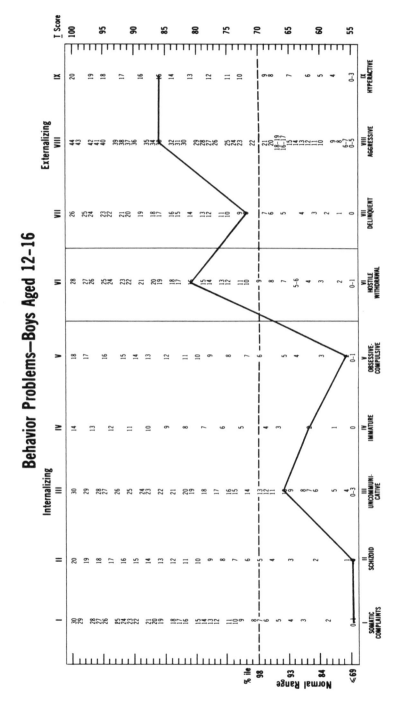

Figure 10-2. Profile of a 12-year-old boy whose behavior problems could qualify him for DSM-III diagnoses of Attention Deficit Disorder with Hyperactivity and Undersocialized Aggressive Conduct Disorder.

Diagnosis in the Broad Sense: Diagnostic Formulations

The CBCL and Profile are designed to contribute to diagnostic formulations by providing differentiated pictures of parents' views of their children's competencies and problems, rather than categorical diagnostic labels. As outlined earlier in the Chapter, the CBCL is a natural part of the diagnostic phase in which information is gathered from parents. The parents' CBCL data can be integrated with the developmental history, clinician's observations of the child and parents, interview impressions, family dynamics, school reports, psychological and achievement test data, and medical findings.

In integrating the different kinds of information, the clinician can use the CBCL and Profile to focus the diagnostic inquiry on questions such as the following:

1. Is the picture obtained from the CBCL and Profile consistent with the referring complaints?

    a. Does the Profile show that the problem behaviors exceed those reported by parents in the normative samples, as indicated by scores above the 98th percentile on the narrow-band scales or the 90th percentile on the total problem scale?

    b. Is deviance concentrated in the areas of the referring complaints or in other areas? For example, "hyperactivity" is a common referring complaint that often masks deviation in other areas among children whose activity levels are not especially deviant.

2. Is a similar picture obtained from both parents and from other adults, or are there clinically important discrepancies?

    a. Discrepancies should be investigated to determine whether they reflect genuine variations in the child's behavior or whether the differences lie in the informants' perceptions.

    b. Differences in perceptions should guide the choice of *whose* behavior and/or perceptions should be the chief targets for change: the child's, one or both parents', the teacher's, or somebody else's.

    c. The choice of intervention should be based on whose perceptions or behavior are to be changed—for example, interventions mainly with the parents, child, school, or some combination thereof.

3. Does the correlation between the child's Profile and the types for that child's sex/age group show that the child is similar to a particular group of clinically-referred children, or is the child's pattern unlike those previously identified?

   a. If the child's Profile has a substantial intraclass correlation with a particular Profile type, is anything known about the typical course and outcome for that type? Or has the clinician accumulated enough personal experience with that type to guide diagnostic formulations and decisions about interventions?[1]

4. What do the competencies shown on the Profile indicate about a child's need for help?

   a. If the child's scores on one or more of the social competence scales are below the normal range (below the 2nd percentile), this suggests that the child's competencies need strengthening.

   b. If the child's scores on the social competence scales are well within the normal range, interventions can focus primarily on the behavior problems.

5. How do the child's cognitive abilities and academic achievement relate to the picture obtained from the CBCL and Profile?

   a. If the child is below the normal range in both ability and achievement, it should not be surprising if he/she obtains a low score on the School scale. Nor should it be surprising if the child has low scores on the other competence scales and an excess of immature behaviors, such as those of the Immature scale for 12–16-year-old boys. However, high scores on other behavior problem scales may reflect the psychological *consequences* of low ability, rather than low ability per se. For example, a child of low ability who must compete with higher ability children may react with various kinds of behavior problems; these might be reflected in high scores on the Depressed, Withdrawal, Aggressive, Delinquent, or Hyperactive scales. In such cases, adjusting the demands placed on the child and providing academic help may be important components of an intervention.

   b. If the child is of very low ability (e.g., IQ below 50), important behavioral areas, such as self-help skills, must be assessed in other ways. The American Association on Mental Deficiency's *Adaptive Behavior Scales* (Lambert & Windmiller, 1981), for example, are specifically designed to assess the self-help skills of the retarded.

---

[1]As explained in Chapter 8, the Profile *types* are based on transformation of the raw behavior problem scale scores to standard scores derived from *clinical* samples; by contrast, the pattern visible on a child's hand-scored or computer-scored Profile shows how a child compares with *normative* groups of agemates. The child's similarity to the clinical type must, therefore, be judged from the intraclass correlation with each type rather than from the visible Profile pattern. Intraclass correlations ≥ .40 with a Profile type indicate substantial similarity. If a child's Profile correlates highly with more than one type, the child should be classified according to the type he/she correlates highest with. Research currently in progress is designed to identify correlates of the various Profile types.

However, if a child is expected to adapt to normal agemates in home and community settings, the CBCL and Profile can also aid in diagnostic formulations and the planning of interventions by pinpointing specific behavior problems that need remediation.

c. If a child's academic achievement is much below expectations for the child's cognitive level, the CBCL and Profile (and Teacher's Report Form) can indicate deviant behavior that is hindering school performance.

6. How do medical factors relate to the picture obtained from the CBCL and Profile?

a. Does the child have a medical condition that could account for behavioral deviance evident on the Profile? Some illnesses directly cause lethargy and withdrawal, whereas other problems, such as depression and hyperactivity, may be by-products of an illness or may be reactions to the constraints of medical treatment or physical handicap.

b. If the child is not known to have a medical problem, do the CBCL or Profile indicate the need for a medical examination? if numerous somatic complaints are reported, for example, possible organic causes should be investigated.

7. Can specific environmental factors explain the picture obtained from the CBCL and Profile?

a. Behavior that the Profile shows to be deviant from normative groups may be typical of a child's family or subcultural group. The behavior may still need changing if it impedes the child's adaptive development, but it may require different interventions than if it were not typical of the child's family or subcultural group.

b. Does the child's environment lack opportunities for developing certain competencies or does it increase the risk of certain problem behaviors? For example, if a child's home is extremely isolated, this may limit the child's opportunities to obtain a high score on the Social scale. However, it is not likely to reduce it to the clinical range (below the 2nd percentile or T score of 30). Similarly, a recent death in the family may explain elevated scores on scales indicative of depression.

In summary, the CBCL and Profile are designed to aid in diagnostic formulations by providing an explicit picture of children's behavior as seen by their parents. This picture provides a focal point around which to organize observations by the clinician, teachers, and others, self-reports by the child, developmental history, cognitive abilities and achievement, medical factors, and environmental variables in arriving at a comprehensive formulation.

INTERVENTIONS

From the behavioral problems and competencies perceived by parents, teachers, clinician, and child, the clinician needs to answer questions like the following:

1. Is the child's behavior really deviant?

    a. If not, then changes in the child may not be needed, but the parents, family system, teacher, or others may need help.

2. If the child's behavior is in need of change, are the problems confined to particular situations or do they occur in many situations?

    a. If the problems are confined to particular situations, intervention may need to focus on those situations and the people involved in them.

    b. If the problems are not confined to particular situations, then the child's overall adaptive pattern may need changing, although interventions may include family therapy, work with parents and teachers, and environmental manipulations, as well as direct work with the child.

3. Which problem areas should receive highest priority for intervention?

    a. The degree of deviance shown by the various scales of the Profile can aid the clinician in deciding whether to focus on those that are most deviant, those that have the most immediate destructive potential (e.g., the behaviors of the Aggressive scale), or social competencies that need strengthening (as shown by the Activities, Social, and School scales).

4. What are the goals of intervention in terms of the child's overall adaptive pattern?

    a. Using the child's Profile pattern to specify goals can help to avoid an excessively narrow focus on diagnostic constructs such as "attention deficit disorder," "depression," or "conduct disorder." Even children who happen to meet DSM criteria for formal diagnoses of this sort often need help in other areas as well.

    b. By considering the child's entire pattern of competencies and problems, clinicians can tailor goals and interventions to the child's specific needs, rather than aiming interventions at diagnostic constructs.

5. Do changes in the child's reported behavior show that the goals of an intervention are met?

    a. By having the CBCL (and related instruments) filled out at intervals during and after intervention, changes in reported behavior can be monitored to determine whether the goals are met.

    b. Although changes in targeted behaviors may occur, it is equally important to know about unanticipated changes in other behaviors. The Profile of a child treated for hyperactivity, for example, may show increases in depression while the targeted hyperactivity declines.

   c. The total behavior problem score and certain items that have strong associations with clinical status can serve as general barometers of the child's functioning. Item *103. Unhappy, sad, or depressed*, in particular, is a good indicator of overall functioning, as it has shown a stronger association with clinical status than any other single CBCL item (Achenbach & Edelbrock, 1981). Other common items that have shown especially strong associations with clinical status include: *8. Can't concentrate, can't pay attention for long; 22. Disobedient at home; 23. Disobedient at school; 25. Doesn't get along with other children; 35. Feels worthless or inferior; 43. Lying or cheating; 45. Nervous, highstrung, or tense*; and *61. Poor school work*.

6. How can experience with previous cases be used to help in choosing an intervention?

   a. As research and clinical experience grow, knowledge of the course, prognosis, and treatment responsiveness of particular Profile patterns can be used to guide the choice of interventions.

   b. As outlined in the section on diagnosis, correlations printed on the computer-scored Profile can be used to determine whether the child resembles particular types identified among other children of the same sex and age.

   c. By having CBCLs sent to parents for completion at regular follow-up intervals (e.g., 6 months, 12 months, 18 months), the clinician can determine outcomes for particular types of cases in his or her own caseload.

PROGRAM ACCOUNTABILITY AND PLANNING

For purposes of accountability and planning, most service programs require periodic documentation of the types of disorders seen and their association with other variables, such as age, sex, socioeconomic status, source of referral, need for particular services, length of treatment, and outcome. Identifying the types of cases that typically have the best and worst outcome may be especially important for the wise use of resources, since cases having consistently poor outcomes should be considered for other types of help. A child guidance clinic or the special educational services of a school district, for example, may need such data in order to formulate and justify annual budgets and to plan for personnel. Such agencies may also need this type of data to document their allocation of resources and changes that occur in caseloads.

In planning new services, agencies such as community mental health centers and state departments of mental health often need survey data from existing facilities and general population samples to determine the prevalence of particular disorders in a catchment area. Similarly, agencies may need prevalence rates to plan services for particular groups, such as children in foster care and the children of welfare clients, mental patients, single parents, and ethnic minorities. Pediatricians and other practitioners may also need to know the prevalence and types of behavior disorders associated with the medical disorders they treat.

Case Registers

One way to obtain a comprehensive picture of all the referrals in a particular area is to establish a *case register*. This is a system whereby all clinical services within an area, such as a city, county, or state, obtain standardized data on all cases and submit the data to a central facility for analysis. When maintained over an extended period, such as a year, a case register provides valuable data on the total number of each type of problem, the types of problems seen in various facilities, seasonal fluctuations, etc.

In the past, efforts to set up case registers for children have depended on formal diagnoses and information culled from records by clerical workers or reluctant clinicians. However, the CBCL and Profile offer standardized data obtained directly from parents without the need for clerical workers or clinicians to abstract information or fill out forms. Completed CBCLs can be sent to a central facility for data processing. Or, where the participating services have access to computer terminals, the data can be key punched at the clinical setting and transmitted automatically to a central computer for scoring and storage. No names or other personal identifying data need to be transmitted, as each service can use its own code numbers. A central computer can also score individual profiles and print them out on each clinical service's own terminal, making the profiles available for immediate clinical use. Similar computerized systems are feasible for schools, where computer terminals available for vocational education can often be used. Another alternative is to punch the data on diskettes via microcomputers which can display the basic information needed for clinical use and then have the punched data read into a central computer for analysis.

If regular follow-ups are done by each clinical service (e.g., at 6-month intervals), the follow-up data can be entered and analyzed to track the cases seen in the area served by the case register. Follow-up data on the course of disorders within a city, county, or state can aid in the long-term planning and justification of agency budgets by answering the frequently asked question, "What happens to these kids later?"

CLINICAL TRAINING

The CBCL and Profile provide a framework within which various phases of clinical training can be organized, as exemplified by the following:

1. Training for intake assessments. If trainees learn to use the CBCL and Profile as part of the intake assessment, they can be taught to use their interviews to follow up on data obtained with these instruments and to focus on matters best dealt with in the interview. Interviewing is expensive: It requires an appointment system, waiting and interview rooms, advance preparation, extended attention, and compilation of the interview data by the clinician. Costs are further increased by the occasional failure of clients to keep appointments. Supervised training interviews are still more costly, because cases must be selected for their training value and both the supervisor and clinical trainee must be involved. It is therefore important to make the best possible use of supervised interview time rather than wasting it to get information that can be obtained more efficiently with the CBCL.

2. Selecting teaching cases. The lack of a well-substantiated system of formal diagnoses for childhood disorders makes it hard to select cases that clearly exemplify particular disorders. Extensive assessment is required to determine whether a child truly fits diagnostic categories like those of the DSM. Even when a child does meet the criteria for a DSM category, viewing the child solely in terms of the category often obscures other important facets of his or her behavior. It can therefore be helpful to use the Profile to select training cases that have relatively pure behavior patterns and also to select those that are hard to classify because they present a mixed or unusual pattern.

3. Comparing data from different sources. A key objective of clinical training is to help trainees grasp the multifaceted and relativistic nature of behavioral problems and competencies. The CBCL and related instruments can be used to compare and contrast behavior reported by a mother, father, teacher, direct observer, and the child. This can help the clinical trainee form a more comprehensive picture of the child than by soliciting unstructured descriptions. It can also pinpoint discrepancies that need exploration to determine whether they reflect differences in the child's behavior in different situations or idiosyncracies of the informants' judgment.

4. Having trainees fill out the CBCL. To sharpen trainees' skills in assessing behavioral problems and competencies, they can be asked to fill out the CBCL in the course of evaluating children. Their ratings can then be compared with ratings by parents and experienced clinicians, and the reasons for discrepancies can be explored. This is especially useful for training child care workers and others who function as surrogate parents for disturbed children. Where multiple workers care for the same child, the Profiles scored from their ratings can be compared to provide better perspectives on variations in the child's behavior and on discrepancies in views of the child.

5. Having trainees evaluate intervention effects. By obtaining ratings at intervals, the trainee can learn to document the effects of an intervention and determine whether other people observe the same effects as the trainee believes are occurring.

SETTINGS FOR USE OF THE CBCL AND PROFILE

This section summarizes some of the ways in which the CBCL and Profile can be used in different situations. It is intended only to illustrate various uses rather than provide a complete listing.

Outpatient Mental Health Services

As discussed earlier in this chapter, the CBCL forms a natural part of intake procedures into child guidance clinics, community mental health centers, private practices, and other outpatient services. Parents can fill it out at home or in a waiting room with no investment of professional time. Clerical workers can score the Profile by hand or key punch the data for scoring by computer. The clinician can use the CBCL and Profile as a takeoff point for interviewing, including exploration of differences between parents. The competencies and problems reported at intake can also be used to aid in decisions about interventions, to compare parents' perceptions with those of other informants, and as a baseline against which to evaluate change, as assessed by subsequent readministration of the CBCL.

Inpatient Mental Health Services

Although the CBCL and Profile were standardized on outpatient samples, they can also be used in certain inpatient settings. The behavior problem scales of the Revised Profile have been extended upward to a T score of 100 (versus 90 on the First Edition) in order to accommodate the high scores often found among inpatients and to reflect differentiated Profile patterns among children who are high on multiple scales. It should be noted, however, that inpatients often have so many problems that they will be in the clinical range on many of the Profile scales. This is not surprising, as it reflects the fact that they are indeed deviant in multiple areas.

As with outpatient services, the CBCL can be used as part of inpatient intake and evaluation procedures. Once a child has been admitted, child care workers, nurses, psychiatric aides, and other personnel in the child's living quarters can complete the CBCL to record the child's behavior as they see it. In some such settings, however, only the behavior problem portion (pages 3 and

4) will be applicable, as the child will have little opportunity to manifest the social competencies tapped by pages 1 and 2. Nevertheless, low social competence scores on the pre-admission Profile can indicate a need for strengthening competencies.

If the child makes home visits, or has trial placements outside the residential setting, CBCLs can be completed by parents and parent surrogates for comparison with those completed by workers in the treatment setting. Such comparisons can reveal, for example, that improvements seen within the treatment setting may not be borne out in the settings to which a child must ultimately adapt; or that competencies have not improved as problems have declined. In such cases, the child may need special help in adapting to the post-treatment settings. This can involve training parents and others how to behave toward the child as much as it involves changing the child's behavior. For example, parents may need to be taught to support the child's adaptive behavior and avoid situations that might overwhelm it.

Although the CBCL can be used in inpatient settings, it does not include extremely deviant behaviors of the kind shown by autistic, severely retarded, and organically damaged children. More specialized instruments are needed to assess the behavior of these children.

Schools

The Teacher's Report Form and Direct Observation Form (Chapter 12) are counterparts of the CBCL for rating school behavior. However, in the course of referrals for special school services related to behavioral, emotional, and learning problems, it is important to consult with parents and obtain their views of their child's behavior. Because the CBCL has many of the same items as the Teacher's Report Form and Direct Observation Form, it provides a basis for directly comparing parents', teachers', and observers' views of the child's behavior.

If the ratings of school and home behavior are similar, this indicates that the child's behavior problems are not restricted to one setting and that interventions need to promote generalized change. On the other hand, if deviant behavior is reported in only one setting, then an intervention may need to focus mainly on that setting.

Sometimes, both school and home ratings show significant problems, but the problem behaviors differ in the two settings. Suppose, for example, that the profile of an 8-year-old boy scored from his parents' ratings shows deviance mainly on the Depressed scale, whereas the profile scored from his teacher's ratings show deviance mainly in inattentiveness. This may indicate that problems of inattention perceived by the teacher are not due to any basic attention deficit, but to general unhappiness. In another case, aggression seen in school may be accompanied by withdrawal and uncommunicativeness in the home, which would require different interventions than if aggression were consistent across situations.

Where the need for a particular service is already clear — such as special education for a retarded child — it is nevertheless important to have a picture of the child's home behavior. For example, CBCL ratings may show that a retarded child has social skills deficits or behavior problems that interfere with adaptation in the home or neighborhood. If so, a school social worker could help the child's family implement training procedures coordinated with the teacher's efforts to train adaptive behavior. During periodic reevaluations of the child, ratings by parents can continue to aid in determining the most appropriate placements and educational objectives for the child.

Medical Settings

Health maintenance organizations, pediatricians, family practitioners, and other medical personnel must make judgments about the behavior of the children they serve. Many parents, for example, consult their child's physician when they have questions about the child's behavior. Even when parents do not raise questions, children's doctors must be alert for behavior problems that hinder adaptive development or medical management, have medical consequences, or may be caused by medical conditions.

The CBCL and Profile offer an efficient, inexpensive way for medical personnel to obtain parents' reports of their children's behavior and to relate it to norms for the child's sex and age. Pediatricians and family practitioners may find it most convenient to have parents fill out the CBCL in the waiting room when they bring their child for regular physical examinations. A look at the Profile can alert the physician to areas that need exploration and can provide a basis for answering parents' particular concerns. The behavior of children with chronic illnesses or handicaps often requires special attention. Profile data can help to discriminate between age-appropriate problems and those specifically associated with a particular medical condition.

Physicians who specialize in a particular disorder can use the CBCL to accumulate data on the behavior problems associated with various stages in the course and treatment of the disorder. This will enable them to anticipate problems and advise parents. Siblings of children suffering from severe medical problems may also show behavioral reactions that can be assessed with the CBCL and Profile.

Court-Related Uses

Children and adolescents become involved with the legal system in a variety of ways. When offenders are referred to juvenile court, evaluations of their behavior and background can be aided with the CBCL and related instruments. After a court disposition to probation, foster placement, incarceration, etc., these instruments can also be used to assess behavioral change. Ratings of broad samples of behavior can give a much more meaningful picture than a focus on delinquent behavior alone. Some offenders may be deviant only in terms of delinquent behavior, for example, whereas the delinquent behavior of others is only an incidental aspect of deviance in other areas.

In questions of legal custody and foster placement, profiles scored from CBCLs completed by the different adults involved can be compared to determine how each adult sees the child. For example, if a foster placement has been made because of the child's behavior problems, profiles scored from CBCLs completed by the natural parents and foster parents can be compared to determine whether the child's behavior appears to change. If not, more than a change of home environment is likely to be needed. Agencies responsible for foster children can also use the CBCL to survey needs for mental health services within their caseload. And profiles obtained from CBCLs completed by mothers and fathers in custody cases can assist in determining which parent is the better informed and more realistic about their child by comparing each parent's report with what else is known about the child.

SUMMARY

Good clinical practice requires a good research base, and good research requires close links with clinical practice. The CBCL and Profile are designed to bridge research and clinical practice.

The CBCL can be completed by parents as a natural part of the intake procedure in many settings. Where feasible, it is desirable to have both parents independently complete the CBCL to highlight areas of agreement and disagreement. Data from the CBCL and Profile can then be used as a take-off point for clinical interviewing. As data become available from other sources, the clinician can compare them with the picture presented by each parent via the CBCL and Profile.

The Profile can contribute to *formal diagnosis* by showing the degree of a child's deviance in behaviors that parents are more likely to observe than clinicians. It also enables the clinician to compare the degree of deviance for dimensions of behavior problems corresponding to diagnostic categories such as hyperactivity, conduct disorders, and depression.

The Profile can contribute to *diagnostic formulations* by providing an individualized picture of the child's problems and competencies, as seen by parents. This picture is broader and more detailed than that provided by formal diagnostic categories.

Comparisons of the problems and competencies perceived by parents, teacher, clinician, and child can guide decisions about the type and target of interventions. If the CBCL is used as a baseline measure of the parents' perceptions, it can be readministered during and after the intervention to evaluate change, as seen by the parents.

For purposes of program accountability and planning, CBCL data aggregated across caseloads and catchment areas can be used to document the type, rate, and distribution of behavior disorders. The CBCL can also be used to obtain data for case registers without requiring clinical or clerical time to abstract information or fill out forms.

The CBCL and Profile can help to structure clinical training, including training for intake assessments, selection of teaching cases, comparisons of data obtained on the child from different sources, having trainees fill out the CBCL, and having trainees evaluate intervention effects.

Situations in which the CBCL and Profile can be used include outpatient mental health services, inpatient mental health services, schools, medical settings, and court-related services.

Chapter 11
Research Use of the Child Behavior
Checklist and Profile

In Chapter 10, we discussed the need for basing clinical services more firmly on research and for linking research more closely to clinical practice, in order to improve services to children. Although we designed the CBCL and Profile to link clinical services and research, this does not imply an exclusion of "basic" research in favor of "applied" research. In reference to clinical disorders, the distinction between basic and applied research pertains mainly to different stages or facets of research, rather than to categorical differences in the nature of the research.

Because it concerns so many aspects of children's functioning, research on behavior disorders will always need to draw on methods, theory, and findings from other fields, such as developmental psychology, biology, and psychopharmacology. Yet, to advance beyond a potpourri of theoretical concepts and fragmented empirical findings, the field must evolve its own research paradigms.

Because behavior disorders involve so many different variables, they are unlikely to be completely explained by a single theory, such as psychoanalysis or learning theory. Instead, multiple theories, each dealing with different phenomena, need to be integrated within a developmental framework. Such a framework requires methodological paradigms that can be shared by researchers studying various questions under various conditions.

The CBCL and Profile enable researchers of diverse theoretical persuasions to share a common methodology, even though they may also use methods specialized to their own purposes. With the exception of very severe and unusual conditions such as autism, these instruments can be used to study most behavior disorders in children aged 4 through 16, when parents or parent surrogates are available as informants. By portraying multiple dimensions of behavioral problems and competencies, the Profile provides a more comprehensive picture of each child's reported behavior than do instruments limited to a single dimension. Although unidimensional instruments are often used to assess disorders thought to be univocal, children showing deviance on these instruments may be even more deviant in other ways. For example, some children who obtain high scores on a measure of childhood depression may be still more deviant in ways not assessed by the measure of depression. It is therefore important to complement specialized assessment with the more comprehensive assessment offered by the Profile.

Because creative research blends existing concepts and methods in new ways, we cannot anticipate all possible research uses of our instruments. Instead, we will outline general research applications to initial assessment, assessment of changes in reported behavior, selection of subjects, and the generation of new hypotheses.

EPIDEMIOLOGICAL RESEARCH

Knowledge of the prevalence and distribution of particular types of behavior disorders is important for planning services, developing hypotheses about etiological factors, identifying secular trends, and interpreting findings on particular samples in the light of data from larger populations. Where the disorders themselves must be defined in terms of behavioral phenotypes, epidemiological data are needed to provide normative distributions of problem behavior. Cutoff points on these distributions can then be established for discriminating among various groups.

Population Studies

Although several home interview surveys have included questions about children's behavior (reviewed by Achenbach & Edelbrock, 1981), they did not link normative data to syndromes derived empirically from clinical samples. Nor did they compare prevalence rates in nonclinical survey samples with rates for clinical samples. Most survey findings therefore shed little light on clinical syndromes and maladaptation severe enough to warrant clinical referral.

As reported in detail by Achenbach and Edelbrock (1981), our own survey employed all 118 behavior problems and 20 social competence items of the CBCL. The data from our samples of nonreferred children were used to norm the scales of the Profile and to establish cutoff points on the total behavior problem and competence scores that discriminate well between re-ferred children and nonreferred children.

The general methodology used by Achenbach and Edelbrock (1981) can be employed to obtain epidemiological data in other localities and in relation to other assessment procedures, such as teacher ratings, self-ratings, and diagnostic interviews with children and parents. For example, a researcher may wish to determine whether the rates for overall behavior problems or for certain specific problems differ significantly in a particular community from the rates we found. Or it may be important to determine whether rates are elevated in particular subgroups, such as children from certain neighborhoods or ethnic groups, or children who are disadvantaged or handicapped. Agencies that serve children, such as schools, may also wish to obtain local norms for use as a baseline against which to judge ratings for individual children nominated for special help.

Case Registers

In Chapter 10, we discussed case registers in relation to accountability and planning for clinical services. Case registers that record uniform data on all people referred for services within a delimited area can also be extremely valuable for research in general. Registers of tumors and infectious diseases, for example, provide data on geographical, socioeconomic, ethnic, age, sex, occupational, and secular variations. These data are used to develop hypotheses about etiologies and outcomes and can aid in testing such hypotheses.

Although case registers have also been valuable for the study of adult mental disorders such as schizophrenia (cf. Schulsinger, Mednick, & Knop, 1981), the few attempts to establish case registers for children's disorders have been severely handicapped by a lack of standardized assessment data (e.g., Wing, Baldwin, & Rosen, 1972). Except for broad distinctions between mental retardation, organic brain syndromes, and behavior disorders, tabulations of clinical diagnoses have been of limited value for several reasons:

1. Clinical diagnoses of children's behavior disorders have not shown adequate reliability or validity (see Achenbach, 1982, Chapter 15).
2. There has been little consistency between the child diagnostic categories of successive editions of the DSM and other nosologies.
3. Diagnoses are often shaped by third party payment criteria or by clerical workers who must translate clinicians' comments into official diagnostic codes.

For purposes of a case register, the CBCL can provide data that are easily and uniformly obtained across diverse clinical settings. These data are supplied directly by parents rather than clinicians and clerical workers. Although the Profile provides standardized scales, norms, and types with which to analyze the CBCL data, the basic data are molecular enough to be aggregated in other ways according to the researcher's aims. In other words, the data are not irretrievably buried in *a priori* diagnostic categories.

Because the CBCL does not depend on clinicians or clerical workers to follow uniform protocols for obtaining, interpreting, or coding data, it avoids problems of enforcing uniformity across different clinical services. Because clinicians can make immediate use of CBCL data, they are more likely to participate than if data obtained for a case register are of no immediate use to participants. An added incentive can be provided by having the case register facility score profiles for the clinical services. For example, each service can keypunch its own CBCL data from terminals connected to a case register computer and obtain printouts of the scored profiles. The services can assign code numbers to their own cases and retain the original forms completed by parents, thereby avoiding submission of personally identifiable data.

The CBCL can thus form an easy starting point for a case register. Agreement to supply CBCL data may pave the way for obtaining more difficult data, such as interview assessments and clinical diagnoses requiring conformity to a rigid protocol in all settings. A case register employing the CBCL can also provide the basis for periodic follow-ups to determine the course and outcome for referred children. For example, each participating service can have parents fill out the CBCL at 6-month intervals. These data can then be used to compare changes in children who differ in initial Profile patterns.

ETIOLOGICAL STUDIES

Several strategies are possible for using the CBCL and Profile in research on the etiology of behavior disorders. One general strategy is to use the Profile to discriminate among children who differ in reported behavior and then to determine whether they differ in possible etiological factors as well. The initial phenotypic discrimination can be made in any of the following ways:

1. By grouping children according to their correlations with the Profile types identified through cluster analysis (detailed in Chapter 8).

2. By grouping children according to the Internalizing–Externalizing dichotomy. This can be done either by using a criterion such as a difference of 10 T score points between these two scales or using the Internalizing–Externalizing clusters of Profile types shown in Chapter 8.

3. By grouping children according to a criterion of particular interest to the researcher, such as a high score on one particular scale and a low score on another.

4. By using relations between the social competence and behavior problem scores, such as distinguishing between children who have similar behavior problem patterns but different social competence patterns.

A second general strategy is to start with children assumed to differ in certain etiological factors and then see whether they differ in scores or patterns on the Profile. Using the Profile as a dependent variable can tell us whether hypothesized (or confirmed) differences in etiology lead to phenotypic differences; or, conversely, whether the phenotypes derived from parent ratings are too multidetermined to reflect specific etiological factors. If the Profile does not correlate with etiological differences confirmed by other means, it should be asked whether this is because (*a*) the Profile is insensitive to differences in phenotypes differing in etiology or (*b*) different etiologies produce the same behavioral phenotypes. To answer this question, it would be necessary to determine whether any other measure could detect differences in behavior that correlate with etiological differences.

A third strategy is to manipulate variables thought to affect the etiology of particular disorders to see whether Profile scores or patterns differ before and after the manipulation. If the manipulation is known to affect the etiological condition—for example, a drug already proven to ameliorate an organic abnormality—then the manipulation can test the sensitivity of the Profile to changes in the etiological abnormality. On the other hand, if an unproven intervention is tried in hope of ameliorating abnormalities (etiological or otherwise), the Profile can be used as a dependent variable in order to assess change in response to the intervention. The specificity of a particular intervention's effect can also be assessed by determining whether children differing in initial Profile type or other distinguishing characteristics show different degrees or types of change in response to the intervention. For example, does stimulant medication have different effects on children who score high only on the

Hyperactive scale and those who score high on the Aggressive scale as well as the Hyperactive scale?

Heuristic Implications

The hierarchies, distributions, and correlates of Profile patterns can have a heuristic value for generating hypotheses. For example, the hierarchy of Profiles for girls aged 12-16 (Figure 8-13) shows that Profile type A (Anxious-Obsessive) and type B (Somatic Complaints) jointly form a higher-order cluster before ultimately joining two other Profile types to form a global Internalizing cluster. This suggests that Profiles A and B have something in common that differentiates them both from profiles in general and from other Internalizing profiles. The figures in Chapter 8 show that profiles for some of the other sex/age groups likewise join together before forming global Internalizing and Externalizing clusters.

In certain sex/age groups, there are Profile types that never join the Internalizing or Externalizing clusters. An example is Profile type D (Sex Problems) for girls 6-11, which evidently has little in common with either the three Profile types that form the Internalizing cluster or the three that form the Externalizing cluster. Analysis of the correlates of this Profile type showed that it was accompanied by higher scores on the Activities scale than any other Profile types were (Edelbrock & Achenbach, 1980). This suggests that these girls differ from other clinically-referred girls not only in their specific patterns of reported problems and their dissimilarity to the two traditional broad band groupings, but also in displaying greater involvement and competence in the sports, nonsports activities, jobs, and chores that make up the Activities scale. These initial findings could provide leads for more intensive research on etiological factors that differentiate the Sex Problems type from the others found for 6-11-year-old girls.

OUTCOME STUDIES

A fundamental question in the developmental study of pscyhopathology is: "What typically happens to children having Disorder X?" If we knew what the typical outcomes were with and without particular interventions, we would be better able to decide which children actually need professional help, what kind they need, and how to advise parents. We would also be able to focus research efforts on disorders found to have poor outcomes.

The question of outcome can be addressed in numerous ways. However, the different approaches all share a need for standardized assessment of children's initial characteristics and outcome characteristics.

Longitudinal General Population Studies

One strategy is to start with large general population samples and then to trace the course and outcome of disorders in these samples. Unfortunately, this is seldom practical: The low baserates and lack of clear pathognomonic signs for most disorders would make it necessary to have very precise assessments of enormous samples in order to find enough children manifesting different disorders. Furthermore, longitudinal assessments of large general population samples are hampered by family moves, loss of subjects' cooperation, and the difficulty of sustaining research personnel and funding.

Even when such research is feasible, causal relations and developmental consistencies are hard to infer from a mass of correlational data in which many statistical associations can arise by chance. Life-span developmental designs have been devised to strengthen the basis for inference. But such designs require multiple cohorts and cannot fully disentangle variance associated with age, cohort, and time-of-assessment (see Achenbach, 1980; Adam, 1978). Experimental tests of causal relations would, of course, be highly desirable, but are seldom feasible in large-scale longitudinal studies.

Children at Risk

An alternative to the general population longitudinal strategy is to start with samples of children who are at risk either because of significant adaptational problems or other factors, such as having a psychotic, alcoholic, or abusive parent. This can increase the yield of "cases" for longitudinal study. It may, however, have the disadvantage of limiting generalizations to groups identified in the same way. For example, individuals who become psychotic without having a psychotic parent may be quite different from psychotic individuals who do have a psychotic parent. Yet, until we have a better understanding of children who are clearly at risk, we may not be able to launch effective research on those having less obvious signs of trouble.

If we start with children already referred for mental health services or known to be at statistically high risk in light of factors such as parental psychosis, the simplest strategy is to assess them initially with the CBCL and other measures of interest. (Where a parental condition such as psychosis is the risk factor, it is, of course, important to have the CBCL filled out by the unaffected parent or another adult who knows the child well.) Thereafter, the subjects should be reassessed at regular intervals with the CBCL and other measures that are sensitive to change. Where feasible, it is better to obtain relatively frequent assessments rather than a single outcome assessment after a long interval. Frequent reassessments make it possible to track the course of change, which may vary in ways not detectable from a single outcome assessment.

Frequent reassessments also reduce loss of subjects, since addresses and personal contacts can be continually updated. If subjects are nevertheless lost, the reassessments up to the time of loss provide valuable data that would be unavailable if only a single long-term follow-up were planned.

Although frequent reassessments may seem more costly than a single follow-up, it is not expensive to mail instruments like the CBCL at regular intervals (e.g., six months) and to call families who fail to respond by mail. More expensive in-person contacts can be reserved for longer intervals (e.g., one or two years), while the intervening postal or telephone contacts save the expense of locating subjects who might disappear if sought only at longer intervals.

Identifying Cases with the Worst Outcomes

When treatment outcomes are studied, uncontrolled variations in the interventions may confound the interpretation of course and outcome. Controlling intervention conditions is the province of experimental treatment studies, to be discussed later in the chapter. However, experimental control of treatment is often so difficult that it is only worth attempting as a sequel to nonexperimental studies. For example, suppose a follow-up study shows that children with a particular Profile pattern at intake typically have much worse outcomes than children with other Profile patterns. Such a finding indicates that the poor outcome group needs more or different help. If the finding were replicated for similar children who have received different interventions, we would conclude that more effective interventions must be sought for these children. The interventions that seem effective in nonexperimental studies should ultimately be tested via experimental treatment research.

Research Spanning Two or More Sex/Age Profiles

Recall that the purpose of performing separate factor analyses for each sex at ages 4-5, 6-11, and 12-16 was to reflect differences in the patterning and prevalence of reported behavior problems. As reported in Chapter 2, we indeed found some syndromes that were restricted to one sex or a particular age group. Furthermore, even syndromes that were fairly similar across sex/age groups showed variations in their precise composition and the distributions of their scores among the groups. To obtain an accurate picture of how the behavior reported on the CBCL compares with that reported for a child's peers, the child should therefore be scored on the version of the Profile standardized for his/her sex/age group.

Nevertheless, users must often make comparisons across different sex/age groups. This can be done in the following ways:

1. Crossing from One Age Range to the Beginning of the Next. If children are to be studied longitudinally over a period in which they advance from one age range to the beginning of the next, the form of the Profile on which they were initially scored can continue to be used. For example, if a sample of 4-5-year-olds is reassessed when they reach 6, they can continue to be scored on the Profile for 4-5-year-olds. This is because the precise age demarcations of the Profile are necessarily arbitrary. For most research purposes, it is preferable to use the same scoring system from the initial to the final assessment, provided that the subjects have advanced no more than about a year into the next age range.

2. Crossing from the Top of One Age Range into the Next. If children are at the top of one age period at the beginning of a study and advance well into the next age period by the end of the study, the Profile for the later age period can be used throughout. For example, if children are studied from age 11 to 15, the Profile for 12–16-year-olds can be used throughout. (Note that, because the CBCL is the same for all ages from 4 through 16, the raw data will always be obtained in the same way. The decision to score the Profile for a slightly younger or older age range than the child's actual age can be made after the data are obtained with the CBCL.)

3. Samples that Include Children from Two Age Ranges. If a cross-sectional or longitudinal study begins with children who overlap two age periods somewhat, the researcher can score them all on the Profile most appropriate for most of the subjects. For example, if a sample includes children aged 11 through 14, the Profile for 12–16-year-olds can be used for the entire sample.

4. Combining Diverse Ages and Both Sexes. If a researcher needs to combine wider age spans or both sexes, this can be done by analyzing those scores that are based on similar items for all the groups to be included.

a. The scores for total behavior problems, total social competence, and social competence scales are based on identical items for all groups, except for the omission of the School scale for 4–5-year-olds.

b. The Aggressive scale and Somatic Complaints scale are reasonably similar among the groups, while versions of the Delinquent, Hyperactive, Schizoid, Depressed, and Withdrawal scales exist for most of the groups.

c. To take account of sex/age differences in the prevalence of reported behaviors even where the items are identical, the T scores computed for a child's sex/age group should be used. If Internalizing scores for children of both sexes at ages 6–11 and 12–16 were to be analyzed together, for example, the 6–11-year-old boys' raw Internalizing scores should first be converted to T scores derived from the table or computer program for 6–11-year-old boys; the 6–11-year-old girls' raw Internalizing scores should be converted to T scores derived from the table or computer program for 6–11-year-old girls, and so forth.

Age Changes in Phenotypes. Although the age changes in syndromes may be a nuisance, they also present opportunities to assess relations between phenotypes that differ with age. For example, if 10-year-old boys having the Hyperactive Profile pattern (Profile type E for 6–11-year-old boys) are followed until the age of 13, do they all still show the Hyperactive pattern (type D for 12–16-year-olds)? Or do they have some other pattern, such as the Immature-Aggressive type C? Or does one subgroup retain the Hyperactive pattern while another subgroup evolves into the Immature-Aggressive pattern? If so, what predicts these different developmental courses?

By grouping children according to their Profile patterns at one age, and then comparing them again at a later age, we can test not only whether there is stability in their Profiles, but whether they continue to share particular Profile characteristics, even though their Profiles change between the initial and follow-up ratings. In fact, because the determinants and functions of particular behaviors are likely to change with age, complete stability of specific behaviors would be unusual. Research designed to detect systematic *changes* in behavior from one developmental period to another may therefore be more productive than research seeking only stabilities in behavior.

Use of the Profile Outside Its Normative Age Range. Because the CBCL is designed for ages 4 through 16, it can continue to be used for follow-ups until subjects are at least 16 years old. Although the Profile has been standardized only through age 16, ratings obtained through about the age of 18 can continue to be scored on the Profile for purposes of comparing changes in subgroups within a cohort on whom ratings were obtained earlier. However, because we did not seek normative data on 17- and 18-year-olds, it is not known how any particular raw score compares with scores that would be obtained by representative samples of nonreferred adolescents of these ages. It is also possible that the composition of the scales does not reflect the patterning of behavior as well for adolescents over the age of 16 as for those on whom the scales were derived. As discussed in Chapter 12, we have devised the Youth Self-Report Form to span ages 11–18.

The value of the Profile prior to age 4 is likewise limited by the lack of data on the prevalence and patterning of behavior, although it may be satisfactory for children close to their fourth birthday. As discussed in Chapter 12, we are developing an additional checklist for ages 2 and 3.

EXPERIMENTAL INTERVENTION STUDIES

The most powerful strategy for testing causal relations is usually to manipulate the hypothesized causal or independent variable in order to see whether it affects the dependent variable of interest. In testing the effects of therapy for a particular disorder, for example, children having the disorder are divided into an experimental group that receives the therapy and a control group that is similar in all respects except for the therapy that is being tested. Alternatively, two or more similar groups receive different therapies in order to find out which is the most effective. Where the therapy is expected to be ameliorative rather than curative, it may be alternated with a no-therapy or placebo condition in the same subjects in order to compare their functioning with and without the therapy.

For behavior disorders of childhood, drug therapies provide exceptionally good opportunities for experimental tests of efficacy: The active drug can be compared with a placebo administered under identical conditions, while the subjects, people administering the drugs, and evaluators of outcome are all blind as to the drug condition. Certain behavioral interventions have also been subjected to extensive experimental testing, although precise control of the conditions of administration and evaluations of efficacy are more difficult than with drug therapies. Experimental testing of psychotherapy is still more difficult, because of the long duration, variations in procedures from case to case, and greater emphasis on general well-being than on specific target behaviors. Other interventions, such as parent guidance or training, group experiences, and special educational environments also involve wider variations in implementation and outcome variables.

Because experimental tests are difficult and expensive, they should be preceded by careful study and specification of the target variables, as well as preliminary assessments of the candidate interventions to determine whether they warrant an experimental test. For example, as discussed earlier, nonexperimental outcome studies may be used to identify Profile patterns that have poor outcomes after conventional mental health services. Further study of the poor-outcome groups is needed to design interventions specifically aimed at their unique characteristics. If non-experimental evaluations of these interventions show that they are feasible and seem to produce better results than conventional services, it may then be time for an experimental comparison with alternative approaches or with no-treatment control conditions, or both.

Use of the Profile in Experimental Studies

As with nonexperimental longitudinal and outcome studies, experimental studies can use Profile scores and patterns to compare changes in reported behavior occurring under different experimental conditions. The Profile can also be used for initially selecting and matching subjects. For example, in order to insure that children receiving a particular therapy are similar with respect to their reported behaviors, the correlation of their Profiles with a target Profile type can be used as a selection criterion. The size of the correlation required for admission to the study can be stipulated by the researcher according to the "purity" of groups desired and the number of available subjects (see Chapter 8 for details).

If one therapy group is to be compared with another therapy group or a no-treatment control group, the groups can be matched for Profile pattern. One procedure is to randomly assign to each condition subjects having the target Profile in order to create groups that are reasonably similar with respect to Profile patterns and other key variables (*randomized groups design*).

If it is feasible to find closely matched individual subjects, small groups (or "blocks") can be formed that contain as many very similar subjects as there are treatment and control conditions. For example, if there were two treatments and a no-treatment control condition, each block would contain three subjects. A random procedure is then used to select the individual from each block who will receive each treatment condition (*randomized blocks design*). In both the randomized groups and randomized blocks designs, the objective is to insure that the subjects receiving different conditions are as similar as possible with respect to Profile pattern and other variables.

Relations between Experimental Conditions and Profile Type. The simplest experimental treatment studies assess the effects of one or more interventions on a particular type of disorder. However, it is often important to determine whether different types of children or disorders show different responses to a particular treatment. In this case, a two-factor experimental design can be used in which children grouped according to Profile type form two or more levels of one factor, while an experimental and a control condition form two levels of the second factor. It can thus be determined whether the outcomes are better in the experimental condition than in the control condition for all Profile types studied, or whether the experimental condition has different effects on different Profile types.

A further elaboration of this design is to study the effects of two or more treatments on two or more Profile types in order to see which treatment works best for which type. Possible outcomes would include the following:

1. A *main effect of treatment,* whereby one treatment works better than the others for all Profile types.

2. A *main effect of Profile type,* whereby one Profile type has a better outcome than the others, regardless of treatment.

3. An *interaction of Profile type-by-treatment*, whereby one Profile type has its best outcome under one treatment condition, but another Profile type has its best outcome under a different treatment condition.

Any of these findings could provide a much better basis for *prescribing* specific treatments for specific Profile types than we now have.

TAXONOMIC AND TAXOMETRIC RESEARCH

In contrast to the categorical concepts of traditional nosologies, our approach to taxonomy is designed to take advantage of quantification in the following ways:

1. The quantitative *derivation of taxa* through factor analysis and cluster analysis.

2. The quantitative *assessment of the attributes* of an individual that serve as criteria for classification within the taxonomy.

3. The quantitative *specification of the degree* to which the individual fits various taxa.

Because it applies quantitative methods to the process of discriminating among individuals and taxa and to assigning individuals to the taxa, our approach can be viewed as "taxometric." (See Meehl & Golden, 1982, for an extended discussion of taxometric concepts.) A taxometric approach harnesses the power of quantitative methods in deriving taxonic criteria and in detecting relations between taxonic criteria and other variables.

In the absence of definitive knowledge about the underlying causes or structures of disorders, the value of taxa depends largely on their ability (*a*) to organize molecular data into more molar and meaningful units, and (*b*) to discriminate among individuals who are then found to differ in other important ways. A taxonic system based on parents' ratings cannot capture all important distinctions between children, but it can form a bridgehead from which to advance research on the taxonic value of other sources of data.

For example, teachers are often second only to parents as important judges of children's behavior. As described in Chapter 12, we have developed the Teacher's Report Form to obtain teachers' ratings of many of the same behaviors that parents rate on the CBCL. Our factor analyses of teachers' ratings have yielded some factors that are similar to those obtained from parents' ratings and some that are different. In the teachers' ratings, for example, a large number of items involving inattentiveness loaded on a factor that was separate from a factor defined largely by overactivity, whereas these items formed a single factor in the parents' ratings. Conversely, somatic complaints formed a separate factor in the parents' ratings but not in the teachers' ratings.

It is not surprising that teachers are more sensitive to covariation in attentiveness, whereas parents are more sensitive to covariation in somatic complaints. Yet, even if teachers and parents are not sensitive to exactly the same behavior patterns and even if children's behavior is not the same at school and home, a particular Profile pattern scored from parents' ratings may be consistently associated with a particular Profile pattern scored from teachers' ratings. For example, children whose parent-scored Profile correlates highly with the Somatic Complaints Profile type might be found to have teacher profiles elevated mainly on the Inattentive scale.

The degree to which a child's Profile must match a particular parent-scored Profile type in order to predict the teacher-scored Profile pattern can also be assessed. For example, the strength of association between parent and teacher Profile patterns can be compared for children who have relatively "pure" versions of a parent Profile type (e.g., intraclass correlation $\geq .40$) and children who have less "pure" versions (e.g., intraclass correlation of .20 to .39). The assessment of relations between Profiles scored from parent and teacher ratings can be used not only for predictive purposes but also to gain a better understanding of the different facets of children's behavior in different situations. Other forms of assessment, such as cognitive measures, personality tests, interviews, and developmental histories can likewise be tested as potential correlates of Profile patterns.

OPERATIONS RESEARCH

In Chapter 10, we discussed the use of the CBCL and Profile in program accountability and planning. Most clinical services require at least periodic documentation of the types of disorders seen and their association with other variables. More extensive documentation can be achieved through follow-up studies of outcomes for various kinds of cases and through case registers of all referrals within a delimited area.

Efforts of this sort exemplify *operations research*, which has been defined as "the application of scientific methods, techniques, and tools to problems involving the operations of a system so as to provide those in control of the operations with optimum solutions to the problems" (Churchman, Ackoff, & Arnoff, 1957, pp. 8–9). The CBCL and Profile are applicable to various kinds of operations research in addition to the documentation of reported behavior patterns in caseloads, follow-up studies, and case registers. In fact, one reason for developing the CBCL and Profile was to overcome a major obstacle to operations research in mental health systems:

> ". . . present information systems do not reflect the movement of different populations through the system, since an adequate client classification mechanism has not yet been developed and implemented. Presently, one can only simulate the system as if it were treating a homogeneous population of clients. This assumption of homogeneity may have caused a continuing misallocation of valuable resources" (Lyons, 1980, p. 256).

The scores and patterns provided by the CBCL offer a basis for classifying clients as they enter, move through, and leave mental health services. By comparing the type, duration, and outcome of services for children classified according to their Profile scores and patterns, it can be determined whether services, costs, and outcomes vary according to the problems actually reported for the children.

Another form of operations research involves cross-referencing among criteria that serve various functions within a system. For example, the Profile may be used to obtain an initial picture of a child's behavior and to monitor changes in the behavior, as perceived by parents. However, DSM-III diagnoses may also be required for purposes of third party payment. Operations research might therefore be designed to determine whether relations between Profile patterns and DSM-III diagnoses are sufficiently consistent for one to predict the other or whether they jointly provide a better understanding of children.

In Chapter 10, we discussed descriptive similarities between the syndromes of the Profile and DSM-III syndromes (see Table 10-1). Some Profile patterns resemble the behavioral pictures required for certain DSM diagnoses, such as the Hyperactive Profile pattern and the DSM diagnosis of Attention Deficit Disorder with Hyperactivity. Yet, this does not necessarily mean that children with the Hyperactive Profile — and *only* these children — will be diagnosed Attention Deficit with Hyperactivity.

One obstacle to finding associations between DSM diagnoses and other variables is that DSM diagnoses of children's disorders are often of low reliability. Even when made from standard case history materials read by each diagnostician, DSM-III diagnoses have proven to be less reliable than DSM-II diagnoses, which were themselves of low reliability (Mattison, Cantwell, Russell, & Will, 1979; Mezzich & Mezzich, 1979). If Profile patterns are to be cross-referenced with DSM diagnoses, the reliability of such diagnoses must first be assured. This may require considerable training of the diagnosticians and the exclusion or aggregation of diagnostic categories that remain unreliable despite careful training. For example, the overlapping content of the DSM's Oppositional and Conduct Disorders may make them impossible to discriminate reliably.

Other forms of operations research may focus on client characteristics important to a particular clinical setting, such as variations in behavior problem patterns and outcomes for children referred by different sources (e.g., pediatricians versus schools versus courts), seasonal fluctuations in the types of problems seen, and differences between children from different geographical areas (e.g., rural versus urban) or economic groups (e.g., welfare versus private fee-paying).

SUMMARY

The CBCL and Profile are designed to be used in many types of research, both "basic" and "applied." These instruments enable researchers to share a common methodology while also using methods specialized for their own purposes. In this chapter, we outlined applications related to initial assessment, assessment of changes in reported behavior, selection of subjects, and the generation of hypotheses.

If disorders are defined in terms of behavioral phenotypes, *epidemiological data* are needed to provide normative distributions of problem behavior and to establish cutoff points for discriminating among various groups. The methodology we employed to obtain our normative data can be applied to other populations. The epidemiological data thus obtained can be analyzed in terms of our behavior problem and competence scales, as well as in terms of individual items and total scores. The CBCL and Profile are also suited to case register research, and they provide an easy starting point from which to add more difficult procedures.

In studies of *etiology*, one strategy is to use the Profile to discriminate between children who differ in reported behavior and then compare them with respect to possible etiological factors. A second strategy is to start with children assumed to differ in etiological factors and then use the Profile as a dependent variable to see if such children differ in reported behavior. A third strategy is to manipulate variables thought to affect the etiology of particular disorders in order to see whether Profile scores or patterns vary with the manipulation. The hierarchies, distributions, and correlates of Profile patterns can also play a heuristic role in generating hypotheses about the etiologies of disorders and the links among them.

The CBCL and Profile are applicable to various types of *outcome studies*, including longitudinal general population studies, studies of children at-risk, and the identification of cases having the worst outcomes. The social competence scales, total social competence score, some of the narrow-band behavior problem scales, Internalizing score, Externalizing score, and total behavior problem score can be analyzed across sex/age groups by using the T scores derived from the normative samples for each subject's sex and age. Procedures were outlined for linking analyses of the entire Profile across age periods.

Experimental intervention studies can use the Profile to select subjects who are similar with respect to reported behavior, to classify subjects into groups on whom interventions will be compared, and to assess outcomes.

The Profile is designed to advance taxonomic research by capitalizing on quantitative methods to derive taxa, to assess the criterial attributes of individuals, and to specify the degree to which individuals fit each taxon. This *taxometric* approach can be used to test the Profile's power to discriminate among individuals who differ in other important ways. In can also be used to test the taxonic power of other types of data, such as teachers' ratings, and to augment the typology of Profiles by enlarging its taxa to include other forms of data found to be consistently associated with them.

Operations research can make use of the Profile to improve the functioning of mental health service systems by classifying children as they enter, move through, and leave mental health services. Within a system, the Profile can be cross-referenced with criteria that serve other functions, such as DSM diagnoses, and can be used to assess differences in presenting patterns, course, and outcome that are related to important client characteristics.

Appendix F contains a bibliography of research using the CBCL and Profile.

Chapter 12
Instruments to Supplement the Checklist and Profile

Although we chose parents' reports as our starting point, we have repeatedly stressed that no single source or type of data is adequate for comprehensive assessment of children. The subjective perspectives of the informants, their relationships to and influences on the children rated, and the situations in which they see the children can all affect behavioral ratings. We have therefore sought to supplement the picture obtained from parents with data from other informants. Because so many factors differentially affect the informants, they are not necessarily expected to agree closely with one another. Nor is one informant intended to serve as a reliability or validity criterion for the others. Instead, data contributed by each type of informant are to be judged for their ability to contribute information not readily obtainable in other ways. In this chapter, we will summarize instruments we have developed to obtain data from teachers, direct observers, and children themselves.

THE TEACHER'S REPORT FORM OF THE CHILD BEHAVIOR CHECKLIST

Next to parents, teachers are usually the second most important adults in children's lives. School is a central arena for the development of social as well as academic skills. Behavioral problems and competencies not evident to parents may be of great concern to teachers. Teachers' reports are often needed, as teachers frequently instigate clinical referrals or must be consulted about the school functioning of children referred by others.

In order to obtain teachers' views of children's behavior, we developed the Teacher's Report Form (TRF) of the Child Behavior Checklist. Page 1 of the TRF (Figure 12-1) is designed to obtain demographics, information on the context in which the teacher knows the child, previous special services, repetition of grades, and ratings of academic performance. Page 2 (Figure 12-2) requests teachers' ratings on four general adaptive characteristics (Items VIII-1 through 4), plus standardized test data and other information teachers can provide.

Pages 3 and 4 of the TRF (Figures 12-3 and 12-4) list behavior problem items in the same format as employed on the Child Behavior Checklist. However, teachers are asked to base their ratings on the previous 2 months, rather than the 6-month rating period specified on the CBCL. The TRF employs a shorter rating period for two reasons: (*a*) Because teachers usually know a child for only one academic year, a 6-month rating period would restrict teachers' ratings to the last 3 months of the school year. (*b*) The low frequency behaviors that may be picked up by parents' ratings over 6-month

CHILD BEHAVIOR CHECKLIST - TEACHER'S REPORT FORM

CHILD'S AGE	CHILD'S SEX ☐ Boy ☐ Girl	RACE	CHILD'S NAME
GRADE	THIS FORM FILLED OUT BY ☐ Teacher		
DATE	☐ Counselor ☐ Other (specify) _____		SCHOOL

PARENTS' TYPE OF WORK (Please be specific — for example, auto mechanic, high school teacher, homemaker, laborer, lathe operator, shoe salesman, army sergeant.)

FATHER'S
TYPE OF WORK _____

MOTHER'S
TYPE OF WORK _____

I. How long have you known this pupil?

II. How well do you know him/her? ☐ Very Well ☐ Moderately Well ☐ Not Well

III. How much time does he/she spend in your class per week?

IV. What kind of class is it (Please be specific, e.g., regular 5th grade, 7th grade math, etc.)

V. Has he/she ever been referred for special class placement, services, or tutoring?

  ☐ No   ☐ Don't Know   ☐ Yes — what kind and when?

VI. Has he/she ever repeated a grade?

  ☐ No   ☐ Don't Know   ☐ Yes — grade and reason

VII. Current school performance — list academic subjects and check appropriate column:

Academic subject	Far below grade	Somewhat below grade	At grade level	Somewhat above grade	Far above grade
1. _____	☐	☐	☐	☐	☐
2. _____	☐	☐	☐	☐	☐
3. _____	☐	☐	☐	☐	☐
4. _____	☐	☐	☐	☐	☐
5. _____	☐	☐	☐	☐	☐
6. _____	☐	☐	☐	☐	☐

3/81 Edition

Figure 12-1.   Page 1 of the Teacher's Report Form.

VIII. Compared to typical pupils of the same age:	Much less	Somewhat less	Slightly less	About average	Slightly more	Somewhat more	Much more
1. How hard is he/she working?	□	□	□	□	□	□	□
2. How appropriately is he/she behaving?	□	□	□	□	□	□	□
3. How much is he/she learning?	□	□	□	□	□	□	□
4. How happy is he/she?	□	□	□	□	□	□	□

IX. **Most recent achievement test scores** (If available):

Name of test	Subject	Date	Percentile or grade level obtained

X. **IQ, readiness, or aptitude tests** (If available):

Name of test	Date	IQ or equivalent scores

XI. **Please feel free to write any comments about this pupil's work, behavior, or potential, using extra pages if necessary**

PAGE 2

Figure 12-2. Page 2 of the Teacher's Report Form.

Below is a list of items that describe pupils. For each item that describes the pupil **now or within the past 2 months,** please circle the **2** if the item is **very true** or **often true** of the pupil. Circle the **1** if the item is **somewhat** or **sometimes true** of the pupil. If the item is **not true** of the pupil, circle the **0**.

0	1	2	1.	Acts too young for his/her age
0	1	2	^{a}2.	Hums or makes other odd noises in class
0	1	2	3.	Argues a lot
0	1	2	^{a}4.	Fails to finish things he/she starts
0	1	2	5.	Behaves like opposite sex
0	1	2	^{a}6.	Defiant, talks back to staff
0	1	2	7.	Bragging, boasting
0	1	2	8.	Can't concentrate, can't pay attention for long
0	1	2	9.	Can't get his/her mind off certain thoughts; obsessions (describe): _____
0	1	2	10.	Can't sit still, restless, or hyperactive
0	1	2	11.	Clings to adults or too dependent
0	1	2	12.	Complains of loneliness
0	1	2	13.	Confused or seems to be in a fog
0	1	2	14.	Cries a lot
0	1	2	^{a}15.	Fidgets
0	1	2	16.	Cruelty, bullying, or meanness to others
0	1	2	17.	Day-dreams or gets lost in his/her thoughts
0	1	2	18.	Deliberately harms self or attempts suicide
0	1	2	19.	Demands a lot of attention
0	1	2	20.	Destroys his/her own things
0	1	2	^{b}21.	Destroys property belonging to others
0	1	2	^{a}22.	Difficulty following directions
0	1	2	23.	Disobedient at school
0	1	2	^{a}24.	Disturbs other pupils
0	1	2	^{b}25.	Doesn't get along with other pupils
0	1	2	26.	Doesn't seem to feel guilty after misbehaving
0	1	2	27.	Easily jealous
0	1	2	28.	Eats or drinks things that are not food (describe): _____
0	1	2	29.	Fears certain animals, situations, or places other than school (describe): _____
0	1	2	30.	Fears going to school

0	1	2	31.	Fears he/she might think or do something bad
0	1	2	32.	Feels he/she has to be perfect
0	1	2	33.	Feels or complains that no one loves him/her
0	1	2	34.	Feels others are out to get him/her
0	1	2	35.	Feels worthless or inferior
0	1	2	36.	Gets hurt a lot, accident-prone
0	1	2	37.	Gets in many fights
0	1	2	38.	Gets teased a lot
0	1	2	^{b}39.	Hangs around with others who get in trouble
0	1	2	40.	Hears things that aren't there (describe): _____
0	1	2	41.	Impulsive or acts without thinking
0	1	2	42.	Likes to be alone
0	1	2	43.	Lying or cheating
0	1	2	44.	Bites fingernails
0	1	2	45.	Nervous, highstrung, or tense
0	1	2	46.	Nervous movements or twitching (describe): _____
0	1	2	^{a}47.	Overconforms to rules
0	1	2	^{b}48.	Not liked by other pupils
0	1	2	^{a}49.	Has difficulty learning
0	1	2	50.	Too fearful or anxious
0	1	2	51.	Feels dizzy
0	1	2	52.	Feels too guilty
0	1	2	^{b}53.	Talks out of turn
0	1	2	54.	Overtired
0	1	2	55.	Overweight
			56.	Physical problems without known medical cause:
0	1	2	a.	Aches or pains
0	1	2	b.	Headaches
0	1	2	c.	Nausea, feels sick
0	1	2	d.	Problems with eyes (describe): _____
0	1	2	e.	Rashes or other skin problems
0	1	2	f.	Stomachaches or cramps
0	1	2	g.	Vomiting, throwing up
0	1	2	h.	Other (describe): _____

Figure 12-3. Page 3 of the Teacher's Report Form. Items marked *a* replace CBCL items, while those marked *b* differ slightly from CBCL items.

0 = Not True   1 = Somewhat or Sometimes True   2 = Very True or Often True

0 1 2 57. Physically attacks people
0 1 2 58. Picks nose, skin, or other parts of body (describe): _____

0 1 2 a59. Sleeps in class
0 1 2 a60. Apathetic or unmotivated

0 1 2 61. Poor school work
0 1 2 62. Poorly coordinated or clumsy

0 1 2 b63. Prefers being with older children
0 1 2 b64. Prefers being with younger children

0 1 2 65. Refuses to talk
0 1 2 66. Repeats certain acts over and over; compulsions (describe): _____

0 1 2 a67. Disrupts class discipline
0 1 2 68. Screams a lot

0 1 2 69. Secretive, keeps things to self
0 1 2 70. Sees things that aren't there (describe): _____

0 1 2 71. Self-conscious or easily embarrassed
0 1 2 a72. Messy work

0 1 2 a73. Behaves irresponsibly (describe): _____

0 1 2 74. Showing off or clowning

0 1 2 75. Shy or timid
0 1 2 a76. Explosive and unpredictable behavior

0 1 2 a77. Demands must be met immediately, easily frustrated
0 1 2 a78. Inattentive, easily distracted

0 1 2 79. Speech problem (describe): _____

0 1 2 80. Stares blankly

0 1 2 a81. Feels hurt when criticized
0 1 2 82. Steals

0 1 2 83. Stores up things he/she doesn't need (describe):

0 1 2 84. Strange behavior (describe): _____

0 1 2 85. Strange ideas (describe): _____

0 1 2 86. Stubborn, sullen, or irritable

0 1 2 87. Sudden changes in mood or feelings
0 1 2 88. Sulks a lot

0 1 2 89. Suspicious
0 1 2 90. Swearing or obscene language

0 1 2 91. Talks about killing self
0 1 2 a92. Underachieving, not working up to potential

0 1 2 93. Talks too much
0 1 2 94. Teases a lot

0 1 2 95. Temper tantrums or hot temper
0 1 2 b96. Seems preoccupied with sex

0 1 2 97. Threatens people
0 1 2 a98. Tardy to school or class

0 1 2 99. Too concerned with neatness or cleanliness
0 1 2 a100. Fails to carry out assigned tasks

0 1 2 b101. Truancy or unexplained absence
0 1 2 102. Underactive, slow moving, or lacks energy

0 1 2 103. Unhappy, sad, or depressed
0 1 2 104. Unusually loud

0 1 2 105. Uses alcohol or drugs (describe): _____

0 1 2 a106. Overly anxious to please

0 1 2 a107. Dislikes school
0 1 2 a108. Is afraid of making mistakes

0 1 2 109. Whining
0 1 2 a110. Unclean personal appearance

0 1 2 111. Withdrawn, doesn't get involved with others
0 1 2 112. Worrying

113. Please write in any problems the pupil has that were not listed above:

0 1 2 _____

0 1 2 _____

0 1 2 _____

PLEASE BE SURE YOU HAVE ANSWERED ALL ITEMS

Figure 12-4. Page 4 of the Teacher's Report Form. Items marked *a* replace CBCL items, while those marked *b* differ slightly from CBCL items.

periods, such as running away and firesetting, do not have counterparts on the TRF.

The 24 TRF items marked in Figures 12-3 and 12-4 with *a* replace CBCL items (such as *Allergy; Asthma; Bowel movements outside toilet*) with behaviors that teachers would be better able to report (such as *Hums or makes odd noises in class; Fails to finish things he/she starts; Defiant, talks back to staff*). The nine items marked *b* are similar to those of the CBCL except for slight changes of wording to make them more appropriate for the school environment (e.g., CBCL Item *25. Doesn't get along with other children* versus TRF item *25. Doesn't get along with other pupils*). The remaining 85 items, plus the open-ended items (56h. and 113.) are identical on the two forms.

Scoring Profiles for the TRF

At this writing, we are constructing scoring profiles for the TRF. The teachers' ratings for academic performance, Items VIII-1 through 4 on page 2 of the TRF, and the mean of these four items are displayed on a profile that shows how the child's scores compare with those of a normative sample of agemates. Like the scales of the Child Behavior Profile, the behavior problem scales of the Teacher Profile are derived from factor analyses of ratings on clinically-referred children and are normed with data from randomly selected nonreferred children. Table 12-1 lists the titles of the behavior problem scales of the Teacher Profile for boys aged 6–11, which is the only sex/age group completed to date.

Table 12-1
Teacher Profile Scales for Boys Aged 6–11

Internalizing Scales[a]	Mixed Scales	Externalizing Scales[a]
Anxious	Unpopular	Aggressive
Social Withdrawal	Self-Destructive	Nervous-Overactive
	Obsessive-Compulsive	Inattentive

[a]Scales are listed in descending order of their loadings on second-order Internalizing and Externalizing factors.

The Social Withdrawal, Obsessive-Compulsive, and Aggressive scales resemble those derived from parents' ratings of 6- to 11-year-old boys. The Inattentive and Nervous-Overactive scales include items that are combined in the Hyperactivity scale derived from parents' ratings. The Inattentive items form an especially strong syndrome to which teachers are likely to be more sensitive than parents. The Anxious, Unpopular, and Self-Destructive scales have no direct counterparts in the parents' ratings of 6- to 11-year-old boys. Nor do the Schizoid, Depressed, Uncommunicative, Somatic Complaints, or Delinquent scales derived from parents' ratings have clear counterparts in the teachers' ratings of 6- to 11-year-old boys, largely because teachers are less likely to observe these behaviors.

Second-order factor analysis of the scales derived from teachers' ratings yielded broad-band Internalizing and Externalizing groupings like those of the parents' scales, although three of the teachers' scales were not clearly associated with either broad-band grouping, as shown in Table 12-1. Further details of the Teacher Profile for boys aged 6 to 11 are presented by Edelbrock and Achenbach (1983). Edelbrock, Costello, and Kessler (1983) report its relation to psychiatric diagnoses of Attention Deficit Disorder, while Reed and Edelbrock (1983) report its relations to direct observations of children's school behavior. TRF forms, completed versions of the scoring profiles, templates, instructions, and a computer entry and scoring program are available from Dr. Achenbach at the University of Vermont. A *Manual* will be prepared when all versions of the Teacher Profile have been completed.

THE DIRECT OBSERVATION FORM OF THE CHILD BEHAVIOR CHECKLIST

The CBCL and TRF summarize a child's behavior as seen by important adults over a period of months. This approach has the advantage of reflecting the adult's view of the child's behavior based on diverse interactions, observations, and kinds of information about the child. Under some circumstances, however, it is feasible and desirable to obtain more structured samples of a child's behavior as recorded by more neutral observers who do not interact with the child. The constraints imposed by structured observational methods, the situations and intervals in which observations are made, and the observer's lack of ongoing relationship with the child make direct observations a supplement rather than a substitute for reports by important adults in the child's everyday life.

To obtain direct observational data in situations such as school classrooms, lunchrooms, recess, and group activities, we have developed the Direct Observation Form (DOF) of the Child Behavior Checklist. The general procedure is for an experienced observer to make a narrative description of behavior occurring over a 10-minute period and then to rate the child on the 96 behavior problem items of the DOF. As shown in Figures 12-5 and 12-6, the 96 items adjoin space for writing the narrative, enabling the observer to keep all the items in view while writing the narrative.

The ratings are made on a 4-point scale, with each point defined as indicated in Figure 12-5. A 4-point scale is used to capitalize on the finer-grained discriminations that experienced observers may be able to make during delimited time samples than parents or teachers are likely to make when judging behavior over a period of months. Eleven items having no direct counterparts on the TRF are marked with an *a*, while 36 items differing only slightly from items of the TRF are marked with a *b*. The remaining 49 items are similar to those of the TRF. Thirty-three items of the TRF have no direct counterparts on the DOF, because they were not likely to be ratable by an observer (e.g., poor school work) or were inappropriate for rating during structured time

For each item that describes the child's behavior **during the observational period**, circle the
    0 if the item was not observed
    1 if there was a very slight or ambiguous occurrence
    2 if there was a definite occurrence with mild to moderate intensity **and** less than three minutes duration
    3 if there was a definite occurrence with severe intensity **or** greater than three minutes duration
For each behavior problem observed, score only the item that most specifically describes the behavior

0 1 2 3	b_1	Acts too young for age	0 1 2 3	39.	Overconforms to rules
0 1 2 3	b_2	Makes odd noises	0 1 2 3	40.	Too fearful or anxious
0 1 2 3	b_3	Argues	0 1 2 3	41.	Physically attacks people
0 1 2 3	4	Behaves like opposite sex	0 1 2 3	42.	Picks nose, skin, or other parts of body (specify):
0 1 2 3	5.	Defiant or talks back to staff			
0 1 2 3	6	Bragging, boasting			
0 1 2 3	b_7	Doesn't concentrate or doesn't pay attention for long			
0 1 2 3	b_8	Can't get mind off certain thoughts; obsessions (specify) _____	0 1 2 3	b_{43}	Falls asleep
			0 1 2 3	44.	Apathetic or unmotivated
			0 1 2 3	45.	Refuses to talk
		_____	0 1 2 3	b_{46}	Disrupts group
0 1 2 3	b_9	Doesn't sit still, restless, or hyperactive	0 1 2 3	b_{47}	Screams
0 1 2 3	10	Clings to adults or too dependent	0 1 2 3	48.	Secretive, keeps things to self
0 1 2 3	11	Confused or seems to be in a fog	0 1 2 3	49.	Sees things that aren't there (specify): _____
0 1 2 3	b_{12}	Cries			
0 1 2 3	13	Fidgets	0 1 2 3	50.	Self-conscious or easily embarrassed
0 1 2 3	b_{14}	Cruelty, bullying, or meanness	0 1 2 3	a_{51}	Sexual problems (specify): _____
0 1 2 3	b_{15}	Daydreams or gets lost in thoughts			
0 1 2 3	b_{16}	Deliberately harms self			
0 1 2 3	b_{17}	Demands or tries to get attention of staff	0 1 2 3	b_{52}	Shows off or clowns
0 1 2 3	b_{18}	Destroys own things	0 1 2 3	b_{53}	Shy or timid behavior
0 1 2 3	19	Destroys property belonging to others	0 1 2 3	b_{54}	Explosive behavior
0 1 2 3	b_{20}	Disobedient	0 1 2 3	55.	Demands must be met immediately, easily frustrated
0 1 2 3	b_{21}	Disturbs other children	0 1 2 3	56.	Inattentive, easily distracted
0 1 2 3	22	Doesn't seem to feel guilty after misbehaving	0 1 2 3	57.	Stares blankly
0 1 2 3	b_{23}	Shows jealousy	0 1 2 3	b_{58}	Acts like feelings are hurt when criticized
0 1 2 3	24	Eats or drinks things that are not food (specify):	0 1 2 3	59.	Steals
			0 1 2 3	60.	Stores up things he/she doesn't need (specify):
0 1 2 3	b_{25}	Shows fear of specific situations or stimuli (specify) _____	0 1 2 3	61.	Strange behavior (specify): _____
			0 1 2 3	62.	Strange ideas (specify): _____
0 1 2 3	b_{26}	Says no one likes him/her			
0 1 2 3	b_{27}	Says others are out to get him/her	0 1 2 3	63.	Stubborn, sullen, or irritable
0 1 2 3	b_{28}	Expresses feelings of worthlessness or inferiority	0 1 2 3	64.	Sudden changes in mood or feelings
0 1 2 3	b_{29}	Gets hurt, accident prone	0 1 2 3	b_{65}	Sulks
0 1 2 3	b_{30}	Gets in physical fights	0 1 2 3	66.	Suspicious
0 1 2 3	b_{31}	Gets teased	0 1 2 3	67.	Swearing or obscene language
0 1 2 3	32	Hears things that aren't there (specify): _____	0 1 2 3	68.	Talks about killing self
			0 1 2 3	69.	Talks too much
			0 1 2 3	b_{70}	Teases
0 1 2 3	33	Impulsive or acts without thinking	0 1 2 3	71.	Temper tantrums or hot temper
0 1 2 3	a_{34}	Isolates self from others	0 1 2 3	72.	Seems preoccupied with sex
0 1 2 3	35	Lying or cheating	0 1 2 3	73.	Threatens people
0 1 2 3	36	Bites fingernails	0 1 2 3	74.	Too concerned with neatness or cleanliness
0 1 2 3	37	Nervous, highstrung, or tense	0 1 2 3	75.	Underactive, slow moving, or lacks energy
0 1 2 3	38	Nervous movements or twitching (specify): ___	0 1 2 3	76.	Unhappy, sad, or depressed
			0 1 2 3	77.	Unusually loud

PAGE 2

Figure 12-5. **Items 1–77 of the Direct Observation Form. Items marked** *a* **have no direct counterparts on the Teacher's Report, while those marked** *b* **differ slightly from Teacher's Report items.**

0 1 2 3	78. Overly anxious to please	0 1 2 3	a90. Runs out of class (or similar setting)
0 1 2 3	79. Whining	0 1 2 3	91. Behaves irresponsibly (specify): _____
0 1 2 3	80. Withdrawn, doesn't get involved with others		
0 1 2 3	81. Worrying		
0 1 2 3	a82. Thumb-sucking	0 1 2 3	a92. Bossy
0 1 2 3	a83. Fails to express ideas clearly	0 1 2 3	b93. Plays with younger children
0 1 2 3	a84. Impatient	0 1 2 3	a94. Complains
0 1 2 3	a85. Tattles	0 1 2 3	b95. Afraid to make mistakes
0 1 2 3	b86. Compulsions, repeats behavior over & over	0 1 2 3	a96. Acts like poor loser
	(specify): _____		97. Other problems (specify):
		0 1 2 3	
0 1 2 3	a87. Easily led by peers	0 1 2 3	
0 1 2 3	b88. Clumsy, poor motor control	0 1 2 3	
0 1 2 3	b89. Doesn't get along with peers	0 1 2 3	

Narrative (continued on page 4 if necessary):

ON-TASK BEHAVIOR

Boxes represent ten 5-second intervals, spaced one minute apart. If the child's behavior was on-task, cross out the box.
To compute a total on-task score, count one point for each box crossed out and sum the ones to yield a score ranging from 0 to 10.

1	2	3	4	5	6	7	8	9	10

PAGE 3

Figure 12-6. Items 78–97 of the Direct Observation Form. Items marked a have no direct counterparts on the Teacher's Report, while those marked b differ slightly from Teacher's Report items.

samples (e.g., unclean personal appearance). Items corresponding to those of the TRF are not necessarily in the same numerical order on the two forms.

On-Task Score

Beside rating the 96 behavior problem items, the observer scores on-task behavior in the following way: At the end of each 1-minute interval, the observer spends 5 seconds judging whether the child is mainly on-task during that 5 seconds. If so, the observer crosses out the number corresponding to that interval. At the end of the 10-minute observation period, the crossed-out intervals are summed to yield a score ranging from 0 to 10 for on-task behavior. The precise definition of on-task behavior should be based on the situation in which observations are made; examples would be school work during classroom observations and nondisruptive social interaction during group activities.

Averaging Scores from Multiple Observation Periods

We have found that the variability of disturbed children's behavior from morning to afternoon and day-to-day necessitates observations on several different occasions in order to obtain representative samples of behavior. The scores for each of the several observation periods can be averaged to obtain the child's final scores. We have found that averaging ratings from six 10-minute observational periods spread across different mornings and afternoons yields stable behavioral scores for disturbed children. Although six sessions may sound like a lot, they total only an hour of observation time. Depending on the goals of the user, it may be desirable to confine all the observations to one type of setting, such as the classroom, or to make observations in several settings, such as classroom, lunchroom, and recess.

Training and Use

Elaborate training is not required for using the DOF, but observers should be thoroughly familiar with all the items and should practice making the narrative descriptions, scoring the items, and discussing disagreements with another observer who rates the same sessions. It is important to follow the scoring rules listed on page 2 of the DOF and to avoid scoring more than one item for a particular behavior.

Reliability, Stability, and Validity

We have obtained high inter-observer reliability for total behavior problem scores without extensive training of the observers. (The total behavior problem score is the sum of 1s, 2s, and 3s for all the behavior problem items.) In a residential treatment center for severely disturbed children, we found a Pearson correlation of .96 ($p < .001$) between the total behavior problem scores obtained by two research assistants across 16 observation sessions. There was virtually no difference between the mean total scores obtained by the two observers (31.06 versus 31.00, t = .06, ns). A Pearson correlation of .71 ($p < .001$) was found between on-task scores across the 16 observation sessions (means = 7.13 versus 8.06, t = 1.63, ns).

In the same residential setting, the Pearson correlation for 6-month stability of the total behavior problem score (averaged over six 10-minute sessions at Time 1 and Time 2) was .55 for classroom observations and .59 for observations during recess ($N = 36$, $p < .001$ for both). Six-month stability of the on-task score was .51 for classroom observations ($p = .002$) and .60 for recess observations ($p < .001$). These correlations are similar to the 6-month stability of .57 ($p < .001$) for CBCL ratings of the same children by their mother or child care worker (depending on whether the child was in full-time residence). Both classroom scores and the CBCL ratings showed significant improvements over the 6-month period (t = 4.31 for observed behavior problems and 4.13 for on-task, both $p < .001$; t = 2.46 for CBCL total problem score, p = .019). The recess observations showed nonsignificant trends in the same direction. Classroom observation scores thus yield about the same stability in rank ordering and the same degree of improvement as the CBCL ratings, whereas recess observation scores yield similar stability in rank ordering but nonsignificant evidence of improvement.

In a sample of 25 public school boys referred for special services for behavior problems, Reed and Edelbrock (1983) found a Pearson correlation of .92 ($p < .001$) between total behavior problem scores obtained by two graduate student observers, when the scores were averaged over 60 minutes of observation (six 10-minute sessions) for each child. Taking each 10-minute observation session as a unit, the overall Pearson r was .86 ($p < .001$). The Pearson correlation between on-task scores was .83 across 60 minutes of observation for each child and .71 between on-task scores computed across all the individual 10-minute observation sessions (both $p < .001$).

Reed and Edelbrock also reported evidence of discriminative validity. As rated by undergraduate observers blind to the boys' status, 15 boys identified by their teachers as having problems received significantly higher total behavior problem scores than 15 nonproblem boys (means = 41.5 versus 27.0, t = 4.3, $p < .001$). (See Reed & Edelbrock for further analyses of the DOF and its relations to the TRF ratings.)

Research is in progress to determine whether the DOF is worth scoring on a differentiated profile like those for the CBCL and TRF. In the meantime, the DOF can be used by school psychologists, special educators, and other practitioners to obtain a picture of the specific behaviors of children in need of help, and by clinicians and researchers wishing to supplement the picture obtained from parent and teacher ratings.

To provide appropriate baselines for behavior in the specific situations in which children are observed, it is recommended that 10-minute DOF observations also be made of two similar children of the same sex prior to and following each 10-minute observation of a target child. The scores obtained by the target child can then be compared with the average of the scores obtained by the two control children in order to assess the target child's deviance from the behavior of peers in the same setting.

Self-explanatory DOF forms can be obtained from Dr. Achenbach.

THE YOUTH SELF-REPORT

The CBCL, TRF, and DOF all describe children's behavior as seen by adults. Adults' reports are essential, because children seldom seek help for their own behavior problems, adults are usually involved in the problems, and adults determine what will be done about the problems. Nevertheless, children's views of their own behavior are also important. Older children, in particular, may be able to provide views and information that parents, teachers, and observers are not privy to.

Clinical interviews are the most common means for obtaining children's reports of their own behavior. Such interviews are usually considered indispensible for helping clinicians form impressions and build rapport. However, clinical impressions and rapport may not yield a clear picture of the child's behavior as the child views it, in a way that can be compared with other people's views. Furthermore, clinical interviews often focus selectively on topics emphasized by the child or interviewer.

To obtain self-reports in a format similar to the CBCL and TRF, we have developed the Youth Self-Report (YSR). The YSR is designed to be filled out by youngsters aged 11 to 18 years. It is simple enough to be filled out by youngsters with a mental age of about 10 and fifth grade reading skills. It can also be read aloud to the respondent if necessary.

As shown in Figures 12-7 and 12-8, the YSR has most of the same social competence items as the CBCL, but they are worded in the first person. Items concerning special class placement, repetition of grades, and school problems are omitted, however, to avoid embarrassing the respondent, and because more accurate information on these items is likely to be available from parents and teachers.

As shown in Figures 12-8, 12-9, and 12-10, the behavior problem items are in the same format as those of the CBCL, except that they are worded in the first person. Beside changes in wording appropriate for first person reports by 11- to 18-year-olds, the 16 items marked with an *a* in Figures 12-8, 12-9, and 12-10 are replacements for CBCL items deemed inappropriate or unlikely to be self-reported in this age range (e.g., CBCL Item 6. *Bowel movements outside toilet*). The replacement items are all benign self-referent statements that give respondents an opportunity to say favorable things about themselves. Note that these 16 items should be *omitted* from the total behavior problem score (sum of 1s and 2s on the remaining 102 behavior problem items, plus open-ended item 56h.). The seven items marked with a *b* in Figures 12-8, 12-9, and 12-10 differ from the corresponding CBCL items in minor ways other than re-wording in the first person. Item 10, for example, is *Can't sit still, restless, or hyperactive* on the CBCL and *I have trouble sitting still* on the YSR.

— for office use only —

IDENTIFICATION #

YOUTH SELF-REPORT — FOR AGES 11-18

YOUR AGE	YOUR SEX ☐ Boy ☐ Girl	GRADE IN SCHOOL	YOUR NAME

YOUR RACE ☐ Black ☐ White ☐ Other (specify) _____	TODAY'S DATE Yr. _____ Mo. _____ Day _____ DATE OF BIRTH Yr. _____ Mo. _____ Day _____	PARENT'S TYPE OF WORK *(Please be specific—for example: auto mechanic, high school teacher, homemaker, laborer, lathe operator, shoe salesman, army sergeant.)* FATHER'S TYPE OF WORK: _____ MOTHER'S TYPE OF WORK: _____

I. **Please list the sports you most like to take part in.** For example: swimming, baseball, skating, skate boarding, bike riding, fishing, etc.

☐ None

	Compared to others of your age, about how much time do you spend in each?			Compared to others of your age, how well do you do each one?		
	Less Than Average	Average	More Than Average	Below Average	Average	Above Average
a. _____	☐	☐	☐	☐	☐	☐
b. _____	☐	☐	☐	☐	☐	☐
c. _____	☐	☐	☐	☐	☐	☐

II. **Please list your favorite hobbies, activities, and games, other than sports.** For example: cards, books, piano, crafts, autos, etc. (Do not include T.V.)

☐ None

	Compared to others of your age, about how much time do you spend in each?			Compared to others of your age, how well do you do each one?		
	Less Than Average	Average	More Than Average	Below Average	Average	Above Average
a. _____	☐	☐	☐	☐	☐	☐
b. _____	☐	☐	☐	☐	☐	☐
c. _____	☐	☐	☐	☐	☐	☐

III. **Please list any organization, clubs, teams or groups you belong to.**

☐ None

	Compared to others of your age, how active are you in each?		
	Less Active	Average	More Active
a. _____	☐	☐	☐
b. _____	☐	☐	☐
c. _____	☐	☐	☐

IV. **Please list any jobs or chores you have.** For example: Paper route, babysitting, making bed, etc.

☐ None

	Compared to others of your age, how well do you carry them out?		
	Below Average	Average	Above Average
a. _____	☐	☐	☐
b. _____	☐	☐	☐
c. _____	☐	☐	☐

Figure 12-7. Page 1 of the Youth Self-Report.

V. **1. About how many close friends do you have?** ☐ None ☐ 1 ☐ 2 or 3 ☐ 4 or more

2. About how many times a week do you do things with them? ☐ less than 1 ☐ 1 or 2 ☐ 3 or more

VI. Compared to others of your age, how well do you:

	Worse	About the same	Better
a. Get along with your brothers & sisters?	☐	☐	☐
b. Get along with other kids?	☐	☐	☐
c. Get along with your parents?	☐	☐	☐
d. Do things by yourself?	☐	☐	☐

VII. Current school performance

☐ I do not go to school

	Failing	Below Average	Average	Above Average
a. English	☐	☐	☐	☐
b. Math	☐	☐	☐	☐
Other subjects: c. _____	☐	☐	☐	☐
d. _____	☐	☐	☐	☐
e. _____	☐	☐	☐	☐
f. _____	☐	☐	☐	☐
g. _____	☐	☐	☐	☐

VIII. Below is a list of items that describe kids. For each item that describes you **now** or **within the past 6 months**, please circle the 2 if the item is **very true** or **often true** of you. Circle the **1** if the item is **somewhat** or **sometimes true** of you. If the item is **not true** of you, circle the **0**.

0 1 2	1. I act too young for my age	0 1 2	14. I cry a lot
0 1 2	2. I have an allergy (describe)	0 1 2	^{a}15. I am pretty honest
		0 1 2	16. I am mean to others
		0 1 2	17. I daydream a lot
	_____	0 1 2	18. I deliberately try to hurt or kill myself
0 1 2	3. I argue a lot	0 1 2	^{b}19. I try to get a lot of attention
0 1 2	4. I have asthma	0 1 2	20. I destroy my own things
0 1 2	5. I act like the opposite sex	0 1 2	21. I destroy things belonging to others
0 1 2	^{a}6. I like animals	0 1 2	22. I disobey my parents
0 1 2	7. I brag	0 1 2	23. I disobey at school
0 1 2	8. I have trouble concentrating or paying attention	0 1 2	24. I don't eat as well as I should
0 1 2	9. I can't get my mind off certain thoughts (describe): _____	0 1 2	25. I don't get along with other kids
		0 1 2	26. I don't feel guilty after doing something I shouldn't
	_____	0 1 2	27. I am jealous of others
0 1 2	^{b}10. I have trouble sitting still	0 1 2	^{a}28. I am willing to help others when they need help
0 1 2	^{b}11. I'm too dependent on adults	0 1 2	29. I am afraid of certain animals, situations, or places, other than school (describe) _____
0 1 2	12. I feel lonely		
0 1 2	13. I feel confused or in a fog		_____

PAGE 2

Figure 12-8. Page 2 of the Youth Self-Report. Items marked *a* replace CBCL items, while those marked *b* differ slightly from CBCL items.

0	1	2	30. I am afraid of going to school
0	1	2	31. I am afraid I might think or do something bad
0	1	2	32. I feel that I have to be perfect
0	1	2	33. I feel that no one loves me
0	1	2	34. I feel that others are out to get me
0	1	2	35. I feel worthless or inferior
0	1	2	36. I accidently get hurt a lot
0	1	2	37. I get in many fights
0	1	2	38. I get teased a lot
0	1	2	39. I hang around with kids who get in trouble
0	1	2	40. I hear things that nobody else seems able to hear (describe) _____
0	1	2	b41. I act without stopping to think
0	1	2	42. I like to be alone
0	1	2	43. I lie or cheat
0	1	2	44. I bite my fingernails
0	1	2	45. I am nervous or tense
0	1	2	46. Parts of my body twitch or make nervous movements (describe)
0	1	2	47. I have nightmares
0	1	2	48. I am not liked by other kids
0	1	2	a49. I can do certain things better than most kids
0	1	2	50. I am too fearful or anxious
0	1	2	51. I feel dizzy
0	1	2	52. I feel too guilty
0	1	2	53. I eat too much
0	1	2	54. I feel overtired
0	1	2	55. I am overweight
			56. Physical problems without known medical cause:
0	1	2	a. Aches or pains
0	1	2	b. Headaches
0	1	2	c. Nausea, feel sick
0	1	2	d. Problems with eyes (describe):
0	1	2	e. Rashes or other skin problems
0	1	2	f. Stomachaches or cramps
0	1	2	g. Vomiting, throwing up
0	1	2	h. Other (describe): _____
0	1	2	57. I physically attack people
0	1	2	b58. I pick my skin or other parts of my body (describe) _____

0	1	2	a59. I can be pretty friendly
0	1	2	a60. I like to try new things
0	1	2	61. My school work is poor
0	1	2	62. I am poorly coordinated or clumsy
0	1	2	63. I would rather be with older kids than with kids my own age
0	1	2	64. I would rather be with younger kids than with kids my own age
0	1	2	65. I refuse to talk
0	1	2	66. I repeat certain actions over and over (describe) _____
0	1	2	67. I run away from home
0	1	2	68. I scream a lot
0	1	2	69. I am secretive or keep things to myself
0	1	2	70. I see things that nobody else seems able to see (describe)
0	1	2	71. I am self-conscious or easily embarrassed
0	1	2	72. I set fires
0	1	2	a73. I can work well with my hands
0	1	2	74. I show off or clown
0	1	2	75. I am shy
0	1	2	76. I sleep less than most kids
0	1	2	77. I sleep more than most kids during day and/or night (describe) _____
0	1	2	a78. I have a good imagination
0	1	2	79. I have a speech problem (describe): _____
0	1	2	a80. I stand up for my rights
0	1	2	81. I steal things at home
0	1	2	82. I steal things from places other than home
0	1	2	83. I store up things I don't need (describe) _____
0	1	2	84. I do things other people think are strange (describe): _____
0	1	2	85. I have thoughts that other people would think are strange (describe) _____
0	1	2	b86. I am stubborn
0	1	2	87. My moods or feelings change suddenly

PAGE 3   *Please see other side*

Figure 12-9. Page 3 of the Youth Self-Report. Items marked *a* replace CBCL items, while those marked *b* differ slightly from CBCL items.

0	1	2	[a]88.	I enjoy being with other people
0	1	2	89.	I am suspicious
0	1	2	90.	I swear or use dirty language
0	1	2	91.	I think about killing myself
0	1	2	[a]92.	I like to make others laugh
0	1	2	93.	I talk too much
0	1	2	94.	I tease others a lot
0	1	2	95.	I have a hot temper
0	1	2	96.	I think about sex too much
0	1	2	97.	I threaten to hurt people
0	1	2	[a]98.	I like to help others
0	1	2	99.	I am too concerned about being neat or clean
0	1	2	100.	I have trouble sleeping (describe) _____
0	1	2	101.	I cut classes or skip school

0	1	2	[b]102.	I don't have much energy
0	1	2	103.	I am unhappy, sad, or depressed
0	1	2	104.	I am louder than other kids
0	1	2	105.	I use alcohol or drugs other than for medical conditions (describe): _____
0	1	2	[a]106.	I try to be fair to others
0	1	2	[a]107.	I enjoy a good joke
0	1	2	[a]108.	I like to take life easy
0	1	2	[a]109.	I try to help other people when I can
0	1	2	110.	I wish I were of the opposite sex
0	1	2	111.	I keep from getting involved with others
0	1	2	112.	I worry a lot

Please write down anything else that describes your feelings, behavior, and interests

PAGE 4   PLEASE BE SURE YOU HAVE ANSWERED ALL ITEMS

Figure 12-10. Page 4 of the Youth Self-Report. Items marked *a* replace CBCL items, while those marked *b* differ slightly from CBCL items.

At this writing, little research has been done with the YSR. Prior to developing the YSR, however, we obtained data from 12- to 17-year-olds who filled out the behavior problem portion of the CBCL at intake into a community mental health center and again at a 6-month follow-up. Despite the third-person wording of the items, the inclusion of the 16 items deleted from the YSR, and the mental health services received in the interim, the Pearson correlation between the total behavior problem scores across the 6-month interval was .69 ($p < 001$, $N = 30$). This indicates considerable stability in the rank ordering of self-ratings of behavior problems by youth referred for mental health services. Furthermore, the total behavior problem scores obtained from the youths' self-ratings on the CBCL showed significant correlations with CBCL ratings of the youths by their mothers and a clinician at both intake and follow-up, as shown in Table 12-2.

Table 12-2
Correlations between CBCL Total Behavior Problem Scores
from Ratings by Clinically-Referred Youth,
their Mothers, and a Clinician

	Intake		*6-Month Follow-up*		
Intake	*Clinician*	*Mother*	*Clinician*	*Mother*	*Youth*
Clinician			.53***	.49***	.40*
Mother	.70***		.38**	.59***	.13
Youth	.55***	.37**	.14	.44**	.69***
6-Month Follow-up					
Mother			.62***		
Youth			.48**	.56**	

Ns range from 27 for Intake Youth × Follow-up Clinician to 73 for Intake Mother × Intake Clinician

*$p < .05$
**$p < .01$
***$p < .001$

Self-ratings of CBCL behavior problem items thus show high enough stability and correlations with other people's views of the subjects to inspire confidence in their meaningfulness. Clinicians who use the YSR report that clinically-referred youths generally like filling it out. It also serves as an effective "ice breaker," in that youths will often talk more freely about themselves and share thoughts about self-reported items, such as suicidal ideation (Item 91), that they would not discuss before. We therefore plan to develop scoring profiles for the YSR analogous to those of the CBCL and TRF. In the meantime, copies of the YSR are available from Dr. Achenbach.

SUMMARY

Because no single source of data is adquate for the comprehensive assessment of children, we have developed companion instruments to supplement the CBCL with data from other key informants.

The Teacher's Report Form (TRF) is designed to obtain teachers' ratings of academic performance, positive adaptive characteristics, behavior problems specific to the school setting, and many of the same behavior problems rated by parents on the CBCL. A profile has been completed for boys aged 6–11, and profiles are being developed for girls aged 6–11, as well as 12–16-year-olds of both sexes.

The Direct Observation Form (DOF) is designed to score behavior problems and on-task behavior from 10-minute observation sessions in classrooms, school lunchrooms, recess, and group activities. Although ratings are made on 4-point scales within structured time samples, many of the items are similar to those of the TRF. High correlations have been found between total DOF problem scores obtained by pairs of observers after minimal training.

The Youth Self-Report (YSR) is designed to obtain self-ratings from 11- to 18-year-olds on most of the CBCL social competence and behavior problem items. Preliminary research indicates good stability in self-ratings by clinically-referred youths over a 6-month period and lower but statistically significant agreement with ratings by parents and a clinician. Although we have not yet constructed scoring profiles for the YSR, informal use with clinically-referred youths indicates that it is a useful clinical tool.

Chapter 13
Answers to Commonly Asked Questions

The purpose of this chapter is to answer questions that have arisen about the CBCL and Profile. Many of these questions were identified via a mail survey that we sent to some 1200 people who had requested our materials. We greatly appreciate the help of those who responded, because they pointed out problems and misunderstandings that we then sought to rectify through the revision of the Profile and explanatory materials, including this *Manual*.

Although we have attempted to answer many of the questions in earlier sections of the *Manual*, we list them here to provide direct answers, supplemented by references to more detailed information where relevant. The questions are grouped according to whether they refer mainly to the content of the CBCL, to scoring the CBCL, to the Profile, or to the Profile types. However, if you have a question that cannot be found under one heading, look under the other headings as well. The Table of Contents and Index may also help you find answers to questions we have not listed here.

QUESTIONS ABOUT THE CBCL

1 . **Why is the CBCL said to have 118 behavior problem items, when the item numbers only go to 113?**

   Answer: Item 56 includes seven specific physical complaints designated as *a* through *g*. Combined with the remaining 111 specifically stated problems, this sums to 118 items. In addition, item 56h provides space for parents to enter any physical problems not otherwise listed, and item 113 provides three spaces for parents to add additional problems of any sort. Total behavior problem scores are computed as the sum of 1s and 2s for the 118 specific problem items + item 56h + the highest score the respondent gives to any additional items written in for number 113. If a 2 is scored for all 118 items, 56h, and 113, the total score would be 240.

2 . **Can the CBCL be filled out by people other than parents?**

   Answer: The CBCL is designed to be filled out by people who know the child well and interact with the child as parents do. Adoptive parents, foster parents, and relatives with whom a child lives are appropriate respondents. For children living in institutions, such as residential treatment centers, child care workers who know the child well would be appropriate respondents for the behavior problem portion of the CBCL. However, they may not know enough of the child's history to complete the social competence portion. As discussed in Chapter 12, we have developed companion instruments to be filled out by teachers, by direct observers, and by 11– to 18-year-olds regarding their own behavior.

3 . What if a parent can't read?

Answer: The CBCL requires only fifth grade reading skills. It can also be administered orally by an interviewer who writes down the parent's answers. Where there is some doubt about a parent's reading skill, embarrassment can be avoided by handing the CBCL to the parent and having the interviewer say he/she will read each item aloud and record the parent's answers on another copy of the CBCL. Parents who can read will usually start answering spontaneously, without waiting for the questions to be read.

4 . What if a parent can read another language, but not English?

Answer: At this writing, we know of translations into the following languages: Chinese, Dutch, French (Canadian), German, Greek, Hebrew, Hindi, Italian, Korean, Spanish, and Swedish. Contact Dr. Achenbach for further information on translations.

5 . Don't certain items involve subjective judgments, such as *35. Feels worthless or inferior* and *52. Feels too guilty?*

Answer: Subjectivity is involved in all ratings of any person by another person. Some items of the CBCL are less subjective than others, but we recognize that the scores obtained on all items reflect parents' judgments about what to report. However, parents are usually in a better position than most other people to judge and report their children's expressions of feelings such as inferiority and guilt.

6. Can the CBCL be used for ages below 4 and over 16?

Answer: We designed the CBCL for ages 4 through 16, because children throughout this age range confront similar challenges in socialization, peer relations, achievement, and adaptive development, and parents are well situated to compare their children's competencies and problems with what is typical for peers. Below the age of 4 and above the age of 16, however, the developmental challenges are different enough to require assessment of behaviors that are not so important between the ages of 4 and 16. We are currently developing a separate checklist for 2- and 3-year-olds. After their offspring pass the age of 16, parents' value as informants may decline as the offspring increasingly separate themselves from home. Although we did not derive or norm scoring scales for the CBCL below the age of 4 or above 16, youngsters who are slightly outside these age limits and whose parents are good informants can be scored on the version of the Profile closest to their age. It must be remembered, however, that our norms are merely rough approximations to what might be obtained for youngsters outside our age limits.

7. Page 3 of the CBCL instructs the respondent to base ratings on the previous 6 months. What if the CBCL is to be readministered over intervals of less than 6 months?

Answer: The 6-month instruction can be changed to suit the interval being used. If the interval is reduced much below 6 months, this may reduce scores on some behavior problem items and scales slightly. Low frequency behaviors such as running away and firesetting, for example, may also be missed if the rating interval is too short. However, if reassessments are planned at intervals of less than 6 months, respondents should use the same shortened interval for the initial ratings as for each follow-up rating. For example, if follow-up ratings are to be done after a 3-month interval, the initial rating should also be based on a 3-month period, so that initial scores will not be higher than the follow-up scores merely because they encompass a longer rating period. Because of the time required for behavioral changes to stabilize and become clearly recognized by parents, rating periods of less than 2 months are probably not worth using.

8. **Is there a short form of the CBCL that takes less time to fill out?**

Answer: There is no short form as such. However, the social competence portion (pages 1 and 2) or behavior problem portion (pages 3 and 4) can be administered alone. Since each of these is brief and each scale's standard scores require that all the constituent items of the scale are considered by the parent, it would not make sense to abbreviate the CBCL any further. A few items can be deleted for certain purposes, however. For example, Item *61. Poor school work* can be deleted for children not in school. Item *78. Smears or plays with bowel movements* is of very low frequency and can be deleted for most groups without affecting scale scores much.

9. **Is there a machine-readable form of the CBCL?**

Answer: Although we did develop an IBM Opscan form to be filled out by the interviewers in our home interview survey (Achenbach & Edelbrock, 1981), we have not developed machine readable forms to be filled out by parents, because (*a*) several items must be described by parents and then judged by a person familiar with the rules for scoring the CBCL; (*b*) machine readable forms would be more difficult and impersonal for parents to fill out; (*c*) machine readable forms would make it difficult to take account of the explanations and qualifications that parents often write on the existing form.

10. **If parents fill out the CBCL, won't this cause them to focus on the child's problems instead of the family system?**

Answer: When parents bring their child for help, they expect to provide information about the child. The CBCL is not likely to instigate an exclusive focus on the child, because data on the family will typically be obtained as well. The clinician's own approach and the specific referral problems usually outweigh the CBCL in determining the degree of focus on the child versus the family system.

SCORING THE CBCL

(Appendix A contains detailed scoring instructions, including criteria for items the respondent is asked to describe.)

1. **What if the respondent scores two different items for exactly the same behavior?**

   Answer: Score only the item that most specifically describes the behavior. For example, if the respondent circled a 2 for Item *1. Acts too young for age* and also circles a 2 for Item *84. Strange behavior,* describing the behavior as "acts very babyish," only Item 1 should be counted.

2. **What if the respondent circles two scores for a particular item or otherwise indicates that the item is true of the child but does not clearly indicate a score of 1 or 2?**

   Answer: Score the item 1.

3. **On *Item 113. Please write in any problems your child has that were not listed above,* what if a respondent describes behavior that is specified elsewhere on the problem list?**

   Answer: Score the item *only* where it is most precisely specified on the problem list, whether or not the respondent has scored it there as well as on Item *113*. For example, if the respondent wrote "very jealous of younger sister," and scored it 2 for Item *113*, only Item *27. Easily jealous* should be scored 2, rather than Item *113,* whether or not the respondent had also scored Item *27*.

4. **How is Item 113 figured in the total score?**

   Answer: If the respondent has entered on Item *113* a problem that is not clearly covered by another item, obtain the total behavior problem score by adding the 1 or 2 scored by the respondent to the sum of 1s and 2s for all other items. If the respondent has entered more than one additional item, count only the one that has received the highest score. Thus, if a respondent has scored one additional item 1 and another item 2, add 2 to the total score. (Adding a maximum of 2 points for Item *113* and 2 for *56h* is intended to limit the amount of variance contributed by items that are not stated for other parents to rate.)

5. **Should CBCLs that have many unanswered items be scored?**

   Answer: The scoring instructions (Appendix A) give rules for dealing with unanswered items. In brief, if one item is omitted from the Activities or Social scale, the mean of the other five items of that scale is substituted for the missing item. If more than one item is missing from either of these scales or any item is missing from the School scale, the respective scale is not scored. On the behavior problem portion, if more than 8 items are left blank (excluding Items *56h* and *113*), do not compute behavior problem scale scores or total scores, unless it is clear that the respondent intends the blanks to be zeroes.

6. **How are the total social competence and behavior problem scores used?**

   Answer: These scores provide global indices of the child's competencies and problems, as seen by the respondent. We have found that behavior problem scores falling at the 90th percentile of the normative groups provide a good cutoff point for discriminating between clinically-referred and nonreferred children (see Chapter 7 for details of the cutoff points for each sex/age group). The total behavior problem score can also be used as a basis for comparing behavior problems in different groups and for assessing change as a function of time or intervention. The total social competence score can be used in similar ways, but is not as susceptible to change, because it is determined partly by historical data, such as repetition of grades in school (see Chapter 7 for details).

7. **The item numbers on some scoring templates do not fit directly over the item numbers on the CBCL.**

   Answer: Templates having white backing on the items were made prior to 1980 for an edition of the CBCL printed at NIMH. The manufacturing process could not control the spacing adequately. Templates without white backing are made for the edition of the CBCL printed at the University of Vermont. The NIMH templates do not fit the University of Vermont edition well. However, the templates without white backing made at the University of Vermont should fit items of the University of Vermont edition of the CBCL within quite close tolerances, although the edges of the templates may not line up with the edges of the CBCL.

THE CHILD BEHAVIOR PROFILE

1. **How can hand scoring be made quicker and easier?**

   Answer: The larger print on the Revised Profile may help, and the time taken to score profiles usually decreases with experience. Certain scores can be omitted if you do not need them, such as the Internalizing and Externalizing scores. If we grouped behavior problem items on the CBCL according to their Profile scales, this might make scoring easier. However, it could create a halo effect on the respondent's ratings and would require different CBCLs for each sex/age group, because items are not on the same scales for all groups. We recommend computer scoring whenever feasible (see Appendix B for details), but we welcome suggestions for making hand scoring easier.

2. **Why are some behavior problem items included on more than one Profile scale?**

   Answer: An item is included on each scale derived from a factor on which the item loaded $\geq .30$ ($\geq .40$ for the Aggressive scale). Chapter 2 explains the rationale for retaining items on more than one scale if they loaded on more than one factor.

3. **Doesn't the presence of some items on Internalizing and Externalizing scales create an artifactual correlation between these groupings?**

   Answer: As explained in Chapter 4, these two groupings are positively correlated even if overlapping items are deleted. Like measures of ability, measures of behavior problems tend to be positively correlated with each other — individuals who have many behavior problems of one type tend to be above average on other types, too. However, Chapter 4 details procedures for categorizing children as Internalizers or Externalizers.

4. **Why are there no norms for the "Other Problems" scale?**

   Answer: The "Other Problems" on each Profile are *not* a scale but merely a list of the items that were either too uncommon to be factor analyzed or that did not load highly enough on any factor to be part of a scale for a particular sex/age group. There are thus no associations among them to warrant treating them as a scale. However, they are included in the total behavior problem score.

5. **Why does the Schizoid scale belong to the Externalizing group on the Profile for 4–5-year-old boys but the Internalizing group on the other Profiles?**

   Answer: As explained in Chapter 4, the Internalizing and Externalizing groupings are derived from second-order factor analyses of the behavior problem scales for each sex/age group. They therefore reflect the correlations actually occurring among the behavior problem scales for each group. Although the scales labeled "Schizoid" for all groups are similar in that they include such items as "Hears things that aren't there," this scale was more highly correlated with the Aggressive and Delinquent scales than with the Internalizing scales among 4–5-year-old boys. We do not know the exact reason, although in Achenbach's (1966) factor analytic study of case history data, boys manifesting a "schizoid" syndrome were found to come from Externalizing as well as Internalizing groupings. This suggests that what is common to the schizoid syndrome for boys may not be consistently subsumed by the Internalizing–Externalizing dichotomy.

6. **Does a high score on the Schizoid scale mean the child has a schizoid personality or is schizophrenic?**

   Answer: None of the scales is intended to be directly equivalent to any clinical diagnosis. The names of the scales are merely intended to summarize the content of the scales. The term "Schizoid" is intended to reflect items such as *Hears things that aren't there*, which are included on this scale in all sex/age groups. However, the version of the scale for 4–5-year-old girls and 6–11-year-old boys includes enough items indicative of anxiety that "anxious" is a plausible alternative label for this scale, especially since some children in these groups can obtain fairly high scores without having any of the items suggestive of weak reality testing. (See Chapter 2 for more information on scale labels.)

7. **Should extremely low scores on any behavior problem scales be considered deviant?**

   Answer: Extremely low scores merely reflect the absence of reported problems. As explained in Chapter 3, the Revised Profile compresses the low end of the behavior problem scales, so that a T score of 55 is the minimum obtainable on any scale. However, nearly all children have at least some behavior problems. The mean problem scores for nonreferred children in our normative samples range from about 17 for 12–16-year-olds to 25 for 4–5-year-olds. In our nonreferred normative samples, the following low behavior problem scores are so uncommon as to suggest that the respondent has not understood the CBCL, is poorly informed about the child, or is not being candid: Total behavior problem scores of 0 to 5 for 4–5-year-olds; 0 to 4 for 6–11-year-olds; 0 to 2 for 12–16-year-olds. The following scores are low enough to hint at a tendency to deny problems, but could accurately reflect the parent's judgment: 6 to 15 for 4–5-year-olds; 5 to 11 for 6–11-year-olds; 3 to 7 for 12–16-year-olds.

8. **Should there be separate norms for mothers' and fathers' ratings or for black and white children?**

   Answer: As detailed in Chapter 6, the mean scale scores obtained from mothers' and fathers' ratings do not differ much, on the average. Ratings by black and white parents matched for socioeconomic status also show minimal differences. Socioeconomic differences are somewhat larger, but are too small compared to the differences between referred and nonreferred children to warrant separate norms. (See Chapter 7 and Achenbach & Edelbrock, 1981, for detailed analyses of differences related to race and socioeconomic status.)

9. **Why are there big gaps between successive raw scores on some scales of the Profile?**

   Answer: On the First Edition of the Profile, large gaps occurred mainly at the low end and between T scores of 70 and 80 on the behavior problem scales, as well as the top end of the School scale. These gaps directly reflected the distributions of scores in the normative samples, where skewed distributions or clusters of individuals at a particular raw score caused a large change in percentiles from one score to the next. As described in Chapter 3, the Revised Profile has eliminated most large gaps by compressing the low end of the behavior problem scales and the top end of the social competence scales, and by assigning scores above the 98th percentile in regular intervals rather than in percentile increments. However, a few large gaps inevitably remain where large proportions of children obtained successive scores. The largest remaining gap is on the Sex Problems scale for boys aged 4–5, where an increase from a raw score of 0 to a raw score of 1 is accompanied by an increase of 12 T score points. This reflects the fact that 72% of the boys in the normative sample obtained a raw score of 0 and 24% obtained a score of 1.

10. **If a child is in one age group at the initial rating and an older group at a later rating, which Profile should be used?**

Answer: Several scales are based on similar items for different age groups. These scales can be used to compare CBCLs filled out at different ages merely by using the *T* scores appropriate for the child's age at each rating. Scales that are similar across most age groups include the social competence scales, total social competence score, Aggressive scale, Internalizing, Externalizing, and total behavior problem score. If a detailed comparison across all scales of the Profile is desired, and a child is close to the limit of one age group at one of the rating points, the child can be scored on the same version of the Profile at both rating points. (The section on Outcome Studies in Chapter 11 provides further information on scoring across age periods.)

11. **How are clinical interpretations of the Profile made?**

Answer: The Profile is intended as a standardized *description* of behavior, as seen by the person filling out the CBCL and compared to reports by parents of children of the same age and sex as the subject. As such, it is to be integrated with everything else that is known about the child, instead of being viewed as a key to hidden entities, as projective tests sometimes are. Rather than being "interpreted," the information from the Profile should be *integrated* with other data to provide a picture of the child consisting partly of the child's standing on dimensions assessable for children in general, such as cognitive level and behavior problem scores, and partly of unique characteristics of the child and family. Specific guidelines and clinical illustrations are provided in Chapter 10.

12. **Is there a "lie" scale for the Profile?**

Answer: Deliberate lying is only one type of bias that can lead to excessively low or high scores, depending on whether the informant denies or exaggerates problems. Social desirability sets, over-scrupulousness, and misunderstandings can also affect ratings. Because of the variety of possible biases and our desire to restrict the CBCL to items that are meaningful in themselves, we did not add items designed to detect the various kinds of biases. Instead, we stress that Profile scores should never be used to make clinical judgments in isolation from other information about the child and the informant; the scores should always be compared with other data in order to identify major distortions and to determine the possible reason for distortions. Extremely low or high total scores for behavior problems or social competence should always be followed up to determine whether they accurately reflect the informant's view of the child, and, if so, whether this view differs markedly from other people's view of the child.

In our answer to Question 7 above, we listed behavior problem scores that are so low as to invite further inquiry. Based on the distributions of behavior problem scores in our clinical samples, the following raw scores are so *high* as to raise questions about exaggeration or misunderstanding: Boys aged 4–5 >129; 6–11 >121; 12–16 >114; girls aged 4–5>108; 6–11 >127; 12–16 >120.

Because the social competence scores have a much smaller range, they do not lend themselves to consideration of response biases as well as the total behavior problem scores do. However, a total social competence score equivalent to a *T* score <13 suggests an unusually negative picture of the child, whereas a social competence score equivalent to a *T* score >78 suggests an unusually favorable picture.

PROFILE TYPES

1. **How can a child have high intraclass correlations with two or more Profile types?**

   Answer: Rather than being mutually exclusive, the Profile types have varying degrees of similarity to one another. As shown in Chapter 8, most of the Profile types are sufficiently similar to some other types to join together in higher-order groupings in the course of cluster analyses. Furthermore, because the individual's similarity to Profile types is quantitatively determined, the same individual can be at least somewhat similar to more than one Profile type. Usually, however, if a child has a high correlation with a Profile type, any other high correlation will be with quite similar Profile types that join with the first Profile in the same higher-order grouping. For example, if a 12-year-old girl has a correlation of .70 with the Anxious-Obsessive type, her second highest correlation is likely to be with the Somatic Complaints type, which joins with the Anxious-Obsessive type to form a higher-order grouping before they both join with a third type to form a broad-band Internalizing grouping (see Figure 8–13).

2. **Does a negative correlation with a type indicate a pattern opposite to that type?**

   Answer: Not necessarily, because the *magnitude* of the child's scores, as well as their pattern, affects the intraclass correlation with the Profile type.

3. **What does it mean if a child's Profile has negative correlations with all the Profile types?**

   Answer: This merely means that the child's Profile does not resemble any of the types identified by our cluster analysis. It does not necessarily mean that there is an error in scoring the child's Profile, nor that the child's reported behavior is unusually deviant or nondeviant.

REFERENCES

Abramowitz, M., & Stegun, I.A. *Handbook of mathematical functions.* Washington, D.C.: National Bureau of Standards, 1968.

Achenbach, T. M. The classification of children's psychiatric symptoms: A factor-analytic study. *Psychological Monographs*, 1966, *80* (Whole No. 615).

Achenbach, T. M. The Child Behavior Profile: I. Boys aged 6–11. *Journal of Consulting and Clinical Psychology,* 1978, *46,* 478–488.

Achenbach, T. M. DSM-III in light of empirical research on the classification of child psychopathology. *Journal of the American Academy of Child Psychiatry,* 1980, *19,* 395–412.

Achenbach, T. M. *Developmental psychopathology* (2nd ed.). New York: Wiley, 1982.

Achenbach, T. M., & Edelbrock, C. S. The classification of child psychopathology: A review and analysis of empirical efforts. *Psychological Bulletin,* 1978, *85,* 1275–1301.

Achenbach, T. M., & Edelbrock, C. S. The Child Behavior Profile: II. Boys aged 12–16 and girls aged 6–11 and 12–16. *Journal of Consulting and Clinical Psychology,* 1979, *47,* 223–233.

Achenbach, T. M., & Edelbrock, C. S. Behavioral problems and competencies reported by parents of normal and disturbed children aged 4 through 16. *Monographs of the Society for Research in Child Development,* 1981, *46,* (Serial No. 188).

Achenbach, T. M., & Lewis, M. A proposed model for clinical research and its application to encopresis and enuresis. *Journal of the American Academy of Child Psychiatry*, 1971, *10,* 535–554.

Adam, J. Sequential strategies and the separation of age, cohort, and time-of-measurement contributions to developmental data. *Psychological Bulletin,* 1978, *85,* 1309–1316.

American Psychiatric Association. *Diagnostic and statistical manual of mental disorders.* Washington, D.C.: Author, 1st edition, 1952; 2nd edition, 1968; 3rd edition, 1980.

Bartko, J. J. On various intraclass correlation reliability coefficients. *Psychological Bulletin,* 1976, *83,* 762–765.

Cattell, R. B. *The scientific use of factor analysis in behavioral and life sciences.* New York: Plenum Press, 1978.

Churchman, C. W., Ackoff, R. L., & Arnoff, E. L. *Introduction to operations research.* New York: Wiley, 1957.

Cohen, J. A coefficient of agreement for nominal scales. *Educational and Psychological Measurement,* 1960, *20,* 37–46.

Cohen, J. *Statistical power analysis for the behavioral sciences* (Rev. Ed.). New York: Academic Press, 1977.

Conners, C. K. Rating scales for use in drug studies with children. *Psychopharmacology Bulletin: Pharmacotherapy with Children.* Washington, D.C.: U.S. Government Printing Office, 1973.

Cronbach, L. J., & Meehl, P. E. Construct validity in psychological tests. *Psychological Bulletin*, 1955, *52*, 281–302.

Davie, R., Butler, N., & Goldstein, H. *From birth to seven: The second report of the National Child Development Study*. London: Longman, 1972.

Doll, E. A. *Vineland Social Maturity Scale*. Circle Pines, MN: American Guidance Service, 1965.

Edelbrock, C. Mixture model tests of hierarchical clustering algorithms: The problem of classifying everybody. *Multivariate Behavioral Research*, 1979, *14*, 367–384.

Edelbrock, C., & Achenbach, T. M. A typology of Child Behavior Profile patterns: Distribution and correlates in disturbed children aged 6 to 16. *Journal of Abnormal Child Psychology*, 1980, *8*, 441–470.

Edelbrock, C., & Achenbach, T. M. The Teacher Version of the Child Behavior Profile: I. Boys aged 6–11. Submitted for publication, 1983.

Edelbrock, C., Costello, A. J., & Kessler, M.D. Empirical corroboration of the Attention Deficit Disorder. *Journal of the American Academy of Child Psychiatry*, 1983, in press.

Edelbrock, C., & McLaughlin, B. Hierarchical cluster analysis using intraclass correlations: A mixture model study. *Multivariate Behavioral Research*, 1980, *15*, 229–318.

Evans, W. R. The Behavior Problem Checklist. Data from an inner city population. *Psychology in the Schools*, 1975, *12*, 301–303.

Feild, H. S., & Armenakis, A. A. On use of multiple tests of significance in psychological research. *Psychological Reports*, 1974, *35*, 427–431.

Guilford, J. P. *Fundamental statistics in psychology and education* (4th ed.). New York: McGrall-Hill, 1965.

Guzé, S. B. Validating criteria for psychiatric diagnosis: The Washington University approach. In M. S. Akiskal & W. L. Webb (Eds.), *Psychiatric diagnosis: Exploration of biological predictors*. New York: Spectrum, 1978.

Hollingshead, A. B. *Two Factor Index of Social Position*. New Haven, CT: Yale University Dept. of Sociology, 1957.

Hollingshead, A. B. *Four Factor Index of Social Status*. New Haven, CT: Yale University Dept. of Sociology, 1975.

Kraepelin, E. *Compendium der Psychiatrie*. Leipzig: Abel, 1883.

Lambert, N., & Windmiller, M. *AAMD Adaptive Behavior Scale. School Edition*. Monterey, CA: Publishers Test Service, 1981.

Lyons, J. P. Operations research in mental health delivery systems. In J. B. Sidowski, J. H. Johnson, & T. A. Williams (Eds.), *Technology in mental health care delivery systems*. Norwood, NJ: Ablex, 1980.

Mash, E. J., & Johnston, C. Parental perceptions of child behavior problems, parenting self-esteem, and mothers' reported stress in younger and older hyperactive and normal children. *Journal of Consulting and Clinical Psychology*, 1983, *51*, 86–99.

Mattison, R., Cantwell, D. P., Russell, A. T., & Will, L. A comparison of DSM-II and DSM-III in the diagnosis of childhood psychiatric disorders. *Archives of General Psychiatry*, 1979, *36*, 1217–1222.

Meehl, P. E. Schizotaxia, schizotypy, schizophrenia. *American Psychologist,* 1962, *17,* 827–838.

Meehl, P. E., & Golden, R. R. Taxometric methods. In P. C. Kendall & J. N. Butcher (Eds.), *Handbook of research methods in clinical psychology.* New York: Wiley, 1982.

Mercer, J. R. Psychological assessment and the rights of children. In N. Hobbs (Ed.), *Issues in the classification of children* (Vol. 1). San Francisco: Jossey–Bass, 1975.

Mezzich, A. C., & Mezzich, J. E. Diagnostic reliability of childhood and adolescence behavior disorders. Presented at American Psychological Association. New York, Sept., 1979.

Milich, R., Roberts, M., Loney, J., & Caputo, J. Differentiating practice effects and statistical regression on the Conners Hyperkinesis Index. *Journal of Abnormal Child Psychology,* 1980, *8,* 549–552.

Miller, L. C. Louisville Behavior Check List for males, 6–12 years of age. *Psychological Reports,* 1967, *21,* 885–896.

Miller, L. C., Hampe, E., Barrett, C. L., & Noble, H. Test-retest reliability of parent ratings of children's deviant behavior. *Psychological Reports,* 1972, *31,* 249–250.

Peterson, D. R. Behavior problems of middle childhood. *Journal of Consulting Psychology,* 1961, *25,* 205–209.

Quay, H. C. Classification. in H. C. Quay & J. S. Werry (Eds.), *Psychopathological disorders of childhood* (2nd ed.). New York: Wiley, 1979.

Quay, H. C., & Peterson, D. R. *Interim Manual for the Revised Behavior Problem Checklist.* Coral Gables, FL: Applied Social Sciences, University of Miami, 1983.

Reed, M. L., & Edelbrock, C. Reliability and validity of the Direct Observation Form of the Child Behavior Checklist. *Journal of Abnormal Child Psychology,* 1983, in press.

Rutter, M., Yule, B., Quinton, D., Rowlands, O., Yule, W., & Berger, M. Attainment and adjustment in two geographical areas. III: Some factors accounting for area differences. *British Journal of Psychiatry,* 1974, *125,* 520–533.

Sakoda, J. M., Cohen, B. H., & Beall, G. Test of significance for a series of statistical tests. *Psychological Bulletin,* 1954, *51,* 172–175.

Schulsinger, F., Mednick, S. A., & Knop, J. *Longitudinal research.* Boston: Nijhoff, 1981.

United States Department of Labor. *Dictionary of Occupational Titles* (3rd ed.). Washington, D.C.: U.S. Government Printing Office, 1965.

Wainer, H. Estimating coefficients in linear models: It don't make no nevermind. *Psychological Bulletin,* 1976, *83,* 213–217.

Wechsler, D. *Manual for the Wechsler Intelligence Scale for Children—Revised.* New York: Psychological Corporation, 1974.

Weissman, M. M., Orvaschel, H., & Padian, N. Children's symptoms and social functioning self-report scales. Comparison of mothers' and children's reports. *Journal of Nervous and Mental Disease,* 1980, *168,* 736–740.

Winer, B. J. *Statistical principles in experimental design* (2nd ed.). New York: McGraw-Hill, 1971.

Wing, L., Baldwin, J. A., & Rosen, B. M. The use of child psychiatric services in three urban areas: an international case-register study. In J. K. Wing & A. M. Hailey (Eds.), *Evaluating a community psychiatric service.* London: Oxford University Press, 1972.

Woolf, H. B. (Ed.) *Webster's New Collegiate Dictionary.* Springfield, MA: Merriam, 1977.

APPENDIX A
INSTRUCTIONS FOR HAND SCORING THE CHILD BEHAVIOR PROFILE

Social Competence Scales

There are some small differences between the entry formats for hand scoring and computer scoring the social competence scales. When using our computer programs, the data should therefore be entered according to the computer-scoring instructions (see Appendix B). If a parent checks more than 1 box where only 1 should be checked, score the average of the 2 boxes checked. Be certain to use a scoring Profile appropriate for the child's sex and age.

Activities Scale

Do *not* score this scale if data are missing for more than 1 of the 6 scores indicated below beside Roman numerals I, II, and IV. The Roman numerals correspond to those on Page 1 of the CBCL and on the *Activities* scale of the Profile scoring form.

I-A. # of Sports.　　　If parent reports 0 to 1 sport — enter 0 on Profile

2 sports — enter 1 on Profile

3 sports — enter 2 on Profile

I.　Please list the sports your child most likes to take part in. For example: swimming, baseball, skating, skate boarding, bike riding, fishing, etc.

I-A = 0 ☐ None

0 a. _____

1 b. _____

2 c. _____

I-B. Mean Score for Participation & Skill in Sports. If parent reports no sports, enter 0.

For each response of *Less Than Average* or *Below Average* — score 0

Average — score 1

More Than Average or *Above Average* — score 2

Excluding blanks and *Don't know* responses, compute the *mean* of these scores by summing them and dividing by the number of scores you have summed. Enter this *mean* on the Profile.

		Compared to other children of the same age, about how much time does he/she spend in each?					Compared to other children of the same age, how well does he/she do each one?			

Don't Know	Less Than Average **0**	Average **1**	More Than Average **2**		Don't Know	Below Average **0**	Average **1**	Above Average **2**
☐	☐	☐	☐		☐	☐	☐	☐
☐	☐	☐	☐		☐	☐	☐	☐
☐	☐	☐	☐		☐	☐	☐	☐

$$\textbf{I-B} = \frac{\textbf{sum of scores}}{\textbf{number of scores}}$$

II-A. # of Nonsports Activities. Do not count listening to radio or TV, goofing off, or the like as activities.

II. Please list your child's favorite hobbies, activities, and games, other than sports. For example: stamps, dolls, books, piano, crafts, singing, etc. (Do not include T.V.)

If 0 or 1 activity — enter 0 on Profile
2 activities — enter 1 on Profile
3 or more activities — enter 2 on Profile

II-A = **0** ☐ None

0 a. _____

1 b. _____

2 c. _____

II-B. Mean of Participation & Skill in Activities. Compute mean as specified for sports in I-B above. Enter this mean on the Profile.

		Compared to other children of the same age, about how much time does he/she spend in each?					Compared to other children of the same age, how well does he/she do each one?			

Don't Know	Less Than Average **0**	Average **1**	More Than Average **2**		Don't Know	Below Average **0**	Average **1**	Above Average **2**
☐	☐	☐	☐		☐	☐	☐	☐
☐	☐	☐	☐		☐	☐	☐	☐
☐	☐	☐	☐		☐	☐	☐	☐

$$\textbf{II-B} = \frac{\textbf{sum of scores}}{\textbf{number of scores}}$$

IV-A. # of Jobs or Chores.   Include paying and nonpaying jobs and chores.

IV. Please list any jobs or chores   If 0 or 1 job — enter 0 on Profile
your child has. For example: 2 jobs — enter 1 on Profile
paper route, babysitting,   3 jobs — enter 2 on Profile
making bed, etc.

IV-A = 0 ☐ None
  0 a. _____
  1 b. _____
  2 c. _____

IV-B. Mean Job Quality. Compute mean as specified in I-B above. Enter this
mean on the Profile.

Compared to other children of the   **IV-B** = $\dfrac{\text{sum of scores}}{\text{number of scores}}$
same age, how well does he/she
carry them out?

Don't Know	Below Average	Average	Above Average
		0	**1**	**2**
☐	☐	☐	☐
☐	☐	☐	☐
☐	☐	☐	☐

Total Score for Activities Scale. Sum the 6 scores just entered on the *Activities*
scale of the Profile. If missing data prevent computation of 1 score,
substitute the *mean* of the other 5 for the missing score in computing the
total. After computing the total, round off to the nearest .5 and mark the
corresponding number in the column of scores appropriate for the child's
age.

Social Scale

Do *not* score this scale if data are missing for more than 1 of the 6 scores indicated below beside Roman numerals III, V, and VI. The Roman numerals
correspond to those on Pages 1 and 2 of the CBCL and on the *Social* scale of
the Profile scoring form.

III-A. # of Organizations.   If 0 or 1 organization — enter 0 on Profile
III. Please list any organizations,   2 — enter 1 on Profile
clubs, teams, or groups your   3 or more — enter 2 on Profile
child belongs to.

III-A = 0 ☐ None
  0 a. _____
  1 b. _____
  2 c. _____

III-B. Mean of Participation in Organizations. Compute mean as specified in I-B above. Enter this mean on the Profile.

Compared to other children of the same age, how active is he/she in each?

$$III-B = \frac{\text{sum of scores}}{\text{number of scores}}$$

Don't Know	Less Active	Average	More Active
	0	**1**	**2**
☐	☐	☐	☐
☐	☐	☐	☐
☐	☐	☐	☐

V-1. # of Friends.

If 0 or 1 friends — enter 0 on Profile
2 or 3 friends — enter 1 on Profile
4 or more friends — enter 2 on Profile

1. About how many close friends does your child have?

☐ None ☐ 1 ☐ 2 or 3 ☐ 4 or more
V-I = **0** **0** **1** **2**

V-2. Contacts with Friends. If parent checks *None* in V-1 — enter 0 on Profile
Less than 1 — enter 0 on Profile
1 or 2 — enter 1 on Profile
3 or more — enter 2 on Profile

2. About how many times a week does your child do things with them?

☐ less than 1 ☐ 1 or 2 ☐ 3 or more
V-2 = **0** **1** **2**

VI-A. Behavior with Others. For Items *a*, *b*, and *c*:

If parent checks *worse* — score 0
about the same — score 1
better — score 2

Excluding any item for which the parent did not check a box, compute the *mean* of these scores and enter it on the Profile.

VI. Compared to other children of his/her age, how well does your child:

	Worse	About the same	Better
a. Get along with his/her brothers and sisters?	**0** ☐	**1** ☐	**2** ☐
b. Get along with other children?	☐	☐	☐
c. Behave with his/her parents?	☐	☐	☐

$$\text{VI-A} = \frac{\textbf{sum of a + b + c}}{\textbf{number of scores}}$$

VI-B. Play/work by self. For Item *d*:

If parent checks *worse* — enter 0 on Profile

about the same — enter 1 on Profile

better — enter 2 on Profile

d. Play and work by himself/
herself?   ☐   ☐   ☐

VI-B =   **0**   **1**   **2**

Total Score for Social Scale. Sum the 6 scores just entered on the *Social* scale of the Profile. If missing data prevent computation of 1 score, substitute the *mean* of the other 5 for the missing score in computing the total. After computing the total, round off to the nearest .5 and mark the corresponding number in the column of scores appropriate for the child's age.

School Scale

Do *not* score if the child is below age 6, not in school, or if data are missing for any of the 4 scores indicated below for Items VII-1 through VII-4, which appear on Page 2 of the CBCL and on the *School* scale of the Profile scoring form.

VII-1. Mean performance. For each academic subject checked

failing — score 0

below average — score 1

average — score 2

above average — score 3

Enter the *mean* of these scores on the Profile. (Academic subjects include reading, writing, arithmetic, spelling, science, English, foreign language, history, social studies, and similar subjects. Do *not* count physical education, art, music, home economics, driver education, industrial arts, typing, or the like.)

VII. 1. Current school performance — for children aged 6 and older:

	Failing	Below average	Average	Above average
☐ Does not go to school	**0**	**1**	**2**	**3**
a. Reading or English	☐	☐	☐	☐
b. Writing	☐	☐	☐	☐
c. Arithmetic or Math	☐	☐	☐	☐
d. Spelling	☐	☐	☐	☐
Other academic sub- e. _____	☐	☐	☐	☐
jects — for example: history, science, foreign f. _____	☐	☐	☐	☐
language, geography. g. _____	☐	☐	☐	☐

VII-1 = sum of scores/number of scores

VII-2 Special Class. For any type of remedial special class (for retarded, emotionally disturbed, learning disabled, perceptual-motor handicapped, reading readiness, resource room, etc.) — enter 0 on Profile

not in remedial class — enter 1 on Profile

    2. Is your child in a special class?

      ☐ No   ☐ Yes — what kind?

VII-2 = 1   **0**

VII-3. Repeated Grade.   If any grades were repeated — enter 0 on Profile

no grades repeated — enter 1 on Profile

    3. Has your child ever repeated a grade?

      ☐ No   ☐ Yes — grade and reason

VII-3 = 1   **0**

VII-4. School Problems. If any school problem is stated that was present in the last 6 months and was not already scored above — enter 0 on Profile

no problem beside those scored above — enter 1 on Profile

    4. Has your child had any academic or other problems in school?

      ☐ No   ☐ Yes — please describe

VII-4 = 1   **0** (for problems present in the past 6 months and not already scored above)

Total Score for School Scale. Sum the 4 scores just entered on the *School* scale of the Profile, unless 1 or more score is missing. After computing the total, round off to the nearest .5 and mark the corresponding number in the column of scores appropriate for the child's age. The numbers you have marked for the three social competence scales can now be connected to form a profile.

Total Social Competence Score (Optional)

A total social competence score can be obtained by summing the totals of the 3 scales. *T* scores for total social competence scores are listed on the following pages.

Behavior Problem Scales

Do *not* score if data are missing for more than 8 items, not counting #56h and 113, unless it is clear that the parent intended blanks to be 0s. If a parent circles two numbers for an item, score the item 1.

Item Scores

Place the Page 3 template for a child of this age and sex over Page 3 of the CBCL. The Roman numerals and letters beside each item number indicate the scales on which the item is scored. If the parent circled 1 or 2 beside an item, enter the 1 or 2 on the appropriate scales of the Profile. Repeat using the Page 4 template on Page 4. Comments written by the parent should be used in judging whether items deserve to be scored, with the following guidelines:

a. For each behavior reported by the parent, only the CBCL item that most specifically describes the behavior should be scored. If the parent's comments show that more than one item has been scored for a particular behavior, or if the parent writes in a behavior for #56h or 113 that is specifically covered elsewhere, count only the most specific item.

b. For extreme behaviors (e.g., sets fires, attempts suicide)—if parent notes that it happened once but circles 0 or leaves it blank, score 1 unless it clearly happened earlier than the interval specified in the rating instructions (e.g., 6 months).

c. For items on which parent notes "used to do this," score as the parent scored it, unless it clearly occurred earlier than the interval specified in the instructions.

d. When in doubt, score item the way the parent scored it, unless it is clear that the parent has scored it inappropriately, especially on the following items:

   9. Obsessions—exclude anything that is clearly not obsessional; e.g., do *not* score "won't take no for an answer."

  28. Eats or drinks things that are not food—do *not* count sweets and junk food.

  40. Hears things and 70. Sees things—do *not* score anxiousness about sounds and sights that others also notice; e.g., afraid noises at night might be burglars; do *not* score experiences while under the influence of drugs or alcohol.

  46. Nervous movements—if "can't sit still" or anything entirely covered by Item 10 is entered here, score *only* Item 10.

 56d. Problems with eyes—do *not* score "wears glasses," "near-sighted," and other ordinary visual problems having an organic basis.

  66. Compulsions—do *not* score noncompulsive behavior; e.g., "keeps hitting brother."

  72. Sets fires—score playing with matches or lighter if parent reports it.

  77. Sleeps more than most—do *not* score "wants to stay in bed," but score difficulties in waking child.

  83. Stores up things—do *not* score hobby collections, such as stamps, dolls, or miniatures.

  84. Strange behavior and 85. Strange ideas—if what the parent describes is specifically covered by another item, score the more specific item instead.

 105. Alcohol or drugs—do *not* score tobacco or medication.

113. **Additional problems**—score only if *not* specifically covered by another item; if parent lists more than 1 "other" item, count only highest toward total behavior problem score.

Scale Scores

To obtain the total raw score for the behavior problem scales, sum the 1s and 2s you have entered for each scale. Then mark the corresponding number in the graphic display above the scale and connect the marked numbers to form a profile. Percentiles based on normal children can be read from the left side of the graphic display. *T* scores can be read from the right side.

Internalizing and Externalizing

Using the box to the right of the Behavior Problems Profile, enter the score (0, 1, or 2) for each behavior problem next to the item's number under the heading *Item*. Sum the scores to get the Total Internalizing score and likewise for the Total Externalizing score. Under the heading *Total*, locate the total you have obtained. The score to the right of that number is the *T* score. (The Internalizing and Externalizing scores can *not* be computed by adding scale totals, because some items appear on more than one scale.)

Total Behavior Problem Score

To compute the total behavior problem score, sum the 1s and 2s on the CBCL and enter the sum to the right of the Profile. If the parent has entered a problem for Item 56h or 113 that is not covered by another item, include the score for 56h or 113. If more than one problem has been entered for item 113, count only the one having the highest score. The total behavior problem score can be cross-checked by subtracting the number of items scored as present from the sum of 1s and 2s. The difference should equal the number of 2s. (The number and sum of items can *not* be computed by adding scale totals, because some items appear on more than one scale.) *T* scores for the total social competence score and total behavior problem score are listed in the tables that follow.

T Scores for Boys Aged 4–5

Social Competence				*Behavior Problems*			
T	*Raw Score*	*T*	*Raw Score*	*T*	*Raw Score*	*T*	*Raw Score*
10	0	44	11.0	30	0	68	48–50
11	.5	46	11.5	31	1	69	51–53
13	1.0	48	12.0	32	2	70	54–55
14	1.5	50	12.5	33	3	71	56–59
15	2.0	52	13.0	34	4–5	72	60–63
16	2.5	53	13.5	35	6	73	64–67
18	3.0	55	14.0	36	7	74	68–71
19	3.5	57	14.5	39	8	75	72–75
20	4.0	60	15.0	41	9–11	76	76–80
21	4.5	62	15.5	42	12	77	81–84
23	5.0	63	16.0	43	13	78	85–88
24	5.5	65	16.5	44	14	79	89–92
25	6.0	68	17.0	45	15–16	80	93–96
26	6.5	70	17.5	46	17	81	97–100
28	7.0	73	18.0	47	18	82	101–104
29	7.5	74	18.5–19.0	48	19	83	105–109
30	8.0	75	19.5–20.0	49	20	84	110–113
36	8.5	76	20.5–21.0	50	21	85	114–117
37	9.0	77	21.5	51	22	86	118–121
38	9.5[a]	78	22.0–22.5	52	23	87	122–125
40	10.0	79	23.0–23.5	53	24–26	88	126–129
41	10.5	80	24.0	54	27–28	89	130–136
				55	29	90	137–146
				56	30	91	147–156
				57	31–32	92	157–166
				58	33–34	93	167–176
				59	35	94	177–186
				60	36	95	187–195
				61	37	96	196–205
				62	38–41	97	206–215
				63	42[b]	98	216–225
				64	43	99	226–235
				65	44–45	100	236–240
				66	46–47		

[a]Lower limit of "normal" range
[b]Upper limit of "normal" range

T Scores for Boys Aged 6–11

Social Competence				*Behavior Problems*			
T	*Raw Score*	*T*	*Raw Score*	*T*	*Raw Score*	*T*	*Raw Score*
10	0	62	23.5	30	0–1	77	82–84
11	.5	64	24.0	32	2	78	85–88
12	1.0–1.5	66	24.5	34	3	79	89–91
13	2.0	69	25.0	36	4	80	92–94
14	2.5	71	25.5	38	5	81	95–98
15	3.0	72	26.0	39	6	82	99–101
16	3.5–4.0	73	26.5	40	7	83	102–104
17	4.5	75	27.0	41	8	84	105–108
18	5.0	77	27.5	42	9	85	109–111
19	5.5	78	28.0–28.5	43	10	86	112–114
20	6.0–6.5	79	29.0–29.5	44	11	87	115–118
21	7.0	80	30.0	45	12	88	119–121
22	7.5			46	13	89	122–128
23	8.0			47	14	90	129–138
24	8.5–9.0			48	15–16	91	139–149
25	9.5			49	17	92	150–160
26	10.0			50	18	93	161–170
27	10.5			51	19	94	171–181
28	11.0–11.5			52	20–21	95	182–192
29	12.0			53	22–24	96	193–202
30	12.5			54	25	97	203–213
31	13.0			55	26–27	98	214–224
32	13.5			56	28	99	225–234
33	14.0			57	29–30	100	235–240
36	14.5			58	31–32		
37	15.0–15.5			59	33–34		
39	16.0[a]			60	35		
40	16.5			61	36–38		
41	17.0			62	39		
42	17.5			63	40[b]–42		
44	18.0			64	43–45		
45	18.5			65	46		
47	19.0			66	47–49		
48	19.5			67	50		
50	20.0			68	51–55		
52	20.5			69	56–60		
53	21.0			70	61		
54	21.5			71	62–64		
56	22.0			72	65–68		
58	22.5			73	69–71		
60	23.0			74	72–74		
				75	75–78		
				76	79–81		

[a]Lower limit of "normal" range
[b]Upper limit of "normal" range

T Scores for Boys Aged 12–16

Social Competence

T	Raw Score	T	Raw Score
10	0	61	24.0
11	.5-1.0	62	24.5-25.0
12	1.5	66	25.5
13	2.0	68	26.0
14	2.5-3.0	70	26.5
15	3.5	71	27.0
16	4.0	77	27.5
17	4.5-5.0	78	28.0-28.5
18	5.5	79	29.0-29.5
19	6.0	80	30.0
20	6.5-7.0		
21	7.5		
22	8.0		
23	8.5-9.0		
24	9.5		
25	10.0		
26	10.5-11.0		
27	11.5		
28	12.0		
29	12.5-13.0		
30	13.5		
32	14.0		
34	14.5		
36	15.0		
37	15.5		
38	16.0[a]		
39	16.5		
40	17.0		
42	17.5		
43	18.0		
44	18.5		
45	19.0		
47	19.5		
48	20.0		
49	20.5		
51	21.0		
53	21.5		
54	22.0		
55	22.5		
57	23.0		
60	23.5		

Behavior Problems

T	Raw Score	T	Raw Score
30	0	80	91-92
33	1	81	93-95
37	2	82	96-98
39	3	83	99-101
41	4	84	102-104
43	5	85	105-107
44	6	86	108-109
45	7	87	110-112
46	8	88	113-115
47	9	89	116-122
48	10	90	123-133
49	11	91	134-144
50	12-13	92	145-156
51	14-15	93	157-167
52	16	94	168-178
53	17	95	179-189
54	18	96	190-200
55	19-20	97	201-212
56	21-22	98	213-223
57	23	99	224-234
58	24-25	100	235-240
59	26-27		
60	28-30		
61	31-33		
62	34-37		
63	38[b]		
64	39-44		
65	45-49		
66	50-52		
67	53-56		
68	57-62		
70	63-64		
71	65-67		
72	68-70		
73	71-72		
74	73-75		
75	76-78		
76	79-81		
77	82-84		
78	85-87		
79	88-90		

[a]Lower limit of "normal" range
[b]Upper limit of "normal" range

T Scores for Girls Aged 4–5

	Social Competence				Behavior Problems		
T	*Raw Score*	*T*	*Raw Score*	*T*	*Raw Score*	*T*	*Raw Score*
10	0	78	22.5	30	0-2	77	79-80
11	.5	79	23.0-23.5	33	3	78	81-83
13	1.0	80	24.0	34	4	79	84-86
14	1.5			35	5	80	87-88
15	2.0			37	6	81	89-91
16	2.5			39	7	82	92-93
18	3.0			41	8-9	83	94-96
19	3.5			42	10	84	97-98
20	4.0			43	11	85	99-101
21	4.5			44	12	86	102-103
23	5.0			45	13-15	87	104-106
24	5.5			46	16	88	107-108
25	6.0			47	17	89	109-115
26	6.5			48	18-19	90	116-127
28	7.0			49	20-22	91	128-139
30	8.0			50	23	92	140-151
33	8.5			51	24	93	152-163
34	9.0			52	25-26	94	164-175
37	9.5			53	27-28	95	176-186
39	10.0[a]			54	29-30	96	187-198
40	10.5			55	31	97	199-210
42	11.0			56	32	98	211-222
44	11.5			57	33	99	223-234
46	12.0			58	34	100	235-240
47	12.5			59	35		
49	13.0			60	36-40		
50	13.5			61	41		
52	14.0			62	42[b]-45		
54	14.5			63	46-48		
56	15.0			64	49-50		
58	15.5			65	51		
60	16.0			66	52		
61	16.5			67	53		
63	17.0			68	54-56		
65	17.5			69	57-59		
68	18.0			70	60-63		
71	18.5			71	64-65		
73	19.0			72	66-68		
74	19.5-20.0			73	69-70		
75	20.5			74	71-73		
76	21.0			75	74-75		
77	21.5-22.0			76	76-78		

[a]Lower limit of "normal" range
[b]Upper limit of "normal" range

T Scores for Girls Aged 6–11

	Social Competence				Behavior Problems		
T	Raw Score	T	Raw Score	T	Raw Score	T	Raw Score
10	0	62	24.0	30	0	79	89–92
11	.5	63	24.5	32	1	80	93–96
12	1.0	64	25.0	35	2	81	97–100
13	2.0	67	25.5	36	3	82	101–104
14	2.5–3.0	70	26.0	38	4	83	105–108
15	3.5	71	26.5	40	5	84	109–112
16	4.0	75	27.0	41	6	85	113–116
17	4.5–5.0	77	27.5	43	7–8	86	117–120
18	5.5	78	28.0–28.5	44	9	87	121–124
19	6.0	79	29.0–29.5	45	10	88	125–128
20	6.5–7.0	80	30.0	46	11–12	89	129–134
21	7.5			47	13–14	90	135–144
22	8.0			48	15	91	145–154
23	8.5–9.0			49	16	92	155–164
24	9.5			50	17–18	93	165–174
25	10.0			51	19	94	175–184
26	10.5–11.0			52	20	95	185–194
27	11.5			53	21	96	195–204
28	12.0			54	22–23	97	205–214
29	12.5–13.0			55	24	98	215–224
30	13.5			56	25–26	99	225–234
32	14.0			57	27	100	235–240
35	14.5–15.0			58	28–29		
36	15.5			59	30–32		
37	16.0			60	33		
39	16.5[a]			61	34–35		
40	17.0			62	36		
42	17.5			63	37[b]–41		
43	18.0			64	42–43		
44	18.5			66	44		
46	19.0			67	45–48		
47	19.5			68	49–51		
49	20.0			69	52–53		
51	20.5			70	54–56		
52	21.0			71	57–60		
55	21.5			72	61–64		
56	22.0			73	65–68		
58	22.5			74	69–72		
59	23.0			75	73–76		
61	23.5			76	77–80		
				77	81–84		
				78	85–88		

[a]Lower limit of "normal" range
[b]Upper limit of "normal" range

T Scores for Girls Aged 12–16

Social Competence				*Behavior Problems*			
T	*Raw Score*	*T*	*Raw Score*	*T*	*Raw Score*	*T*	*Raw Score*
10	0	62	24.5	30	0	83	101–103
11	.5	63	25.0	33	1	84	104–107
12	1.0–1.5	65	25.5	35	2	85	108–110
13	2.0	68	26.0	38	3	86	111–114
14	2.5	69	26.5	40	4	87	115–117
15	3.0–3.5	72	27.0	41	5	88	118–121
16	4.0	77	27.5	43	6	89	122–128
17	4.5	78	28.0–28.5	44	7	90	129–138
18	5.0–5.5	79	29.0–29.5	46	8	91	139–149
19	6.0	80	30.0	47	9	92	150–160
20	6.5			48	10	93	161–170
21	7.0			49	11	94	171–181
22	7.5–8.0			50	12	95	182–192
23	8.5			51	13	96	193–202
24	9.0			52	14–15	97	203–213
25	9.5–10.0			54	16–17	98	214–224
26	10.5			55	18–19	99	225–234
27	11.0			56	20–21	100	235–240
28	11.5–12.0			57	22–24		
29	12.5			58	25		
32	13.0			59	26–27		
33	13.5–14.0			60	28–29		
34	14.5–15.0			61	30–31		
35	15.5			62	32–33		
37	16.0			63	34–38 (37[b])		
38	16.5[a]			64	39–40		
40	17.0			65	41–43		
41	17.5			66	44–45		
43	18.0			67	46–48		
44	18.5			68	49–52		
45	19.0			69	53–55		
47	19.5			70	56–58		
48	20.0			71	59–62		
49	20.5			72	63–65		
51	21.0			73	66–69		
52	21.5			74	70–72		
54	22.0			75	73–76		
55	22.5			76	77–79		
57	23.0			77	80–83		
58	23.5			78	84–86		
59	24.0			79	87–90		
				80	91–93		
				81	94–96		
				82	97–100		

[a]Lower limit of "normal" range
[b]Upper limit of "normal" range

APPENDIX B
COMPUTER ENTRY AND SCORING PROGRAMS FOR THE CBCL AND PROFILE

Revised May, 1988

Earlier printings of this *Manual* described FORTRAN programs that we provided for scoring the CBCL and Teacher's Report Form. Except under unusual circumstances, we will no longer provide or support FORTRAN programs, because microcomputers have become so widespread, our microcomputer programs are easier to use, and the microcomputer programs can be used to enter and store data for transfer to larger mainframe computers.

We currently provide microcomputer programs on $5^1/4''$ and $3^1/2''$ diskettes for IBM–PC and PS/2 compatible computers with MS- or PC-DOS operating systems and on $5^1/4''$ diskettes for Apple II, IIc, IIe, and II+ using either DOS 3.3 or ProDOS. These programs provide interactive entry and verification of data that is keypunched from the information provided on the CBCLs completed by parents and other informants. The programs are not designed for direct entry of data by the informants themselves. The entered raw data can be stored and can be scored on the Child Behavior Profile. The scored data can also be stored on a diskette.

The scoring programs compute raw scores for all items, raw scale scores, T scores for all scales, and intraclass correlations between a child's profile pattern and the profile types identified for that child's age and sex, as described in Chapter 8. The correlations with the profile types are printed across the bottom of the page on which the behavior problem portion of the profile is printed. Printing of profiles requires a printer that can produce 132 columns in regular or compressed mode.

Note that there are some differences between the data entry formats for the hand-scored and computer-scored formats. They produce the same results on the Child Behavior Profile, however. Write to Dr. Achenbach for the current status and prices of programs for scoring the CBCL for Ages 4-16, CBCL for Ages 2-3, Teacher's Report Form, Direct Observation Form, Youth Self-Report, and Semistructured Clinical Interview for Children.

INPUT DATA FORMAT[a]

Social Competence Section

Card 1

Col. #	Field Name	Col. #	Field Name
1–10	Subject ID #	48	Total # of Organiz.: 0–3
11–12	Card # (usually 01)	49	How Active in Org. A: 1–3,9
13	Sex: 1 = Boy; 2 = Girl	50	How Active in Org. B: 1–3,9
14–15	Age in years	51	How Active in Org. C: 1–3,9
16[b]	Race or ethnicity: 1 = White; 2 = Black; 3 = Mixed or Other; 4 = Am. Indian; 5 = Chicano; 6 = Puerto Rican; 7 = Oriental	52	Total # of Jobs: 0–3
		53	How Well Does Job A: 1–3,9
		54	How Well Does Job B: 1–3,9
		55	How Well Does Job C: 1–3,9
17–22[b]	Date Filled Out	56	# of Friends: 1 = None; 2 = 1; 3 = 2 or 3; 4 = 4 or more
23–28[b]	Date of Birth		
29–30[b]	Socioeconomic Status (Hollingshead Score)	57	Times/Week with Friend: 1 = less than 1; 2 = 1 or 2; 3 = 3 or more
31[b]	Filled Out By: 1 = Mother; 2 = Father; 3 = Other	58	Gets Along with Sibs: 1–3,9
		59	Gets Along w/Peers: 1–3,9
32–33[b]	Agency #	60	Gets Along w/Parents: 1–3,9
34	Total # of Sports: 0–3	61	Play/Work by Self: 1–3,9
35	Time in Sport A: 1 = Below Average; 2 = Average; 3 = Above Average; 9 = Don't know	62	Academic Performance, Subject A: 1 = Failing; 2 = Below Ave.; 3 = Average; 4 = Above Average
36	Time in Sport B: 1–3,9	63	Subject B: 1–4,9
37	Time in Sport C: 1–3,9	64	Subject C: 1–4,9
38	Skill in Sport A: 1–3,9	65	Subject D: 1–4,9
39	Skill in Sport B: 1–3,9	66	Subject E: 1–4,9
40	Skill in Sport C: 1–3,9	67	Subject F: 1–4,9
41	Total # of Activities: 0–3	68	Subject G: 1–4,9
42	Time in Activity A: 1–3,9	69	Special Class: 1 = yes; 2 = no
43	Time in Activity B: 1–3,9	70	Repeated Grade: 1 = yes; 2 = no
44	Time in Activity C: 1–3,9		
45	Skill in Activity A: 1–3,9	71	Other Acad. Prob.: 1 = yes; 2 = no
46	Skill in Activity B: 1–3,9		
47	Skill in Activity C: 1–3,9	72–74	* * * (To indicate end of Social Competence card.)

[a]Our scoring programs have used this format since April, 1981. We can provide the listing of a program that translates data from our earlier 5-column ID to the above 10-column ID format.
[b]Optional – not required for scoring profile.

Behavior Problem Section

Card 2

Col. #	Field Name
1–10	Subject ID #
11–12	Card # (usually 02)
13	Sex: 1 = Boy; 2 = Girl
14–15	Age in Years
16–80	Behavior Problem Items 1–58 from Checklist

Card 3

Col. #	Field Name
1–10	Subject ID #
11–12	Card # (usually 03)
13	Sex: 1 = Boy; 2 = Girl
14–15	Age in Years
16–70	Behavior Problem Items 59–113 from Checklist
71–73	E N D (to mark end of Behavior Problem section)

Documentation accompanying the program includes details of output format.

APPENDIX C
FACTOR LOADINGS OF ITEMS ON BEHAVIOR
PROBLEM SCALES[a]

Boys Aged 4–5:   10-Factor Varimax Rotation

Internalizing Scales
I. Social Withdrawal

111.	Withdrawn	.58	13.	Confused	.40
65.	Won't talk	.53	45.	Nervous	.36
80.	Stares blankly	.50	17.	Daydreams	.36
42.	Likes to be alone	.47	75.	Shy, timid	.35
18.	Harms self	.45	91.	Suicidal talk	.31
46.	Twitches	.40	87.	Moody	.30
				Eigenvalue	3.71

II. Depressed

52.	Feels guilty	.63	69.	Secretive	.36
112.	Worrying	.63	9.	Obsessions	.35
35.	Feels worthless	.62	14.	Cries much	.35
33.	Feels unloved	.61	89.	Suspicious	.34
103.	Sad	.58	111.	Withdrawn	.34
32.	Needs to be perfect	.58	29.	Fears	.33
71.	Self-conscious	.56	83.	Hoarding	.33
34.	Feels persecuted	.53	75.	Shy, timid	.33
88.	Sulks	.52	96.	Sex preoccupation	.32
50.	Anxious	.51	27.	Jealous	.31
12.	Lonely	.46	47.	Nightmares	.31
31.	Fears own impulses	.41	102.	Slow-moving	.30
87.	Moody	.37		Eigenvalue	6.96

III. Immature

1.	Acts too young	.57	28.	Eats nonfood	.38
62.	Clumsy	.55	77.	Much sleep	.38
36.	Accident prone	.50	79.	Speech problem	.37
38.	Is teased	.47	14.	Cries much	.36
13.	Confused	.42	11.	Clings to adults	.35
8.	Can't concentrate	.42	64.	Prefers young kids	.32
				Eigenvalue	3.66

IV. Somatic Complaints

56c.	Nausea	.71	56g.	Vomits	.53
56f.	Stomach problems	.68	56b.	Headaches	.53
56a.	Pains	.62	24.	Doesn't eat well	.31
				Eigenvalue	3.57

[a]Items are designated with the numbers they bear on the CBCL and summaries of their content. For actual wording of items, see the CBCL.

Mixed Scale
V. Sex Problems

110.	Wishes to be opposite sex	.60	73.	Sex problems	.44
5.	Acts like opposite sex	.57	60.	Plays with sex parts too much	.42
59.	Plays with sex parts in public	.51	31.	Fears own impulses	.37
				Eigenvalue	2.84

Externalizing Scales
VI. Schizoid

70.	Sees things	.65	100.	Can't sleep	.42
67.	Runs away	.58	53.	Overeats	.38
40.	Hears things	.52	18.	Harms self	.34
76.	Sleeps little	.50	66.	Compulsions	.33
85.	Strange ideas	.49		Eigenvalue	3.82

VII. Aggressive

95.	Temper	.69	87.	Moody	.56
16.	Cruel to others	.69	41.	Impulsive	.55
22.	Disobeys at home	.66	74.	Shows off	.55
3.	Argues	.64	10.	Hyperactive	.55
86.	Stubborn	.64	19.	Demands attention	.55
21.	Destroys others' things	.63	104.	Loud	.54
37.	Fights	.63	26.	Lacks guilt	.48
68.	Screams	.62	94.	Teases	.48
97.	Threatens	.59	15.	Cruel to animals	.47
20.	Destroys own things	.58	43.	Lies, cheats	.46
57.	Attacks people	.57	109.	Whining	.45
27.	Jealous	.57	45.	Nervous	.43
25.	Poor peer relations	.56		Eigenvalue	11.06

VIII. Delinquent

72.	Sets fires	.51	82.	Steals outside home	.36
106.	Vandalism	.51	91.	Suicidal talk	.33
39.	Bad friends	.49	38.	Is teased	.32
90.	Swearing	.39	36.	Accident prone	.32
37.	Fights	.37	96.	Sex preoccupation	.31
81.	Steals at home	.37	34.	Feels persecuted	.30
				Eigenvalue	3.36

Boys Aged 6–11: 12-Factor Varimax Rotation

Internalizing Scales
I. Schizoid or Anxious

40.	Hears things	.55	50.	Anxious	.36
70.	Sees things	.50	47.	Nightmares	.31
29.	Fears	.44	59.	Plays with sex parts in public	.30
30.	Fears school	.41			
11.	Clings to adults	.37	75.	Shy, timid	.30
				Eigenvalue	2.53

II. Depressed

35.	Feels worthless	.68	14.	Cries much	.39
52.	Feels guilty	.67	50.	Anxious	.39
32.	Needs to be perfect	.58	71.	Self-conscious	.39
33.	Feels unloved	.55	34.	Feels persecuted	.34
112.	Worrying	.52	88.	Sulks	.32
103.	Sad	.51	45.	Nervous	.31
31.	Fears own impulses	.48	89.	Suspicious	.30
91.	Suicidal talk	.46	18.	Harms self	.30
12.	Lonely	.40		Eigenvalue	4.94

III. Uncommunicative

65.	Won't talk	.61	80.	Stares blankly	.33
69.	Secretive	.50	71.	Self-conscious	.32
75.	Shy, timid	.42	13.	Confused	.32
103.	Sad	.36	86.	Stubborn	.30
				Eigenvalue	2.97

IV. Obsessive-Compulsive

85.	Strange ideas	.52	46.	Twitches	.37
100.	Can't sleep	.52	83.	Hoarding	.37
76.	Sleeps little	.45	66.	Compulsions	.36
84.	Strange behavior	.43	54.	Overtired	.36
9.	Obsessions	.42	13.	Confused	.35
92.	Walks, talks in sleep	.40	93.	Excess talk	.34
80.	Stares blankly	.40	47.	Nightmares	.33
17.	Daydreams	.38	50.	Anxious	.33
				Eigenvalue	4.03

V. Somatic Complaints

56f.	Stomach problems	.64	49.	Constipated	.41
56b.	Headaches	.58	51.	Dizziness	.39
56c.	Nausea	.56	77.	Sleeps much	.32
56a.	Pains	.50	54.	Overtired	.31
56g.	Vomits	.44		Eigenvalue	3.08

Mixed Scale
VI. Social Withdrawal

48.	Unliked	.59	38.	Is teased	.36
25.	Poor peer relations	.59	64.	Prefers young kids	.33
111.	Withdrawn	.56	34.	Feels persecuted	.32
42.	Likes to be alone	.46	102.	Slow moving	.31
				Eigenvalue	3.05

Externalizing Scales
VII. Hyperactive

8.	Can't concentrate	.65	41.	Impulsive	.40
1.	Acts too young	.58	64.	Prefers young kids	.40
61.	Poor school work	.56	10.	Hyperactive	.36
62.	Clumsy	.48	79.	Speech problem	.31
13.	Confused	.45	20.	Destroys own things	.30
17.	Daydreams	.43		Eigenvalue	3.75

VIII. Aggressive

3.	Argues	.71	68.	Screams	.49
22.	Disobedient at home	.66	90.	Swearing	.46
95.	Temper	.64	25.	Poor peer relations	.45
86.	Stubborn	.63	88.	Sulks	.45
37.	Fighting	61	7.	Brags	.45
16.	Cruel to others	.60	43.	Lies, cheats	.43
97.	Threatens people	.57	27.	Jealous	.43
94.	Teases	.56	87.	Moody	.43
74.	Shows off	.55	19.	Demands attention	.41
104.	Loud	.51	93.	Excess talk	.41
23.	Disobeys at school	.51	48.	Unliked	.40
57.	Attacks people	.50		Eigenvalue	8.77

IX. Delinquent

82.	Steals outside home	.70	67.	Runs away	.48
81.	Steals at home	.67	39.	Bad friends	.44
21.	Destroys others' things	.57	43.	Lies, cheats	.44
106.	Vandalism	.54	20.	Destroys own things	.42
72.	Sets fires	.50	90.	Swears	.37
101.	Truant	.48	23.	Disobedient at school	.31
				Eigenvalue	4.52

Boys Aged 12–16:   13-Factor Varimax Rotation

Internalizing Scales

I. Somatic Complaints

56c.	Nausea	.74	56d.	Eye problems	.39
56a.	Pains	.68	102.	Slow moving	.38
56f.	Stomach problems	.68	36.	Accident prone	.38
56b.	Headaches	.68	49.	Constipated	.35
54.	Overtired	.56	112.	Worrying	.31
51.	Dizziness	.55	50.	Anxious	.30
56g.	Vomits	.46	80.	Stares blankly	.30
56e.	Rashes	.42		Eigenvalue	5.30

II. Schizoid

52.	Feels guilty	.54	51.	Dizziness	.34
31.	Fears own impulses	.50	32.	Needs to be perfect	.33
99.	Too neat	.42	30.	Fears school	.32
5.	Acts like opposite sex	.41	11.	Clings to adults	.32
40.	Hears things	.39	112.	Worrying	.30
				Eigenvalue	2.96

III. Uncommunicative

69.	Secretive	.61	102.	Slow moving	.38
75.	Shy, timid	.57	88.	Sulks	.37
65.	Won't talk	.56	89.	Suspicious	.36
111.	Withdrawn	.53	86.	Stubborn	.36
42.	Likes to be alone	.53	87.	Moody	.33
103.	Sad	.50	112.	Worrying	.31
71.	Self-conscious	.49	13.	Confused	.30
80.	Stares blankly	.38		Eigenvalue	4.24

IV. Immature

14.	Cries much	.58	108.	Wets bed	.34
109.	Whining	.56	19.	Demands attention	.33
11.	Clings to adults	.39	1.	Acts too young	.30
64.	Prefers young kids	.35		Eigenvalue	2.55

V. Obsessive-Compulsive

9.	Obsessions	.52	31.	Fears own impulses	.34
66.	Compulsions	.52	17.	Daydreams	.32
85.	Strange ideas	.48	7.	Brags	.31
83.	Hoarding	.47	104.	Loud	.30
84.	Strange behavior	.34		Eigenvalue	2.86

Mixed Scale

VI. *Hostile Withdrawal*

48.	Unliked	.69	12.	Lonely		.40
25.	Poor peer relations	.64	1.	Acts too young		.38
38.	Is teased	.54	21.	Destroys others'		.38
35.	Feels worthless	.49		things		
64.	Prefers young kids	.47	33.	Feels unloved		.36
34.	Feels persecuted	.47	62.	Clumsy		.31
111.	Withdrawn	.42	37.	Fights		.30
20.	Destroys own things	.41		Eigenvalue		4.30

Externalizing Scales

VII. *Delinquent*

82.	Steals outside home	.68	21.	Destroys others'		
81.	Steals at home	.66		things		.44
39.	Bad friends	.64	105.	Alcohol, drugs		.43
106.	Vandalism	.58	23.	Disobeys at school		.43
43.	Lies, cheats	.58	67.	Runs away		.41
101.	Truant	.52	20.	Destroys own things		.40
72.	Sets fires	.46	61.	Poor school work		.31
				Eigenvalue		4.94

VIII. *Aggressive*

97.	Threatens people	.71	27.	Jealous	.52
95.	Temper	.70	87.	Moody	.51
16.	Cruel to others	.64	10.	Hyperactive	.46
22.	Disobeys at home	.62	41.	Impulsive	.46
90.	Swearing	.61	37.	Fights	.46
68.	Screams	.60	88.	Sulks	.45
3.	Argues	.59	19.	Demands attention	.45
57.	Attacks people	.58	45.	Nervous	.44
86.	Stubborn	.58	89.	Suspicious	.42
94.	Teases	.57	93.	Excess talk	.41
104.	Loud	.53	34.	Feels persecuted	.40
				Eigenvalue	8.53

IX. *Hyperactive*

8.	Can't concentrate	.61	23.	Disobeys at school	.38
10.	Hyperactive	.48	1.	Acts too young	.36
61.	Poor school work	.45	62.	Clumsy	.36
44.	Bites nails	.40	41.	Impulsive	.34
45.	Nervous	.40	74.	Shows off	.34
				Eigenvalue	3.05

Girls Aged 4–5: 8-Factor Varimax Rotation

Internalizing Scales

I. Somatic Complaints

56a.	Pains	.55	54.	Overtired	.36
56f.	Stomach problems	.55	71.	Self-conscious	.35
56c.	Nausea	.49	102.	Slow moving	.34
56g.	Vomits	.47	68.	Screams	.32
56b.	Headaches	.44	75.	Shy, timid	.32
11.	Clings to adults	.40	92.	Walks, talks in sleep	.31
56e.	Rashes	.40	77.	Much sleep	.31
14.	Cries much	.38	24.	Doesn't eat well	.30
51.	Dizziness	.36		Eigenvalue	4.61

II. Depressed

32.	Needs to be perfect	.64	34.	Feels persecuted	.40
52.	Feels guilty	.62	48.	Unliked	.38
112.	Worrying	.61	71.	Self-conscious	.37
31.	Fears own impulses	.54	9.	Obsessions	.35
35.	Feels worthless	.54	88.	Sulks	.33
33.	Feels unloved	.52	25.	Poor peer relations	.30
103.	Sad	.41	50.	Anxious	.30
87.	Moody	.40	38.	Is teased	.30
				Eigenvalue	5.20

III. Schizoid or Anxious

100.	Can't sleep	.64	109.	Whining	.36
76.	Sleeps little	.56	45.	Nervous	.34
40.	Hears things	.52	84.	Strange behavior	.33
70.	Sees things	.51	34.	Feels persecuted	.32
50.	Anxious	.50	11.	Clings to adults	.31
29.	Fears	.47	14.	Cries much	.31
19.	Demands attention	.40	9.	Obsessions	.30
				Eigenvalue	4.31

IV. Social Withdrawal

13.	Confused	.65	1.	Acts too young	.39
79.	Speech problem	.56	69.	Secretive	.39
62.	Clumsy	.56	8.	Can't concentrate	.37
80.	Stares blankly	.55	46.	Twitches	.36
17.	Daydreams	.54	66.	Compulsions	.34
102.	Slow moving	.53	56.	Accident prone	.31
111.	Withdrawn	.46	18.	Harms self	.30
65.	Won't talk	.39		Eigenvalue	4.92

Mixed Scale
V. Obese

53.	Overeats	.56	5.	Acts like opposite sex	.35
55.	Overweight	.51	48.	Unliked	.34
38.	Is teased	.48	94.	Teases	.31
85.	Strange ideas	.36	47.	Nightmares	.30
				Eigenvalue	3.22

Externalizing Scales
VI. Aggressive

21.	Destroys others' things	.71	43.	Lies, cheats	.55
16.	Cruel to others	.70	94.	Teases	.52
37.	Fights	.68	104.	Loud	.52
22.	Disobeys at home	.67	86.	Stubborn	.52
57.	Attacks people	.65	90.	Swearing	.51
26.	Lacks guilt	.59	25.	Poor peer relations	.51
20.	Destroys own things	.59	87.	Moody	.46
68.	Screams	.57	3.	Argues	.45
95.	Temper	.57	48.	Unliked	.44
97.	Threatens	.55	41.	Impulsive	.42
15.	Cruel to animals	.55	67.	Runs away	.41
				Eigenvalue	10.77

VII. Sex Problems

96.	Sex preoccupation	.63	60.	Plays with sex parts too much	.44
110.	Wished to be opposite sex	.50	59.	Plays with sex parts in public	.33
73.	Sex problems	.50	39.	Bad friends	.31
5.	Acts like opposite sex	.47		Eigenvalue	3.06

VIII. Hyperactive

10.	Hyperactive	.55	61.	Poor school work	.43
23.	Disobeys at school	.50	93.	Excess talk	.42
74.	Shows off	.46	41.	Impulsive	.41
8.	Can't concentrate	.43	104.	Loud	.40
				Eigenvalue	3.32

Girls Aged 6-11:   12-Factor Varimax Rotation

Internalizing Scales

I. Depressed

112.	Worrying	.67	30.	Fears school	.44
35.	Feels worthless	.66	32.	Needs to be perfect	.41
50.	Anxious	.57	71.	Self-conscious	.41
52.	Feels guilty	.55	45.	Nervous	.35
31.	Fears own impulses	.49	11.	Clings to adults	.34
103.	Sad	.49	111.	Withdrawn	.32
33.	Feels unloved	.47	38.	Is teased	.31
34.	Feels persecuted	.46	75.	Shy, timid	.31
12.	Lonely	.46	88.	Sulks	.30
				Eigenvalue	5.41

II. Social Withdrawal

111.	Withdrawn	.63	88.	Sulks	.36
42.	Likes to be alone	.57	75.	Shy, timid	.34
69.	Secretive	.53	13.	Confused	.31
102.	Slow moving	.48	87.	Moody	.30
65.	Won't talk	.46	80.	Stares blankly	.30
103.	Sad	.43		Eigenvalue	3.56

III. Somatic Complaints

56c.	Nausea	.65	56d.	Eye problems	.39
56a.	Pains	.65	92.	Walks, talks in sleep	.38
56f.	Stomach problems	.60	47.	Nightmares	.37
56b.	Headaches	.52	2.	Allergy	.37
56g.	Vomits	.46	54.	Overtired	.33
51.	Dizziness	.45	77.	Sleeps much	.31
56e.	Rashes	.39		Eigenvalue	4.00

IV. Schizoid-Obsessive

70.	Sees things	.56	67.	Runs away	.39
40.	Hears things	.53	100.	Can't sleep	.36
84.	Strange behavior	.52	76.	Sleeps little	.36
85.	Strange ideas	.46	91.	Suicidal talk	.35
9.	Obsessions	.44	66.	Compulsions	.34
18.	Harms self	.44		Eigenvalue	3.68

Externalizing Scales

V. Hyperactive

8.	Can't concentrate	.65	13.	Confused	.44
1.	Acts too young	.58	10.	Hyperactive	.43
61.	Poor school work	.56	80.	Stares blankly	.39
17.	Daydreams	.50	38.	Is teased	.36
62.	Clumsy	.48	48.	Unliked	.35
64.	Prefers young kids	.47	79.	Speech problem	.31
41.	Impulsive	.44	23.	Disobeys at school	.30
				Eigenvalue	4.40

VI. Sex Problems

96.	Sex preoccupations	.59	60.	Plays with sex parts	
73.	Sex problems	.54		too much	.33
63.	Prefers older kids	.38	93.	Excess talk	.30
52.	Feels guilty	.34		Eigenvalue	2.48

VII. Delinquent

81.	Steals at home	.72	39.	Bad friends	.48
82.	Steals outside home	.65	67.	Runs away	.33
43.	Lies, cheats	.56	90.	Swears	.32
				Eigenvalue	2.93

VIII. Aggressive

95.	Temper	.71	27.	Jealous	.54
3.	Argues	.66	88.	Sulks	.52
22.	Disobeys at home	.64	74.	Shows off	.48
86.	Stubborn	.64	41.	Impulsive	.48
68.	Screams	.60	93.	Excess talk	.47
104.	Loud	.59	23.	Disobeys at school	.46
16.	Cruel to others	.58	33.	Feels unloved	.46
37.	Fights	.57	109.	Whining	.43
94.	Teases	.57	48.	Unliked	.43
87.	Moody	.56	7.	Brags	.42
97.	Threatens people	.55	14.	Cries much	.42
25.	Poor peer relations	.54	21.	Destroys others' things	.42
19.	Demands attention	.54		Eigenvalue	10.02

IX. Cruel

5.	Acts like opposite sex	.45	57.	Attacks people	.38
16.	Cruel to others	.44	37.	Fights	.30
15.	Cruel to animals	.43	20.	Destroys own things	.30
21.	Destroys others' things	.41		Eigenvalue	2.48

Girls Aged 12–16:   11-Factor Varimax Rotation

Internalizing Scales

I. Anxious Obsessive

50.	Anxious	.66	47.	Nightmares	.39
52.	Feels guilty	.59	27.	Jealous	.38
112.	Worrying	.59	45.	Nervous	.37
14.	Cries much	.51	34.	Feels persecuted	.35
35.	Feels worthless	.49	100.	Can't sleep	.35
32.	Needs to be perfect	.48	29.	Fears	.33
31.	Fears own impulses	.47	76.	Sleeps little	.33
12.	Lonely	.46	33.	Feels unloved	.32
71.	Self-conscious	.43	30.	Fears school	.31
9.	Obsessions	.43		Eigenvalue	5.46

II. Somatic Complaints

56c.	Nausea	.68	51.	Dizziness	.53
56f.	Stomach problems	.66	56g.	Vomits	.52
56a.	Pains	.65	56d.	Eye problems	.42
56b.	Headaches	.64	30.	Fears school	.34
				Eigenvalue	3.94

III. Schizoid

40.	Hears things	.52	96.	Sex preoccupation	.35
80.	Stares blankly	.49	70.	Sees things	.32
85.	Strange ideas	.47	47.	Nightmares	.31
17.	Daydreams	.40	29.	Fears	.30
84.	Strange behavior	.38		Eigenvalue	3.09

IV. Depressed Withdrawal

111.	Withdrawn	.63	88.	Sulks	.45
103.	Sad	.57	86.	Stubborn	.38
69.	Secretive	.56	71.	Self-conscious	.38
42.	Likes to be alone	.55	77.	Sleeps much	.38
75.	Shy, timid	.55	80.	Stares blankly	.37
102.	Slow moving	.53	54.	Overtired	.33
65.	Won't talk	.53		Eigenvalue	4.38

Mixed Scale

V. Immature-Hyperactive

1.	Acts too young	.57	83.	Hoarding	.38
64.	Prefers young kids	.54	10.	Hyperactive	.38
62.	Clumsy	.52	11.	Clings to adults	.37
8.	Can't concentrate	.50	48.	Unliked	.34
38.	Is teased	.48	80.	Stares blankly	.32
58.	Picking	.44	17.	Daydreams	.31
25.	Poor peer relations	.43	98.	Thumbsucking	.30
13.	Confused	.38		Eigenvalue	4.39

Externalizing Scales

VI. Delinquent

39.	Bad friends	.69	81.	Steals at home	.44
43.	Lies, cheats	.66	82.	Steals outside home	.40
101.	Truant	.63	90.	Swears	.39
61.	Poor schoolwork	.60	8.	Can't concentrate	.38
105.	Alcohol, drugs	.59	22.	Disobeys at home	.35
23.	Disobeys at school	.59	69.	Secretive	.32
67.	Runs away	.51	63.	Prefers older kids	.31
41.	Impulsive	.50	26.	Lacks guilt	.31
				Eigenvalue	5.23

VII. Aggressive

95.	Temper	.68	93.	Excess talk	.52
104.	Loud	.63	87.	Moody	.51
86.	Stubborn	.61	88.	Sulks	.50
68.	Screams	.60	37.	Fights	.49
94.	Teases	.60	7.	Brags	.49
97.	Threatens people	.57	57.	Attacks people	.47
3.	Argues	.56	27.	Jealous	.47
19.	Demands attention	.55	34.	Feels persecuted	.45
16.	Cruel to others	.55	90.	Swears	.43
22.	Disobeys at home	.55	89.	Suspicious	.42
74.	Shows off	.55	33.	Feels unloved	.42
				Eigenvalue	8.52

VIII. Cruel

21.	Destroys others' things	.62	81.	Steals at home	.37
15.	Cruel to animals	.55	97.	Threatens people	.36
57.	Attacks people	.50	48.	Unliked	.35
20.	Destroys own things	.45	25.	Poor peer relations	.32
16.	Cruel to others	.40	106.	Vandalism	.31
37.	Fights	.39	34.	Feels persecuted	.30
				Eigenvalue	3.19

APPENDIX D

Mean Scale Scores for Boys Aged 4-5

| | Lower SES[a] T Score | | Middle SES[a] T Score | | Upper SES[a] T Score | | All SES Combined | | | | | | | | | |
| | | | | | | | T Score | | SD of T | | Raw Score | | SD of Raw | | SE of Mean | | SE of Meas.[b] |
	Clin	Non-clin	Clin	Non-clin	Clin	Non-clin	Clin	Non-clin	Clin	Non-clin	Clin	Non-clin	Clin	Non-clin	Clin	Non-clin	Clin	Non-clin
N	44	41	30	28	26	31					All N = 100	All N = 100						
Activities	37.8	46.0	41.9	50.4	43.4	50.6	40.5	48.6	14.1	7.5	5.0	6.6	2.9	2.1	.3	.2	1.2	.9
Social	34.2	48.9	35.6	50.4	39.7	48.4	36.0	49.1	14.3	7.1	4.2	6.3	2.1	1.3	.2	.1	.6	.4
Total S.C.	35.1	49.2	38.4	53.1	41.8	52.7	37.7	51.4	15.6	10.0	9.1	12.9	4.4	2.5	.5	.3	1.2	.7
Soc. With.	66.1	58.2	69.7	57.9	65.9	57.5	67.3	57.9	9.8	4.9	5.9	1.9	4.5	2.0	.4	.2	2.3	1.0
Depressed	65.2	57.1	67.7	57.6	65.8	58.4	66.0	57.7	10.3	4.7	12.6	5.4	9.1	4.0	.9	.4	5.6	2.5
Immature	68.5	58.3	70.0	57.5	66.6	57.0	68.6	57.7	10.1	4.7	7.9	2.8	4.9	2.4	.5	.2	1.8	.9
Somatic	65.5	58.2	65.7	58.5	64.0	59.1	65.1	58.6	10.5	5.5	2.0	.6	2.4	.9	.2	.1	.5	.2
Sex Probs.	62.1	58.0	62.2	59.9	65.1	61.4	62.7	59.6	8.4	5.6	.9	.3	1.4	.6	.1	.1	1.0	.4
Schizoid	63.3	58.5	64.7	56.2	64.1	59.4	63.8	58.1	8.2	4.8	2.4	.7	2.8	1.3	.3	.1	1.2	.6
Aggressive	75.8	58.6	72.2	57.1	68.4	57.0	72.9	57.7	13.4	5.8	23.9	9.7	11.7	6.4	1.2	.6	3.5	1.9
Delinquent	68.0	59.1	64.2	58.0	63.9	57.3	65.6	58.3	8.8	4.6	3.9	1.1	3.6	1.5	.4	.1	1.4	.6
Internaliz.	65.3	51.9	67.2	50.0	65.4	52.4	65.9	51.6	11.7	9.4	25.1	9.7	15.6	6.8	1.6	.7	6.4	2.8
Externaliz.	69.9	52.9	66.7	50.1	65.5	49.9	67.8	51.2	12.2	9.7	29.7	11.3	15.6	7.8	1.6	.8	4.1	2.1
Total B.P.	69.1	51.9	68.1	49.9	67.0	50.7	68.3	50.9	12.0	9.7	59.8	24.1	30.1	14.2	3.0	1.4	10.0	4.7

[a]Hollingshead (1957) occupational levels 5-7 = lower SES; 3-4 = middle SES; 1-2 = upper SES.
[b]Standard error of measurement = SD $\sqrt{1\text{-reliability}}$ (Guilford, 1965), computed from reliability of raw scores shown in Table 6-1.

Mean Scale Scores for Boys Aged 6-11

	Lower SES[a] T Score		Middle SES[a] T Score		Upper SES[a] T Score		All SES Combined T Score		SD of T		Raw Score		SD of Raw		SE of Mean		SE of Meas.[b]	
	Clin	Non-clin	Clin	Non-clin	Clin	Non-clin	Clin	Non-clin	Clin	Non-clin	Clin	Non-clin	Clin	Non-clin	Clin	Non-clin	Clin	Non-clin
N	118	120	98	95	84	85	All N = 300				All N = 300							
Activities	40.7	47.5	42.8	49.6	45.6	50.6	42.7	49.1	10.3	7.4	6.3	7.9	2.3	1.9	.1	.1	1.4	1.1
Social	38.0	48.4	35.8	48.5	41.4	52.0	38.2	49.4	10.5	6.8	4.8	7.2	1.9	1.7	.1	.1	.8	.7
School	38.5	48.0	39.9	50.7	41.1	51.3	39.7	49.8	9.1	6.8	3.6	4.9	1.2	1.0	.1	.1	.2	.2
Total S.C.	35.1	47.3	36.1	51.7	40.6	55.0	37.0	51.0	9.0	10.0	15.0	20.1	3.7	3.2	.2	.2	1.8	1.6
Schiz. Anx.	64.9	57.4	65.0	57.4	64.4	58.4	64.8	57.7	8.5	4.7	3.5	1.3	2.6	1.4	.1	.1	1.0	.6
Depressed	66.7	57.2	67.0	57.5	66.7	57.4	66.8	57.3	9.1	4.4	10.1	3.2	6.4	3.4	.4	.2	1.9	1.0
Uncommun.	67.8	57.9	68.7	58.0	67.1	57.8	67.9	57.9	10.2	5.3	5.2	2.0	2.9	1.9	.2	.1	1.6	1.1
Obs. Comp.	65.8	57.8	66.0	57.3	63.5	56.7	65.2	57.4	8.2	4.5	7.6	2.9	4.6	2.8	.3	.2	2.0	1.2
Somatic	61.5	58.5	62.3	57.3	60.8	57.8	61.6	57.9	7.4	4.7	1.9	.8	2.3	1.3	.1	.1	.8	.5
Soc. With.	67.1	57.9	68.0	57.9	66.2	57.9	67.1	57.9	8.9	4.9	4.8	1.7	3.1	1.8	.2	.1	1.0	.6
Hyperact.	68.5	58.1	69.3	57.9	67.4	56.4	68.5	57.6	9.3	4.8	9.1	3.2	4.1	2.9	.2	.2	1.2	.8
Aggressive	69.7	57.5	69.6	57.2	66.2	56.7	68.7	57.1	10.7	4.8	19.1	7.3	9.2	5.7	.5	.3	2.1	1.3
Delinquent	69.5	58.5	67.9	57.2	67.5	57.2	68.4	57.7	8.5	4.6	5.3	1.0	4.1	1.7	.2	.1	.9	.4
Internaliz.	65.6	51.4	66.1	51.2	65.2	51.1	65.6	51.2	8.9	9.1	23.1	8.4	12.2	6.7	.7	.4	3.2	1.8
Externaliz.	68.9	51.6	68.6	50.9	66.5	50.1	68.1	51.0	8.7	9.3	30.5	10.8	13.1	8.2	.8	.5	2.9	1.8
Total B.P.	68.9	51.0	68.8	50.5	67.6	49.9	68.5	50.5	8.8	9.6	58.9	21.7	24.0	15.0	1.4	.9	4.2	2.6

[a]Hollingshead (1957) occupational levels 5-7 = lower SES; 3-4 = middle SES; 1-2 = upper SES.
[b]Standard error of measurement = SD $\sqrt{1\text{-reliability}}$ (Guilford, 1965), computed from reliability of raw scores shown in Table 6-1

Mean Scale Scores for Boys aged 12-16

	Lower SES[a] T Score		Middle SES[a] T Score		Upper SES[a] T Score		All SES Combined T Score		SD of T		Raw Score		SD of Raw		SE of Mean		SE of Meas.[b]	
	Clin	Non-clin	Clin	Non-clin	Clin	Non-clin	Clin	Non-clin	Clin	Non-clin	Clin	Non-clin	Clin	Non-clin	Clin	Non-clin	Clin	Non-clin
N	78	92	88	81	84	77					All N = 250		Clin = 250					
Activities	38.7	47.7	41.9	49.7	44.7	50.0	41.9	49.1	11.1	7.2	6.3	8.0	2.5	1.9	.2	.1	1.1	.8
Social	38.1	47.9	35.5	49.5	37.7	49.8	37.1	49.0	9.8	7.3	5.2	7.8	1.9	1.9	.1	.1	.6	.6
School	35.3	47.7	36.2	49.7	39.1	51.5	37.1	49.5	10.4	7.3	3.2	4.9	1.3	1.0	.1	.1	.3	.2
Total S.C.	33.7	48.2	34.6	51.4	37.8	53.7	35.5	50.9	9.2	10.1	14.8	20.7	4.0	3.4	.3	.2	1.1	.9
Somatic	63.8	58.2	64.4	57.2	63.2	57.5	63.8	57.7	8.3	4.5	4.5	1.4	4.6	2.0	.3	.1	1.2	.5
Schizoid	63.3	58.4	63.8	57.3	63.1	57.8	63.5	57.9	7.8	4.7	3.0	1.1	2.8	1.5	.2	.1	1.2	.6
Uncommun.	64.3	57.3	65.7	56.9	65.3	57.7	65.2	57.3	8.3	4.5	9.1	3.2	5.5	3.6	.4	.2	2.3	1.5
Immature	66.6	58.1	65.4	58.0	65.4	58.0	65.8	58.1	8.8	4.8	3.1	.9	2.6	1.3	.2	.1	1.4	.7
Obs.-Comp.	65.1	58.4	64.8	57.5	63.3	56.6	64.4	57.5	8.5	4.8	4.4	1.7	3.1	1.9	.2	.1	3.3	2.0
Host. With.	67.8	57.6	68.4	57.2	67.2	57.4	67.8	57.4	8.6	4.4	8.0	1.8	5.1	2.5	.3	.2	1.8	.9
Delinquent	67.8	57.6	68.4	57.2	67.7	57.4	68.0	57.4	8.4	4.2	6.6	1.2	4.6	2.0	.3	.1	.8	.3
Aggressive	66.7	57.7	66.1	56.9	65.7	57.4	66.2	57.3	9.3	4.6	16.1	5.7	8.9	5.9	.6	.4	3.2	2.1
Hyperactive	72.2	58.2	70.7	57.8	68.7	57.6	70.6	57.9	10.2	5.3	9.0	3.0	4.1	2.9	.3	.2	1.3	.9
Internaliz.	64.5	52.1	65.0	50.4	64.3	51.2	64.7	51.3	8.2	9.0	21.4	7.4	12.3	7.4	.8	.5	5.1	3.1
Externaliz.	65.9	52.4	66.2	50.6	66.2	51.1	66.2	51.4	8.1	8.9	26.5	8.4	13.0	8.4	.8	.5	4.1	2.7
Total B.P.	66.9	51.9	67.1	50.0	66.3	50.3	66.8	50.8	8.6	9.4	53.1	17.5	24.7	15.6	1.6	1.0	8.2	5.2

[a]Hollingshead (1957) occupational levels 5-7 = lower SES; 3-4 = middle SES; 1-2 = upper SES.
[b]Standard error of measurement = SD $\sqrt{1 - \text{reliability}}$ (Guilford, 1965), computed from reliability of raw scores shown in Table 6-1.

Mean Scale Scores for Girls Aged 4-5

	Lower SES[a] T Score		Middle SES[a] T Score		Upper SES[a] T Score		All SES Combined T Score		SD of T		Raw Score		SD of Raw		SE of Mean		SE of Meas.[b]	
	Clin	Non-clin	Clin	Non-clin	Clin	Non-clin	Clin	Non-clin	Clin	Non-clin	Clin	Non-clin All N = 100	Clin N = 100	Non-clin	Clin	Non-clin	Clin	Non-clin
N	44	38	30	37	26	25												
Activities	39.2	49.0	42.7	49.2	48.8	48.6	42.6	49.0	13.0	6.8	5.9	7.2	2.6	1.9	.3	.2	.6	.4
Social	34.0	48.1	38.4	49.8	44.8	48.8	37.6	48.9	12.0	7.4	4.2	6.3	2.0	1.6	.2	.2	.5	.4
Total S.C.	35.2	49.6	39.3	52.6	47.5	51.2	39.4	51.1	12.5	9.9	10.2	13.6	3.8	2.7	.4	.3	1.0	.7
Somatic	66.1	57.5	63.9	57.8	63.0	57.3	64.8	57.6	8.2	4.7	7.8	3.6	4.8	3.0	.5	.3	3.0	1.9
Depressed	66.3	56.9	64.5	58.3	62.0	57.4	64.9	57.5	8.9	5.2	9.3	3.4	6.1	4.1	.6	.4	2.4	1.6
Schiz/Anx.	68.1	57.3	67.1	58.7	65.2	56.3	67.1	57.6	9.2	4.8	9.8	4.0	5.5	3.3	.6	.3	3.3	2.0
Soc. With.	68.6	57.7	66.6	58.2	62.6	56.7	66.6	57.6	9.2	5.2	7.1	2.2	5.4	2.9	.5	.3	1.1	.6
Obese	65.9	57.9	62.5	59.6	61.5	56.7	64.1	58.2	8.9	5.4	3.4	1.5	2.8	1.7	.3	.2	2.1	1.3
Aggressive	71.0	57.1	64.9	58.6	61.1	56.0	67.0	57.4	11.8	4.8	15.2	5.8	10.4	5.2	1.0	.5	2.9	1.5
Sex Probs.	65.1	60.5	64.0	60.8	64.0	60.2	64.5	60.6	7.1	3.5	1.4	.3	2.2	.8	.2	.1	1.5	.6
Hyperact.	69.1	57.6	65.1	58.7	60.9	56.0	66.1	57.6	11.7	4.7	6.2	3.1	3.9	2.3	.4	.2	.9	.5
Internaliz.	69.1	49.7	65.3	51.7	62.3	47.0	66.5	50.8	11.3	10.5	28.7	10.8	14.9	9.3	1.5	.9	3.9	2.5
Externaliz.	66.0	48.7	58.0	50.0	56.1	44.5	61.5	49.8	12.8	8.7	21.2	8.4	13.6	6.6	1.4	.7	3.3	1.6
Total B.P.	71.5	50.9	65.0	52.7	61.5	47.8	67.3	48.2	12.6	10.2	58.8	25.2	29.1	17.1	3.0	1.7	6.5	3.8

[a]Hollingshead (1957) occupational levels 5-7 = lower SES; 3-4 = middle SES; 1-2 = upper SES.

[b]Standard error of measurement = $SD \sqrt{1-\text{reliability}}$ (Guilford, 1965), computed from reliability of raw scores shown in Table 6-1

Mean Scale Scores for Girls Aged 6–11

	Lower SES[a] T Score		Middle SES[a] T Score		Upper SES[a] T Score		All SES Combined T Score		SD of T		Raw Score		SD of Raw		SE of Mean		SE of Meas.[b]	
	Clin	Non-clin	Clin	Non-clin	Clin	Non-clin	Clin	Non-clin	Clin	Non-clin	Clin	Non-clin	Clin	Non-clin	Clin	Non-clin	Clin	Non-clin
N	113	101	111	96	76	103	300											
Activities	39.3	47.5	45.1	49.1	45.9	50.6	43.1	49.1	10.1	6.7	6.5	7.9	2.4	1.8	.1	.1	1.4	1.0
Social	37.0	46.5	37.3	49.4	38.4	50.8	37.5	48.9	10.9	7.1	4.8	7.2	1.9	1.8	.1	.1	.5	.5
School	37.3	48.0	35.0	51.0	38.7	50.6	36.8	49.8	11.1	6.8	3.9	5.3	1.3	.8	.1	.0	.4	.3
Total S.C.	34.4	47.4	37.1	51.3	39.4	54.9	36.7	51.1	10.0	9.7	15.2	20.4	4.0	3.1	.3	.2	1.8	1.4
Depressed	69.3	57.0	69.5	57.1	69.3	57.5	69.3	57.2	10.5	4.5	12.9	4.2	7.0	3.7	.4	.2	2.2	1.2
Soc. With.	70.0	57.7	69.2	57.6	66.1	57.9	68.8	57.7	9.9	4.6	6.4	1.8	4.2	1.9	.2	.1	1.5	.7
Somatic	63.8	58.1	63.2	57.5	62.1	57.2	63.2	57.6	8.1	4.3	4.3	1.7	3.9	2.0	.2	.1	.8	.4
Schiz-Obs.	65.5	58.3	64.6	57.8	63.7	58.0	64.7	58.0	7.6	4.6	2.7	.7	2.6	1.1	.2	.1	1.2	.5
Hyperact.	69.9	58.5	70.4	56.6	67.7	57.0	69.5	57.4	9.6	4.5	10.0	2.8	5.5	2.8	.3	.2	.8	.4
Sex Probs.	64.7	59.4	64.8	57.9	62.4	57.7	64.2	58.3	9.6	5.4	2.3	1.0	1.9	1.1	.1	.1	1.7	1.0
Delinquent	67.7	60.1	67.1	58.5	64.2	58.7	66.6	59.1	8.9	4.3	2.0	.4	2.2	.9	.1	.0	.5	.2
Aggressive	71.2	57.4	69.6	57.0	66.6	57.8	69.5	57.4	10.6	4.7	20.2	7.2	10.1	6.0	.6	.3	2.3	1.3
Cruel	67.9	59.1	64.7	58.3	64.5	58.3	65.8	58.5	8.8	4.4	2.5	.5	2.6	1.0	.1	.1	.6	.2
Internaliz.	67.7	51.9	66.8	50.9	66.0	51.0	67.0	51.3	9.1	9.1	23.7	7.7	12.6	6.3	.7	.4	3.3	1.7
Externaliz.	69.3	52.6	68.3	50.4	65.8	50.0	68.1	51.0	9.5	9.4	32.5	10.7	15.7	8.6	.9	.5	2.7	1.5
Total B.P.	70.3	52.1	68.8	49.9	66.9	49.9	68.9	50.6	9.5	9.5	58.4	19.9	26.2	14.2	1.5	.8	4.5	2.5

[a] Hollingshead (1957) occupational levels 5–7 = lower SES; 3–4 = middle SES; 1–2 = upper SES.
[b] Standard error of measurement = SD $\sqrt{1-\text{reliability}}$ (Guilford, 1965), computed from reliability of raw scores shown in Table 6-1.

Mean Scale scores for Girls Aged 12-16

	Lower SES[a] T Score		Middle SES[a] T Score		Upper SES[a] T Score		All SES Combined T Score		SD of T		Raw Score		SD of Raw		SE of Mean		SE of Meas.[b]	
	Clin	Non-clin	Clin	Non-clin	Clin	Non-clin	Clin	Non-clin	Clin	Non-clin	Clin	Non-clin	Clin	Non-clin	Clin	Non-clin	Clin	Non-clin
N	80	87	86	84	84	79	All N = 250											
Activities	40.2	47.5	41.8	49.1	44.7	50.8	42.3	49.1	10.0	7.1	6.2	7.9	2.4	1.9	.2	.1	1.3	1.0
Social	39.6	46.8	37.7	50.2	40.4	50.2	39.2	49.0	9.6	6.9	5.1	7.5	2.0	2.0	.1	.1	.3	.3
School	37.7	49.2	35.4	49.6	39.4	50.5	37.5	49.7	10.6	6.7	3.9	5.3	1.3	.8	.1	.0	.4	.2
Total S.C.	36.5	47.3	35.1	51.6	39.1	54.1	36.9	50.9	9.8	10.0	15.4	20.8	4.2	3.4	.3	.2	1.3	1.0
Anx. Obs.	67.0	56.9	68.0	57.4	66.7	57.6	67.2	57.3	8.7	4.3	11.7	3.6	6.8	3.7	.4	.2	3.5	1.9
Somatic	67.8	59.1	67.9	58.1	66.3	58.7	67.3	58.6	9.1	4.7	2.9	.6	2.9	1.1	.2	.1	1.3	.5
Schizoid	64.7	59.0	65.8	57.8	63.9	58.1	64.8	58.3	8.2	4.7	2.7	.9	2.5	1.2	.2	.1	1.4	.7
Dep. With.	68.0	57.6	69.7	57.7	68.0	57.3	68.6	57.5	9.6	4.4	9.4	3.0	5.0	2.8	.3	.2	1.9	1.1
Im. Hyper.	66.5	57.7	67.8	57.2	64.7	57.1	66.4	57.3	9.0	4.4	7.2	2.3	4.9	2.5	.3	.2	2.1	1.1
Delinquent	69.7	57.7	72.9	57.2	68.2	57.1	70.3	57.3	9.0	4.8	11.5	2.4	6.4	3.3	.4	.2	1.1	.6
Aggressive	65.0	57.0	67.0	57.2	65.2	56.7	65.7	57.0	8.9	4.0	15.5	5.1	9.1	5.2	.6	.3	2.4	1.4
Cruel	67.1	58.7	68.9	59.0	67.2	58.5	67.8	58.8	8.4	3.6	4.0	.5	4.0	1.1	.3	.1	1.1	.3
Internaliz.	63.8	50.1	65.4	49.4	63.7	49.8	64.3	49.8	8.4	8.0	24.4	7.0	12.7	6.5	.8	.4	5.5	2.8
Externaliz.	63.3	50.0	65.8	49.5	62.7	48.6	64.0	49.4	8.6	7.5	26.9	7.3	14.2	7.6	.9	.5	2.8	1.5
Total B.P.	68.0	51.9	70.0	50.1	67.3	49.9	68.5	50.6	9.4	9.5	55.8	16.6	26.3	14.1	1.7	.9	9.5	5.1

[a]Hollingshead (1957) occupational levels 5-7 = lower SES; 3-4 = middle SES; 1-2 = upper SES.
[b]Standard error of measurement = SD $\sqrt{1\text{-reliability}}$ (Guilford, 1965), computed from reliability of raw scores shown in Table 6-1.

APPENDIX E

Pearson Correlations Among *T* Scores for Boys Aged 4–5
Clinical Sample above Diagonal, Nonclinical Sample below Diagonal

	Activ.	Social	Total S.C.	Soc. Withdr.	De-pressed	Imma-ture	Somatic	Sex Prob.	Schizoid	Aggres-sive	Delin-quent	Intern-alizing	Extern-alizing	Total B.P.
Activ.		.52	.86	-.08	-.01	-.22	.07	.01	-.09	-.15	-.12	-.09	-.16	-.13
Social	.63		.82	-.20	-.12	-.26	-.06	.06	-.14	-.36	-.31	-.22	-.38	-.29
Total S.C.	.79	.49		-.15	-.05	-.26	.01	.05	-.09	-.25	-.18	-.16	-.27	-.22
Soc. Withdr.	-.11	-.15	-.19		.72	.67	.39	.17	.51	.50	.58	.83	.59	.72
Depressed	-.15	-.25	-.23	.45		.63	.42	.39	.49	.53	.65	.87	.60	.77
Immature	-.23	-.08	-.20	.59	.58		.33	.21	.43	.52	.60	.81	.59	.70
Somatic	.05	.09	.03	.14	.11	.18		.12	.31	.38	.37	.51	.41	.47
Sex Prob.	.15	-.03	.07	.06	.39	.04	.13		.34	.20	.30	.33	.28	.36
Schizoid	-.08	-.04	-.06	.41	.30	.33	.24	-.13		.50	.53	.54	.62	.62
Aggressive	-.21	-.13	-.15	.65	.57	.61	.09	.11	.39		.73	.62	.94	.82
Delinquent	-.16	.03	-.12	.50	.46	.67	.29	.06	.22	.56		.66	.78	.74
Internaliz.	-.18	-.11	-.17	.65	.75	.67	.40	.35	.41	.58	.55		.74	.91
Externaliz.	-.18	-.03	-.10	.61	.56	.56	.22	.21	.47	.76	.63	.76		.93
Total B.P.	-.16	-.10	-.13	.66	.69	.63	.31	.32	.48	.70	.61	.90	.93	

Note—$N = 100$ in each sample; correlations $> .16$ are significant at $p < .05$.

Pearson Correlations Among *T* Scores for Boys Aged 6-11
Clinical Sample above Diagonal, Nonclinical Sample below Diagonal

	Activ.	Social	School	Total S.C.	Schiz./Anx.	De-pressed	Un-comm.	Obsess-Comp.	Som-atic	Soc. Withdr.	Hyper-active	Aggres-sive	Delin-quent	Intern-alizing	Extern-alizing	Total B.P.
Activ.		.30	.13	.74	.04	.13	-.02	-.00	.07	-.04	-.23	.00	-.12	.07	-.12	-.03
Social	.16		.07	.71	-.21	-.24	-.14	-.26	-.03	-.39	-.35	-.37	-.28	-.28	-.42	-.43
School	.13	.21		.43	.01	.01	-.05	-.03	.05	-.08	-.39	-.11	-.14	-.00	-.21	-.11
Total S.C.	.70	.64	.46		-.07	-.08	-.10	-.15	.05	-.30	-.44	-.39	-.26	-.13	-.39	-.29
Schiz./Anx.	-.03	-.04	.01	-.05		.57	.47	.55	.40	.33	.22	.28	.03	.69	.26	.53
Depressed	.11	-.13	-.05	-.03	.44		.63	.59	.38	.54	.25	.58	.20	.86	.50	.76
Uncommun.	-.04	-.11	-.12	-.12	.36	.58		.51	.31	.43	.38	.41	.27	.70	.46	.63
Obsess-Comp.	-.04	-.20	-.20	-.19	.37	.54	.43		.45	.49	.49	.50	.29	.79	.54	.74
Somatic	-.05	-.05	-.01	.02	.22	.24	.26	.32		.16	.07	.17	.04	.54	.15	.41
Soc. Withdr.	.03	-.20	-.11	-.12	.37	.54	.44	.54	.29		.44	.65	.37	.55	.64	.70
Hyperactive	-.02	-.31	-.38	-.28	.19	.44	.42	.64	.12	.46		.41	.44	.38	.66	.58
Aggressive	-.02	-.27	-.17	-.17	.15	.58	.44	.64	.20	.50	.57		.60	.58	.89	.83
Delinquent	-.13	-.19	-.19	-.23	.10	.27	.41	.42	.28	.33	.46	.55		.25	.73	.58
Internaliz.	.03	-.20	-.13	-.14	.53	.70	.59	.68	.50	.57	.53	.55	.44		.59	.86
Externaliz.	.03	-.29	-.29	-.25	.24	.51	.49	.61	.24	.51	.68	.71	.63	.73		.89
Total B.P.	.03	-.27	-.21	-.20	.42	.63	.56	.66	.40	.60	.63	.66	.57	.91	.92	

Note—*N* = 300 in each sample; correlations > .09 significant at *p* < .05.

Pearson Correlations Among T Scores for Boys Aged 12–16
Clinical Sample above Diagonal, Nonclinical Sample below Diagonal

	Activ.	Social	School	Total S.C.	Som-atic	Schizoid	Un-comm.	Imma-ture	Obsess-Comp.	Host. Withdr.	Delin-quent	Aggres-sive	Hyper-active	Intern-alizing	Extern-alizing	Total B.P.
Activ.		.26	.23	.76	.01	-.03	.09	-.02	-.02	-.10	-.17	-.09	-.12	-.01	-.10	-.07
Social	.18		.20	.69	-.18	-.27	-.33	-.33	-.23	-.47	-.11	-.31	-.28	-.36	-.31	-.36
School	.14	.19		.55	.00	.02	-.08	-.18	-.10	-.31	-.40	-.19	-.38	-.12	-.34	-.26
Total S.C.	.67	.67	.51		-.06	-.12	-.24	-.21	-.13	-.35	-.27	-.24	-.32	-.19	-.30	-.27
Somatic	-.05	-.12	-.21	-.15		.65	.52	.37	.41	.41	.08	.34	.27	.73	.29	.61
Schizoid	-.05	-.09	-.07	-.10	.55		.52	.44	.45	.41	.02	.30	.23	.71	.24	.56
Uncomm.	-.09	-.19	-.13	-.20	.61	.62		.29	.49	.52	.32	.53	.32	.80	.53	.71
Immature	-.07	-.15	-.10	-.17	.33	.39	.50		.44	.67	.19	.55	.58	.60	.53	.64
Obsess-Comp.	.03	-.19	-.18	-.16	.47	.48	.61	.52		.54	.27	.56	.45	.70	.53	.70
Host. Withdr.	-.08	-.23	-.17	-.23	.51	.44	.63	.65	.61		.49	.66	.63	.69	.70	.81
Delinquent	-.15	-.25	-.34	-.34	.32	.27	.48	.36	.48	.49		.44	.52	.30	.71	.53
Aggressive	-.13	-.34	-.17	-.31	.49	.38	.69	.63	.71	.74	.67		.67	.63	.87	.82
Hyperactive	-.23	-.29	-.44	-.41	.41	.22	.51	.58	.48	.60	.62	.71		.50	.79	.71
Internaliz.	-.05	-.25	-.19	-.24	.67	.65	.74	.60	.68	.65	.48	.66	.54		.64	.90
Externaliz.	-.17	-.32	-.29	-.40	.47	.39	.58	.59	.61	.65	.70	.78	.71	.91		.76
Total B.P.	-.13	-.30	-.25	-.35	.62	.55	.67	.58	.66	.69	.62	.73	.63	.92	.76	

Note—$N = 250$ in each sample; correlations $> .10$ significant at $p < .05$.

Pearson Correlations Among T Scores for Girls Aged 4–5
Clinical Sample above Diagonal, Nonclinical Sample below Diagonal

	Activ.	Social	Total S.C.	Som-atic	De-pressed	Schiz/ Anxious	Soc. Withdr.	Obese	Aggres-sive	Sex Probs.	Hyper-active	Intern-alizing	Extern-alizing	Total B.P.
Activ.		.37	.85	-.11	-.06	-.16	-.31	-.07	-.25	-.01	-.15	-.20	-.18	-.21
Social	.17		.75	-.35	-.39	-.27	-.33	-.40	-.51	-.17	-.40	-.47	-.45	-.54
Total S.C.	.72	.71		-.32	-.25	-.29	-.41	-.26	-.47	-.12	-.33	-.42	-.41	-.46
Somatic	-.02	-.28	-.21		.51	.61	.44	.36	.46	.21	.28	.75	.52	.69
Depressed	.02	-.36	-.20	.67		.59	.51	.50	.57	.33	.45	.79	.60	.75
Schiz./Anx.	-.05	-.31	-.25	.55	.68		.39	.30	.51	.23	.48	.76	.56	.72
Soc. Withdr.	.00	-.16	-.12	.50	.64	.44		.40	.49	.43	.54	.72	.52	.70
Obese	-.06	-.30	-.19	.32	.64	.43	.55		.52	.47	.36	.48	.53	.57
Aggressive	-.03	-.26	-.18	.50	.69	.54	.59	.67		.47	.78	.64	.93	.83
Sex Probs.	.09	.06	.11	-.06	.26	.15	.13	.50	.31		.45	.38	.52	.50
Hyperactive	-.06	-.13	-.13	.30	.42	.46	.58	.47	.68	.38		.54	.81	.72
Internaliz.	.03	-.24	-.15	.66	.75	.69	.69	.54	.62	.18	.54		.71	.93
Externaliz.	-.02	-.02	-.15	.45	.59	.48	.54	.64	.78	.42	.70	.74		.88
Total B.P.	.02	-.25	-.15	.63	.73	.63	.67	.65	.74	.30	.64	.92	.88	

Note—$N = 100$ in each sample; correlations $> .16$ are significant at $p < .05$.

Pearson Correlations Among T Scores for Girls Aged 6-11
Clinical Sample above Diagonal, Nonclinical Sample below Diagonal

	Activ.	Social	School	Total S.C.	De-pressed	Soc. Withdr.	Som-atic.	Schiz.-Obsess.	Hyper-active	Sex Probs.	Delin-quent	Aggres-sive	Cruel	Intern-alizing	Extern-alizing	Total B.P.
Activ.		.27	.10	.73	.01	-.09	.05	-.08	-.17	-.02	-.15	-.12	-.12	-.01	-.17	-.12
Social	.14		.16	.73	-.15	-.18	-.05	-.09	-.32	-.09	-.23	-.28	-.30	-.16	-.33	-.28
School	.12	.20		.46	-.11	-.10	-.11	-.12	-.54	-.05	-.19	-.15	-.15	-.13	-.32	-.26
Total S.C.	.69	.68	.44		-.11	-.21	-.02	-.13	-.42	-.06	-.25	-.26	-.26	-.14	-.37	-.29
Depressed	.01	.00	-.06	-.04		.66	.47	.42	.40	.47	.21	.53	.28	.86	.55	.74
Soc. Withdr.	-.03	.02	-.21	-.09	.70		.41	.36	.46	.33	.26	.48	.30	.76	.55	.69
Somatic	.01	.05	-.14	-.02	.35	.37		.34	.25	.26	.10	.25	.15	.65	.28	.52
Schiz.-Obsess.	.01	.00	-.07	.00	.36	.33	.29		.41	.38	.37	.46	.37	.58	.48	.59
Hyperactive	-.05	-.15	-.46	-.24	.43	.49	.29	.33		.32	.46	.59	.48	.49	.77	.70
Sex Probs.	-.10	-.05	-.06	-.13	.41	.31	.20	.21	.36		.38	.57	.41	.48	.57	.58
Delinquent	-.12	-.05	-.25	-.18	.31	.36	.27	.32	.50	.27		.59	.55	.29	.64	.56
Aggressive	-.10	-.13	-.22	-.19	.52	.41	.26	.36	.51	.47	.48		.74	.57	.90	.83
Cruel	-.17	-.19	-.15	-.23	.17	.21	.09	.22	.33	.26	.34	.53		.33	.69	.61
Internaliz.	.01	-.05	-.10	-.09	.71	.69	.61	.57	.47	.41	.39	.49	.25		.65	.87
Externaliz.	-.06	-.22	-.26	-.26	.52	.51	.37	.45	.66	.52	.56	.74	.51	.92		.92
Total B.P.	-.04	-.16	-.22	-.21	.64	.61	.52	.54	.61	.51	.52	.68	.43	.89	.92	

Note—N = 300 in each sample; correlations >.09 significant at p<.05.

Pearson Correlations Among T Scores for Girls Aged 12-16
Clinical Sample above Diagonal, Nonclinical Sample below Diagonal

	Activ.	Social	School	Total S.C.	Anx. Obsess.	Som-atic	Schiz-oid	Depr. Withdr.	Imm. Hyper.	Delin-quent	Aggres-sive	Cruel	Intern-alizing	Extern-alizing	Total B.P.
Activ.		.39	.22	.78	-.06	.00	-.03	-.09	-.06	-.27	-.12	-.12	-.10	-.22	-.15
Social	.21		.20	.75	-.26	-.09	-.15	-.31	-.36	-.26	-.37	-.39	-.30	-.38	-.36
School	.24	.17		.51	-.11	-.19	-.08	-.12	-.23	-.51	-.20	-.21	-.15	-.37	-.28
Total S.C.	.72	.69	.46		-.18	-.10	-.09	-.24	-.25	-.42	-.27	-.30	-.25	-.41	-.33
Anx. Obsess.	.00	-.04	-.03	-.04		.47	.63	.63	.56	.33	.53	.48	.87	.53	.77
Somatic	.09	-.01	-.03	.07	.51		.34	.42	.32	.29	.28	.31	.61	.34	.53
Schizoid	-.05	-.04	-.09	-.06	.57	.36		.53	.57	.30	.45	.34	.69	.46	.64
Depr. Withdr.	.03	-.14	-.07	-.05	.55	.41	.52		.52	.43	.49	.46	.83	.56	.73
Imm. Hyper.	-.04	-.11	-.16	-.11	.61	.33	.57	.57		.41	.53	.63	.61	.61	.72
Delinquent	-.18	-.25	-.34	-.27	.45	.30	.30	.46	.43		.60	.53	.46	.83	.69
Aggressive	-.17	-.12	-.18	-.18	.67	.32	.43	.51	.54	.67		.77	.58	.89	.79
Cruel	-.08	-.10	-.12	-.12	.61	.34	.34	.48	.65	.63	.69		.53	.79	.73
Internaliz.	.06	-.12	-.06	-.01	.73	.56	.66	.71	.58	.47	.58	.52		.65	.89
Externaliz.	-.17	-.16	-.28	-.23	.61	.33	.48	.52	.56	.73	.78	.66	.72		.89
Total B.P.	-.06	-.19	-.21	-.16	.69	.48	.61	.64	.63	.61	.69	.60	.90	.89	

Note—$N = 250$ in each sample; correlations $> .10$ are significant at $p < .05$.

APPENDIX F
Some Studies that have Used the CBCL[a]

Achenbach, T. M. The Child Behavior Profile: I. Boys aged 6-11. *Journal of Consulting and Clinical Psychology,* 1978, *46,* 478-488.

Achenbach, T. M. *Developmental psychopathology, 2nd Edition.* New York: Wiley, 1982

Achenbach, T. M. What is child psychiatric epidemiology the epidemiology of? In F. Earls (Ed.), *Studies of Children. Monographs in Psychosocial Epidemiology,* No. 1. New York: Neale Watson Academic Publications, 1980.

Achenbach, T. M. Assessment and taxonomy of children's behavior disorders. In B. B. Lahey & A. E. Kazdin (Eds.), *Advances in clinical child psychology,* (Vol. 5). New York: Plenum, 1982.

Achenbach, T. M. The role of taxonomy in developmental psychopathology. In M. E. Lamb & A. L. Brown (Eds.), *Advances in developmental psychology,* (Vol. 1). Hillsdale, New Jersey: Erlbaum, 1981.

Achenbach, T. M., & Edelbrock, C. S. The classification of child psychopathology: A review and analysis of empirical efforts. *Psychological Bulletin,* 1978, *85,* 1275-1301.

Achenbach, T. M., & Edelbrock, C. S. The Child Behavior Profile: II. Boys aged 12-16 and girls aged 6-11 and 12-16. *Journal of Consulting and Clinical Psychology,* 1979, *47,* 223-233.

Achenbach, T. M., & Edelbrock, C. S. Taxonomic issues in child psychopathology. In T. H. Ollendick & M. Hersen (Eds.), *Handbook of child psychopathology.* New York: Plenum, 1983.

Achenbach, T. M., & Edelbrock, C. S. Behavioral problems and competencies reported by parents of normal and disturbed children aged 4 through 16. *Monographs of the Society for Research in Child Development,* 1981, *46* (Serial No. 188).

Adcock, K. S. Assessment of the consistency in ratings of children's behavior problems between therapist and parent. M. S. Thesis, Department of Applied Behavioral Sciences, Wright State University, Dayton, OH, August, 1980.

Altrows, I., Roy, G., Nicholson, L., Maunula, S., Grossi, V., & Eller, D. Personality tests and children's behaviour. Presented at the Psychologists' Association of Alberta, Banff, Alberta, October, 1982.

Barkley, R. A. *Hyperactive children. A handbook for diagnosis and treatment.* New York: Guilford, 1981.

Benjamin, P. Y., Levinsohn, M., Drotar, D., & Hanson, E. E. Intellectual and emotional sequelae of Reyes Syndrome. *Critical Care Medicine,* 1982, *10,* 583-587.

[a]Users are advised to do their own literature searches in order to find additional studies.

Bradley, S. J., Doering, R. W., Zucker, K. J., Finegan, J. K., & Gonda, G. M. Assessment of the gender-disturbed child: A comparison to sibling and psychiatric controls. In J. Sampson (Ed.), *Childhood and sexuality: Proceedings of the International Symposium.* Montreal: Éditions Études Vivantes, 1980.

Butnik, S. M. Anxiety and locus of control as correlates of the internalizer-externalizer symptom dimension among a group of emotionally disturbed children. Ph.D. Dissertation, Department of Psychology, Ohio State University, 1980.

Cohen, N. J., Gotlieb, H., Kershner, J., & Wehrspann, W. The relationship between children's internalizing and externalizing symptom patterns and measures of competence: A study of the concurrent validity of the Achenbach Child Behavior Profile. Presented at the American Adacemy of Child Psychiatry, Washington, D.C., October, 1982.

Cohen-Sandler, R., Berman, A. L., & King, R. A. A follow-up study of hospitalized suicidal children. *Journal of the American Academy of Child Psychiatry,* 1982, *21,* 398-403.

Cytryn, L., McKnew, D. H., Bartko, J. J., Lamour, M., Hamovit, J., & Bunney, W. E. Offspring of patients with affective disorders. II. Presented at the American Academy of Child Psychiatry, Chicago, October, 1981.

Durham, T., & Childers, J. A comparison of CBCL Profiles in two clinical samples. Presented at the American Psychological Association, Los Angeles, August, 1981.

Edelbrock, C., & Achenbach, T. M. The Teacher Version of the Child Behavior Profile: I. Boys aged 6–11. Submitted for publication, 1983.

Edelbrock C., & Achenbach, T. M. A typology of Child Behavior Profile patterns: Distribution and correlates in disturbed children aged 6 to 16. *Journal of Abnormal Child Psychology*, 1980, *8,* 441–470.

Edelbrock, C., Costello, A. J., & Kessler, M. D. Empirical corroboration of the Attention Deficit Disorder. *Journal of the American Academy of Child Psychiatry,* 1983, in press.

Feinstein, C. B., Blouin, A. G., Egan, J., & Conners, C. K. Depressive symptomatology in a child psychiatric outpatient population: Correlations with diagnosis. Presented at the American Academy of Child Psychiatry, Dallas, October, 1981.

Feinstein, C. B., Egan, J., Conners, C. K., & Stoney, K. A survey of depressive symptomatology in a child psychiatry outpatient clinic. Presented at the American Academy of Child Psychiatry, Chicago, October, 1980.

Fischer, M., Rolf, J. E., Hasazi, J. E., & Cummings, L. Follow-up of a preschool epidemiological sample: Cross-age continuities and predictions of later adjustment with internalizing and externalizing dimensions of behavior. *Child Development,* 1983, in press.

Frame, C., Matson, J. L., Sonis, W. A., Fialkov, M. J., & Kadzin, A. E. Behavioral treatment of depression in a prepubertal child. *Journal of Behavior Therapy and Experimental Psychiatry,* 1982, *13,* 239–243.

Fuhrman, M., & Kendall, P. C. Cognition in childhood psychopathology: A reply to Schwartz et al. Department of Psychology, University of Minnesota, 1983.

Garrison, S. R., & Stolbert, A. L. Modification of anger in children by affective imagery training. *Journal of Abnormal Child Psychology,* 1983, *11,* 115–130.

Garrison, W., & Earls, F. The Child Behavior Checklist as a screening instrument in a normal population of young children. Presented at the American Academy of Child Psychiatry, Washington, D. C., October, 1982.

Gordon, M., Crouthamel, C., Post, E. M., & Richman, R. A. Psychosocial aspects of constitutional short stature: Social competence, behavior problems, self-esteem, and family functioning. *Journal of Pediatrics,* 1982, *101,* 477–480.

Gordon, M., & Tegtmeyer, P. F. The egocentricity index and self-esteem in children. *Perceptual and Motor Skillss,* 1982, *55,* 335–337.

Gordon, M., & Tegtmeyer, P. F. Oral-dependent content in children's Rorschach protocols. *Perceptual and Motor Skills,* 1983, in press.

Gould, M. S., & Shaffer, D. The characteristics of drop-outs from a child psychiatry clinic. Presented at the American Academy of Child Psychiatry, Washington, D.C., October, 1982.

Gould, M. S., & Shaffer, D. Psychiatric symptoms in the parents of children seen in a child psychiatry clinic. Presented at the American Academy of Child Psychiatry, Washington, D. C., October, 1982.

Hazzard, A., Christensen, A., & Margolin, G. Children's perceptions of parental behaviors. *Journal of Abnormal Child Psychology,* 1983, *11,* 49–59.

Heath, G. A., Hardesty, V. A., Goldfine, P. E., & Walker, A. M. Childhood firesetting: An empirical study. *Journal of the American Academy of Child Psychiatry,* 1983, *22,* 370–374.

Hermann, B. P. Neuropsychological functioning and psychopathology in children with epilepsy. *Epilepsia,* 1982, *23,* 545–554.

Hermann, B. P., Black, R. B., & Chhabria, S. Behavioral problems and social competence in children with epilepsy. *Epilepsia,* 1981, *22,* 703–710.

Hodges, K., Kline, J., Stern, L., Cytryn, L., & McKnew, D. The development of a child assessment interview for research and clinical use. *Journal of Abnormal Child Psychology,* 1982, *10,* 173–189.

Hodges, K., McKnew, D., Cytryn, L., Stern, L., & Kline, J. The Child Assessment Schedule (CAS) diagnostic interview: A report on reliability and validity. *Journal of the American Academy of Child Psychiatry,* 1982, *21,* 468–473.

Holmes, C. S., Hayford, J. T., & Thompson, R. G. Parents' and teachers' differing views of short children's behavior. *Child Care, Health, and*

Development, 1982, *8,* 327–336.

Holmes, C. S., Hayford, J. T., & Thompson, R. G. Personality and behavior differences in groups of boys with short stature. *Children's Health Care,* 1982, *11,* 61–64.

Kazdin, A. E., French, N. H., Unis, A. S., & Esveldt-Dawson, K. Assessment of childhood depression: Correspondence of child and parent ratings. *Journal of the American Academy of Child Psychology,* 1983, *22,* 157–164.

Kendall, P. C., & Fischler, G. L. Behavioral and adjustment correlates of problem solving: Validational analyses of interpersonal cognitive problem-solving measures. *Child Development,* in press.

Klein, G., & Love, A. The profile of the emotionally disturbed and mentally retarded adolescent in the community. Presented at Thistletown Research Day, Toronto, Canada, March, 1983.

Kuhnley, E. J., Hendren, R. L., & Quinlan, D. M. Firesetting by children. *Journal of the American Academy of Child Psychiatry,* 1982, *21,* 560–563.

Lemoine, R. L., & Carney, A. The Louisiana Client-Outcome Evaluation Project: An initial progress report. Baton Rouge, Louisiana: Office of Mental Health and Substance Abuse, Louisiana Department of Health and Human Resources, 1982.

Loeber, R. The stability of antisocial and delinquent child behavior: A review. *Child Development,* 1982, *53,* 1431–1446.

Loeber, R., & Dishion, T. J. Boys who fight: Familial and antisocial correlates. Paper presented at the meeting of the American Psychological Association, Washington, D.C., August, 1982.

Loeber, R., & Schmaling, K. B. Empirical evidence for overt and covert patterns of antisocial conduct problems. Oregon Social Learning Center, Eugene, Oregon, 1983.

Loeber, R., & Schmaling, K. B. The utility of differentiating between mixed and pure forms of antisocial child behavior. Submitted for publication, 1983.

Mash, E. J., & Johnston, C. Parental perceptions of child behavior problems, parenting self-esteem, and mothers' reported stress in younger and older hyperactive and normal children. *Journal of Consulting and Clinical Psychology,* 1983, *51,* 86–99.

Mash, E. J., Johnston, C., & Kovitz, K. A comparison of the mother-child interactions of physically abused and non-abused children during play and task situations. *Journal of Clinical Child Psychology,* in press.

McArdle, J., Brown, C. H., Aist, M. B., & Harris, J. C. Prevalence of behavior problems in 6- to 12-year-old girls and boys in a rural community. Presented at the American Academy of Child Psychiatry, Washington, D.C., October, 1982.

McClure, F. D., & Gordon, M. Performance of disturbed hyperactive and nonhyperactive boys on an objective measure of hyperactivity. *Journal of Abnormal Child Psychology,* submitted.

McCown, D. E. Selected factors related to children's adjustment following sibling death. Ph.D. Dissertation, Department of Human Development and Family Studies, Oregon State University, Corvallis, Oregon, 1982.

McMahon, W. M., Ferre, R. C., Latkowski, M., Peterson, K., & Marriott, S. The Child Behavior Profile: Use with inpatients. Presented at the American Academy of Child Psychiatry, Washington, D.C., October, 1982.

McPherson, S. J. Family counseling for youthful offenders in the juvenile court setting: A therapy outcome study. Ph.D. Dissertation, Division of Counseling and Educational Psychology, University of Oregon, 1980.

Michael, R. L., Klorman, R., Salzman, L. F., Borgstedt, A. D., & Dainer, K. B. Normalizing effects of methylphenidate on hyperactive children's vigilance performance and evoked potentials. *Psychophysiology,* 1981, *18,* 665-677.

Mitchell, M. K. The effects of Hodgkin's disease on the socialization skills of adolescents. M. S. Thesis, School of Nursing, University of Maryland, 1982.

Noam, G., Hauser, S., Jacobson, A., Powers, S., & Miranda, D. Ego development and psychopathology. *Child Development,* 1983, in press.

Offord, D. R., & Boyle, M. H. The setting up of a province-wide survey to determine the prevalence of emotional and behavioral problems. Report No. 7, Department of Psychiatry, McMaster University, Hamilton, Ontario, Canada, 1982.

Olmstead, J. V. Children's service needs assessment family foster care survey. Olympia, WA: Office of Research Analysis and Information Services Division, 1980.

Patterson. G. R. A process analysis of the rejecting mother. In W. Hartup & Z. Rubin (Eds.), *Social Relationships: Their role in children's development.* Harwichport Conference, Harwichport, Massachusetts, 1982.

Paulauskas, S. A cognitive-developmental analysis of self-image disparity in depressed children. Ph.D. Dissertation, Department of Psychology, University of Pittsburgh, 1983.

Plaisted, J. R., Wilkening, G. N., Gustavson, J. L., & Golden, C. J. The Luria-Nebraska Neuropsychological battery—Children's Revision: Theory and Current Research Findings. *Journal of Clinical Child Psychology,* 1983, *12,* 13-21.

Rapoport, J., Elkins, R., Langer, D. H., Sceery, W., Buchsbaum, M. S., Gillin, C., Murphy, D. L., Zahn, T. P., Lake, R., Ludlow, C., & Mendelson, W. Childhood obsessive-compulsive disorder. *American Journal of Psychiatry* 1981, *138,* 1545-1554.

Reed, M. L., & Edelbrock, C. Reliability and validity of the Direct Observation Form of the Child Behavior Checklist. *Journal of Abnormal Child Psychology,* 1983, in press.

Sawyer, M. G., Minde, K., & Zuker, R. The burned child—scarred for life? A study of the psychosocial impact of a burn injury at different developmental stages. *Burns,* 1982, *9,* 205-213.

Schwager, W., Dennie, D., & Smith M. Franco-Ontarian children in Sudbury. A mental health study. Sudbury, Ontario, Department of Sociology and Anthropology, Laurentian University, 1982.

Solodow, W. A longitudinal study of depressive symptoms in children. Ph.D. Dissertation, Department of Psychology, Long Island University, June, 1983.

Sonis, W., Klein, R. P., Blue, J. H., Comite, F., & Culter, G. Social competence and behavior problems in children with precocious puberty. Presented at the Society for Research in Child Development, Detroit, April, 1983.

Stein, S., & Gibbons, C. A comparison: CCW and parent report. Presented at Thistletown Research Day, Toronto, Canada, March, 1983.

Susman, E. J., Nottelmann, E. D., & Blue, J. H. Social competence, mood, and behavior problems in normal adolescents. Presented at the Society for Research in Child Development, Detroit, April, 1983.

Tegtmeyer, P. F., & Gordon, M. The interpretation of white-space responses in children's Rorschach protocols. *Perceptual and Motor Skills,* 1983, in press.

Tesiny, E. P., & Lefkowitz, M. M. The Peer Nomination Inventory of Depression: 1975–present. Presented at the American Psychological Association, Anaheim, CA, August, 1983.

Vanhasselt, V. B., Simon, J., & Mastantuono, A. K. Social skills training for blind children and adolescents—a program description. *Education of the Visually Handicapped,* 1982, *14,* 34–40.

Weissman, M. M., Orvaschel, H., & Padian, N. Children's symptom and social functioning self-report scales. Comparison of mothers' and children's reports. *The Journal of Nervous and Mental Disease,* 1980, *168,* 736–740.

Whitman, S., Hermann, B. P., Black, R. B., & Chhabria, S. Psychopathology and seizure type in children with epilepsy. *Psychological Medicine,* 1982, *12,* 843–853.

Wolf, D. A., & Mosk, M. D. Behavioral comparisons of children from abusive and distressed families. *Journal of Consulting and Clinical Psychology,* 1983, in press.

Zucker, K. J., Finegan, J. K., Doering, R. W., & Bradley, S. J. Human figure drawings of gender-problem children: A comparison to sibling, psychiatric, and normal controls. *Journal of Abnormal Child Psychology,* 1983, 11, 287–298.

Index[a]

[a]Does not include names that appear only in the bibliography of studies related to the CBCL (Appendix F).